Race and the Third Reich

In memory of my father
Donald Stuart Hutton (1930–2004)

Race and the Third Reich

Linguistics,
Racial Anthropology
and Genetics in
the Dialectic of *Volk*

Christopher M. Hutton

polity

First published in 2005 by Polity Press

Polity Press
65 Bridge Street
Cambridge CB2 1UR, UK.

Polity Press
350 Main Street
Malden, MA 02148, USA

ISBN: 0-7456-3176-2
ISBN: 0-7456-3177-0 (pb)

A catalogue record for this book is available from the British Library and has been applied for from the Library of Congress.

Typeset in 10.5 on 12 pt Times
by SNP Best-set Typesetter Ltd, Hong Kong
Printed and bound in Great Britain by MPG Books Ltd, Bodmin, Cornwall

For further information on Polity, visit our website: www.polity.co.uk

Contents

Acknowledgements

I would like to thank the following for their help and encouragement in a variety of ways (the usual disclaimer applies): Barbara Bader, Dominic Blaettler, Kingsley Bolton, Ellis Cashmore, Dafna Clifford, Paul Dennis, Frank Dikötter, Achim Mock, John Myhill, Lefteris Roussos, Gerd Simon, Sally-Ann Spencer, formerly of Polity Press, Jutta Strauss and my colleagues in the Department of English at the University of Hong Kong. Julia Kuehn was an excellent research assistant during the final stages of the writing. Grant Evans offered comments on an earlier draft and gave numerous suggestions for further reading. My gratitude goes to Bill Marshall for inviting me to present a paper on this topic at Glasgow University, and to Patrick Sériot of the University of Lausanne for an invitation to the colloquium: 'Discourse on language under authoritarian regimes' (October 2003). I am grateful to Andrea Drugan of Polity Press for her patience and advice during the writing of this book, and to the staff of the following institutions: the Library of the University of Hong Kong, in particular the Interlibrary Loan Department, the British Library, the Wiener Library, London, the Wellcome Library for the History and Understanding of Medicine, London, the Staatsbibliothek zu Berlin, the Bundesarchiv, Berlin-Lichterfelde, the Zentrum für Antisemitismusforschung, Berlin. Two anonymous reviewers provided praise and criticism respectively. My special thanks go to Louisa for her love and support throughout.

1

Introduction

This book is intended to give an introduction to the major questions addressed in the study of race in Nazi Germany, and to assess their place within its evolving intellectual and ideological landscape. It offers neither institutional history nor detailed biographies of the participants. What is of particular concern here are points of tension, controversy and uncertainty, both among academic theorists of race and between academics and the political authorities. The focus is on the politically and intellectually central concept of *Volk* ('people') and on competing understandings of German identity. This work offers just one particular path out of many through the maze of the Third Reich, and is written with the intention of informing debate about the relationships between race theory, National Socialism and wider trends in European thought. I have focused on those areas where in my view the received popular view is misleading, and have not attempted to summarize the massive scholarly literature on the institutional basis and implementation of the 'Final Solution' and other crimes against humanity committed by the Nazi regime.

Nazism as an ideological system was both dynamic and contentious. There was no single centre of power, and no single figure who determined the political correctness of a particular intellectual direction. National Socialist Germany did not see the rise of a new, clearly identifiable orthodoxy, as the major theoretical positions on race were staked out long before the Nazi seizure of power in 1933. This is not to say that there were no intellectual changes or developments between 1933 and 1945, but these changes tended to take the form of the neutralization or marginalization of particular schools or groups of academics, and the rise of others.

The initial years of the Nazi regime saw intellectuals from many disciplines making bids for a political, social or cultural role, and seeking the patronage of the Party and state with the intention of completing the political revolution of 1933 with an intellectual and ideological one. The mobilization of academic theory involved pulling down the barriers between academic research and 'life', and between humanities, social science and natural science. This was an attack on narrow specialization in favour of a holistic or *ganzheitlich* approach to knowledge, and reflected an ethnocentric suspicion of academic endeavour as an international enterprise. For example, Alfred Rosenberg (1893–1946), official ideologue of the National Socialist Workers Party (NSDAP), was associated with Nordicism, racial mysticism and a holistic approach to knowledge (Rosenberg 1939). However, revolutionary ideological projects were ultimately frustrated by inertia in the system and the pragmatic orientation of the state. There was in any case no consensus about the institution or structures that should replace the socially and politically elitist, conservative-humanistic university and its traditional academic division of labour (Krieck 1932; Rein 1933; Paletschek 2001). Heinrich Himmler's (1900–1945) academic organization, Ancestral Heritage (Ahnenerbe), steadily gained ground against Rosenberg, and evolved away from cultic Germanophilia towards an embrace of mainstream science.

Nazi intellectual policy was caught between suspicion of self-appointed spiritual advisors to the movement and impatience with the apolitical aloofness of the professoriate. True believers who hoped to find in the Nazi revolution the triumph of their particular ideology were often disappointed by the direction of policy or the ruthlessly pragmatic nature of the regime. Bureaucrats such as Walter Gross (1904–1945) of the Race Policy Office recognized that there was a benefit to be obtained from the promotion of scientific researchers who were loyal to the National Socialist cause without being Nazi activists or ideologues. Gross expressed this view in a letter to the Dean of Medicine at the University of Frankfurt in reference to the appointment of the 'apolitical' geneticist Otmar Freiherr von Verschuer. Verschuer's work, said Gross, could contribute to the strengthening of the scientific foundations of the National Socialist doctrine, as well as having propagandistic value (Völklein 1999: 75–6). The 'apolitical' scholar who was loyal to the regime, without seeking to define its ideological direction, frequently prospered, while self-promoting ideologues were often close to the centres of power only for short periods (Sieg 2001: 258). In many cases, the theorists and scholars who gained the upper hand during the Third Reich were able to carry that dominance over into the academic system of the German Federal

Republic. Ash (1999: 287) talks of 'constructed continuities' in scholarly careers that spanned the Weimar era, the Nazi state and the post-war occupation zones which became the German Federal Republic and the German Democratic Republic.

A considerable communication gap exists between specialist studies on Nazi Germany and the wider academic public. To illustrate this one can take the notorious example of the 'Aryan race'. It had been a commonplace among scholars across a range of disciplines from the last decades of the nineteenth century onwards to deny the scientific validity of this concept. If it could be shown that Nazi scholars promoted this 'myth', then we would have a simple model to show how racist ideology undermined science and scholarship. However, while the term 'Aryan' was used in various fundamental ways in Nazi Germany, there was no academic support at all for its use as a strictly racial label, and by 1935 this was accepted as orthodoxy by the political authorities. There was complete unanimity among scholars of race, and in official publications, that the notion of an 'Aryan race' lacked any scientific basis. The case of the category of Aryan illustrates a wider point concerning theories of human identity. Frameworks and paradigms are seldom fully superseded. Models, concepts, myths, folk names are conserved, reanimated and re-enacted in the social imaginary, and paradigms of thought that are pushed to the margins of scholarly inquiry may nonetheless live on in marginal scholarship, popular culture and intellectual folklore. Such concepts often retain strong political affect, as was the case with the category 'Aryan'.

A second example concerns the idealization of the Nordic type, the blond, blue-eyed, long-headed race to which many – or even all – of the great achievements of humanity were ascribed. This ideal of Nordic beauty was central to popular iconography in the Third Reich. But developments in racial anthropology in the early twentieth century had increasingly led to the conclusion that there was no direct correlation between physical type and psychological type, and this was accepted by race theorists in the Third Reich. What was fundamental was the inner racial nature, the psychological and moral qualities which made up the individual. One could not directly read off the racial quality of an individual from their bodily proportions, hair and eye colour. Mind and body were related in a deeper, more complex way, the understanding of which required knowledge of modern genetics.

The 'ideologically distorted science' or 'pseudo-science' model of Nazi thought is thus potentially quite misleading. Early radical attempts by would-be National Socialist ideologues to question received scientific orthodoxy or to subsume science under ideology were ignored, marginalized or repressed: 'Eventually the National Socialist state effectively terminated all the rogue Aryan science or technology movements' (Walker 2003: 1005). Likewise, there was concerted oppression of occultism, spiritualism, clairvoyance and the various strands of New Age Nazism, especially from 1937 onwards (Rabinbach 2004).

This is not to say that failed intellectual projects within Nazism had no impact on policy, or did not play a fundamental role in the evolution of the regime. Radical Nazi ideologues played a central role in neutralizing politically liberal and internationalist strands in various disciplines, and in the 'coordination' (*Gleichschaltung*) of institutions. But the idea of a racial or ethnocentric key to all areas of human knowledge, which was seen by many would-be ideologues as defining intellectual Nazism, eventually faltered. Ultimately the dominant model that emerged in Nazi Germany was the overt separation of ideology from science, and intellectual discussion in Nazi Germany broadly followed wider trends in European and western thought.

The discussions below of racial theorists and theories are not directly concerned with individual motivation and moral interiority. Intellectuals and scholars who operated as committed Nazis were not guaranteed academic power and influence in the long run, while many scholars and scientists who self-consciously distanced their work from 'vulgar' National Socialism had successful careers. A particular intellectual formation could be ideologically functional within the institutional and intellectual politics of the state, without being expressly politicized and in the absence of overt 'Nazi content'.

2

Nazi Ideology: An Attack on 'Difference'?

Introduction

The modern science of race arose out of the Enlightenment, and the term 'anthropology' has a complex history in debates about humanism and the Enlightenment, often under the term 'philosophical anthropology'. *Anthropologie* as used in German (or French) is generally equivalent to 'physical anthropology' or 'biological anthropology' in English, with links to the comparative anatomy and morphology of the human body. It has a wide sense as the 'study of the human species', with special attention being paid to theories of human origin and evolution (i.e. paleoanthropology). Carl von Linné (1707–1778) first placed *homo sapiens* within a zoological order (Fischer 1923: 7), but the figure conventionally identified as the founder of physical anthropology is Johann Friedrich Blumenbach (1752–1840). Blumenbach classified humanity into five basic races: Caucasian, Mongolian, Ethiopian, American and Malay (Heberer et al. 1959: 62). In the discussion that follows, theories of human diversity based on race will be termed 'racial anthropology'. The nativized German term is *Rassenkunde*.

Debates about continuities and discontinuities in ideology between Nazism and wider trends in European thought began with the advent of the regime and continue to this day. Discussion frequently takes on a dualistic character, in which Nazi ideology is assigned the role of the ideological 'evil twin'. Nazism symbolizes godless materialism for the Christian; pseudo-science for the scientist, etc. One such characterization has been of Nazism as a logical fulfilment of Enlightenment modernity. The Enlightenment is commonly understood as standing for reason, progress, rights and ideas of human perfectibility. However, it is also associated with aggressive utopian modernity, with race theory (racial anthropology) and colonialism. These phenomena are understood as embodying pathological forms of oppressive rationality and Eurocentrism.

The view that Enlightenment modernity involves new forms of internalized and institutionalized scrutiny and control is associated with the French philosopher Michel Foucault (1926–1984). Following this, an influential understanding of Nazism sees it as the fulfilment of oppressive state rationality within modernity (Bauman 1989). On this view, the Enlightenment is associated not only with ideas of reason and progress, but also with the classification of human diversity in terms of a fixed set of biological categories laid down at the centre of power. Regimentation, surveillance and technocratic mastery are seen as involving the control and ultimate elimination of difference. Likewise, modern racism has been associated with humanism, to the point that Nazism has been described as the ultimate form of humanism, understood as a flawed, racist universalism.

Within this framework, critics of the Enlightenment have found an opposition between racist humanism, realized in colonialism and Nazism, and respect for the ecology of human diversity (Ede 1995: 232). This expresses itself in a preference for Johann Gottfried von Herder (1744–1803) over Immanuel Kant (1724–1804). On this view, Herder was the defender of the ecology of human diversity, whereas Kant's universalism has a racist subtext. Later critics of the 'zoological' notion of human races looked back approvingly to Herder's view that the race concept, when applied to humanity, implied a 'degradation of man'. Talk of human 'races' associated humankind with the animal sphere (Voegelin [1933] 1998: 84). After all, Kant digressed from his *Anthropology* to denounce Jews as 'usurious' and 'nonproductive' ([1798a] 1978: 101 fn.) and defined 'the pure moral religion' as 'the euthanasia of Judaism' (1798b; Rose 1990: 96).

However, it was Herder who described the Jews as 'a parasitic plant on the stems of other nations' (Herder 1784–91 (III): 97, cited in Rose 1990: 99). Likewise, Johann Friedrich Blumenbach saw Jews as 'an exception to the rules of nature that he himself posited', namely that human racial characteristics naturally varied with geography and climate (Blumenbach [1795] 1969; Efron 1994: 20). The idea of Jews as radically *different* has deep roots in racial anthropology. Anti-Semitism was fundamental to the ideology of *Volk*, and the concept of Jews as 'parasites' on the natural ecology of nations runs through its modern history into Nazism (Wirth 1914: 139; Schwab 1937: 19; Haase-Bessell 1939: 17). These tensions over authenticity of membership of the *Volk* remain fundamental in contemporary ethnic politics.

The *völkisch* idea

German theorists of *Volk* were reacting to political and social forces which were perceived as coming from 'outside'. The French Revolution (1789) and the ensuing Napoleonic Wars (1799–1815), which brought much of Europe under French colonial rule, spread Enlightenment ideals of equality, citizenship and the rule of law to German-speaking Europe. German intellectuals, like their post-colonial successors, were left with the ambivalence of their forced induction into modernity, as Germans were incorporated to varying degrees into the world's first modern Empire. In response, the theorizing of an organically unified *Volk* became a long-term project of German intellectuals. They sought to impose 'hegemonic, exclusive concepts of "national character" [*Nationalcharakter*], "national spirit" [*Nationalgeist*], or "nationalist feeling" [*Nationalgefühl*] on a heterogeneous, multicultural, and multilingual populace living within the borders of the long-disintegrated Holy Roman Empire' (Zantop 1997: 94). Those historical divisions were frequently presented as the products of modernity, in particular the political emancipation and partial assimilation of Jews into German society, as if Jews were the only obstacles to the realization of the otherwise perfect unity of the *Volk*.

German intellectuals developed theories of national identity which stressed racial, linguistic and cultural diversity and expressed a mistrust of universal ideologies which threatened to erase that diversity. Germans were Europeans, but Germany was not part of the 'West'; rather it was a power block between west and east. Theorists in France also reacted against the egalitarian and theoretically race-blind 'citizenship model' of the French state, notably Arthur Comte de Gobineau (1816–1882) and Georges Vacher de Lapouge (1854–1936). In this tradition, National Socialism was later to understand itself as a force for liberation from oppressive western universalism. It was closer to anti-colonial nationalism than to any kind of imperialism (Mühlmann 1936: 445, 445 fn.).

The creation of a German Reich by Bismarck in 1871 was merely a partial fulfilment of this dream of unified *Volk*. Defeat in the First World War led to the demise of this Second Reich and the end of the monarchy. The Treaty of Versailles (1919) left the Rhineland occupied, imposed reparations both in money and raw materials, and stripped Germany of territory in the west, north and east, as well as seizing its colonial possessions. Germany appeared hemmed in, denied access to both its ancestral territories to the east and to the additional colonial territories which were its right as a great European power. Within Germany, the rise of modernity was perceived as reflecting the triumph of a foreign force. Jews were perceived as dominating key areas of national life and culture, and seen as flourishing precisely in the urban environment which was so toxic to the best elements of the German *Volk*. Politically, the Weimar Republic represented the triumph of the Enlightenment, itself often understood as 'Jewish' in spirit. France, with its conception of *citoyen* or 'citizen', was viewed as racially degenerate.

The term used to characterize radical German nationalist thinking is *völkisch*, variously translated as 'ultra-nationalistic', 'racist' or simply rendered as 'folkish' or 'volkish'. The phrase *völkische Bewegung* ('folkish movement') referred to a range of political positions rather than a single organization. It had its roots in the late nineteenth century (Puschner 2001, 2002: 5) and covered a broad spectrum of opinion. It embraced a range of religious beliefs, from nationalist Protestantism to 'New Age' paganism. Some *völkisch* ideologues were strongly anti-Christian, especially anti-Catholic, and saw Christianity as an expression of the Jewish spirit. Jews were juxtaposed to Aryans, in a struggle for the soul of the *Volk*. However, European racial anxiety was as often focused on Africa (the 'black peril') and Asia (the 'yellow peril') as on the European Jews. Slavophobia was rampant in German nationalist circles in the first decades of the twentieth century (Jakesch 1909: 86). The Slavs were seen as threatening through their rising birth-rate, while the Germans were an ageing people 'without youth' ('Volk ohne Jugend', Burgdörfer 1932, 1936: 254).

There was agreement among *völkisch* ideologues that Germany was facing a crisis, and that crisis was grounded in a nexus of historical, geographical, political and biological factors. Increasingly, the focus was on the biological: charts, graphs and statistics were produced which painted a gloomy prospect for the future vitality of the *Volk* (Burgdörfer 1929, 1934, 1936). The *Volk* was beset on all sides. Thinkers such as the nineteenth-century prophet of racial decline Joseph Arthur, Comte de Gobineau and the world historian Oswald Spengler (1880–1936) were understood as having demonstrated the inevitability of the decline of European civilization. In Spengler's case there was the prospect of a new, vital spring following the collapse, but his model was suffused with pessimism in relation to the so-called progress achieved by modernity. Racial ideologues, following Gobineau's lead, argued that racial conflict determined the course of world history at a deep structural level (Garbe 1938: 441), so that the interactions between national states, and the direction of empires, were a question of racial dominance both inside political units and in conflict between them: 'races make history' (Ekkehart 1936: 2).

Biological and evolutionary metaphors were central to political rhetoric, with notions of 'struggle' (*Kampf*), 'selection' (*Auslese*) and 'adverse selection' (*Gegenauslese*) applied both to social questions and to relations between nations. Adverse selection, as applied to human society, took place when the normal laws of natural selection, in which the biologically fittest flourished, were perceived to be negated by social or cultural forces, so that inferior elements were reproducing faster than superior elements. The view was widespread that the superior Aryan or Nordic element was disappearing through regressive selection (*rückschrittliche Auslese*), in that the more enterprising racial element tended to undertake activities that brought it into danger, in particular by moving to the towns and cities. This was the so-called 'Ammon's Law', named after Dr Otto Ammon (1842–1916), who had concluded that the age was witnessing the 'twilight of the Aryan' (*Arierdämmerung*) (Ammon 1893; Gerstenhauer 1913: 20). This law took on new resonance after the casualties of the First World War.

German ultra-nationalism and ideological Nazism was shaped by powerful relativistic tendencies. Intellectuals and cultural activists sought for Germany a political and ideological space in which to set their own moral and intellectual standards. However, the demand for cultural self-determination was difficult to distinguish from xenophobia and anti-Semitism. Jews were seen as having biologically and spiritually occupied the German *Volk* (Banniza von Bazan 1937). This relativism thus shaded off into a dualistic ('Manichaean') understanding of difference. A simple example of this would be Walther Darré's 'The pig as a criterion for Nordic peoples and Semites', in which cultural difference is grounded in climatic and ultimately race-physiological difference: 'It is not inconceivable that the consumption of pork gives rise to a physiological disharmony in [the Semite's] body' ([1927] 1933: 24).

The effect of this dualistic thinking was to create strong narrative compression, in the sense that there was a strong drive to reduce historical and ideological phenomena to simple oppositions, such as Aryan against Semite, Nordic against Jew, Nordic against Negro, Goethe against Newton, *Volk* against *Masse* (Ullmann 1936). A good example of this is offered by the terms 'Aryan' (*arisch*) and 'Nordic' (*nordisch*). These two concepts were often equated in the popular discourses of early twentieth-century German racial narcissism. However, in scholarly writings of the late nineteenth and early twentieth centuries, they were distinct both methodologically and conceptually. On the negative side, there was narrative pressure to relate the Jews to the Negro, and this was done in relation to perceived skin colour and unbridled or destructive sexuality (Gilman 1993: 18–23). There were also claims that Jews had a high proportion of 'Negro blood'. But the Jew and the Negro could also be understood dualistically, as embodying contrasting aspects of the racial negative. The tension between narcissistic identification and methodological separation was even greater when Aryan and/or Nordic were associated with the category 'German'.

Modernity was seen not primarily as a socio-cultural process, but as a biological one. It was associated with the rise of materialistic mass-consumer societies, with democracy and political liberalism. It involved the disruption of the relation of the *Volk* to territory, to landscape and to the political borders of the state, and the disruption of traditional social hierarchies, as found in rural society, between classes and in the roles of men and women. Races, peoples, social groups, languages, cultures that had been clearly distinct and identifiable, held separate by geography or the operation of social or 'caste' boundaries, were now merging and blurring into one another. The pre-modern 'ecology' or 'natural order', in which different racial and cultural variants of humanity had their own 'place', was breaking down. The pure essences of the past were being lost, and a bastardized, mongrel and degraded humanity was emerging from the cities and ports of modern civilization.

A rising tide of biologically mediocre elements (the criminal, indigent, asocial, insane, the racially and genetically undesirable) was seen as threatening to overwhelm socially elite groups. The natural elites were failing to reproduce fast enough to maintain their leadership position in society. On a wider stage, there was fear of the potential rise of non-white peoples and races, a sense of threat from an ill-defined 'east' and from migration and racial mixing. Conflict, struggle and competition were deemed to be the fundamental determinant of the destiny of peoples and nations, and any nation which ignored the lessons of nature was doomed to extinction. Germany needed to reorder its national life on the basis of organic principles; it needed its lost territories returned, and it needed healthy, vital couples to have large numbers of healthy, vital children.

Ideas about the biological fitness of human beings, a fear of the raceless mass or the cultureless mob, were pervasive among writers and intellectuals of many political persuasions in the early twentieth century. Just how pervasive this fear of modernity was among western intellectuals and writers can be seen from the apocalyptic eugenic fantasies of D. H. Lawrence, H. G. Wells, W. B. Yeats and others (Carey 1992). Intellectuals' experience of the slum-dweller involved an attraction-repulsion across class lines parallel to that experienced by white colonialists across the boundary of race. Nietzsche's critique of modernity was an inspiration for thinkers on both the left and the right. Critiques of capitalism and the machine-age looked for a new (or restored) organic-hierarchical social order, or for the liberation of humanity through the completion of the project of modernity.

Eugenics was the new religion of the intellectuals. Eugenic ideas were 'taken up and developed by sexual reformers, pacifists, social-ists and Jewish scientists as keenly as by right-wing intellectuals and politicians' (Weindling 1989: 317). There was a tension between the socialist desire to raise up humanity through modern social and political reforms ('welfare-oriented eugenics', 'eugenics for all') and an elitist 'aristogenics' based on the fear that that very modernity would set loose the destructive forces of the inferior and the vulgar (Weindling 1989: 471, 482). On the right, belief in the basic tenets of political eugenics went together with pessimism concerning funda-mental trends in western society. The modern biological understand-ing of sexual reproduction as involving the entire hereditary history of both the male and the female parent led to increasing anxiety about the quality of the human breeding stock. The distinctive feature of eugenic debates was that traditional social forms as well as modern society were subjected to bio-utilitarian analysis. The merits of we-lfare, warfare, female emancipation, sexual liberation, sexual absti-nence, marriage, urban life, technological advance, capitalism were discussed from the point of view of their contribution to the biologi-cal improvement of humankind.

In modernity there was a sense that life was speeding up and that old boundaries were disappearing. Electricity blurred the boundary between night and day; urban life and the capitalist system put new strains on the human nervous system (Goldstein 1913: 38–50). Modernity, with its vastly increased mobility, also involved an accel-erated process of racial and cultural hybridization, and this posed an intellectual challenge to those disciplines which sought to track the history of races, peoples and languages. Scholars saw much of the evidence, the anthropological, ethnographic and linguistic data that reflected the early order of things, apparently disappearing before their eyes. Their sense of a world rushing headlong towards chaos was complemented by their sense of an intellectual crisis. The essences of the past were rapidly being erased beyond retrieval.

In the early twentieth century, anyone who tried to make overall sense of race and its relations to prehistory, archaeology and linguistics was therefore faced with a formidable task. Human identity was studied in a multidimensional manner. Peoples, races or civilizations could be defined and identified by a whole range of criteria. These included material culture (tools, pottery, weapons, jewellery); bodily adornment (e.g. tattoos); religious or ritual forms (e.g. burial ritual and style, cosmology, myths); style of dwelling; language; race-anthropological features (skull type, hair, eye colour, height, bodily proportion); original homeland, migration patterns; means of subsistence and relationship to the environment (pastoral, agricultural, fishing); diet; lineage structure (e.g. patriarchal versus matriarchal). To create any kind of coherent narrative required creating sets of correlations between these different dimensions. Often this was done by focusing on a subset of dimensions (e.g. skull type and burial-mound type), or homeland and language, and leaving aside others.

The notion that advanced or civilized peoples were all racially mixed (Baur 1922: 6), and that primitive peoples were free of racial mixing, points to the curious vulnerability that racial anthropology ascribed to the racial make-up of advanced or civilized peoples. Primitive peoples, being closer to their natural state, were seen as true to type, though their cultural level was inevitably inferior. In the case of the advanced peoples, the most dangerous form of racial decline was one that affected the intellectual, creative and moral virtues, rather than minor physical problems like short-sightedness which could be corrected by cultural means (Lenz 1923b: 10–11). The consequence of the perceived vulnerability of advanced racial stock to the social and political institutions of modernity was a widespread pessimism, and a consequent willingness to embrace radical political solutions.

Anti-Semitism was fundamental to the world-view of almost all ultra-nationalist (*völkisch*) ideologues and, increasingly in the post-war era, of race theorists. Jews were the essence of modernity, in that they thrived in cities and in modern consumer capitalism. They represented materialism, liberalism, internationalism, Marxism; they embodied the promiscuity of modernity, in that they were citizens of all countries, spoke many languages and lacked any organic relationship to territory and landscape. They were a global people, violating the natural ecology of humankind, which saw different races predominating in different parts of the world. The fact that Jews thrived in modernity gave them unique power and influence over the distressed German *Volk*. Jews were caught between a left-wing and moderate nationalist critique of their incomplete assimilation and a radical *völkisch* attempt to reverse the effects of emancipation (Breuer 2001: 328–9). Within fascistic ecology, Jews were seen as the ultimate 'humans' in their perceived separation from, or destructive relationship to, nature. Carl Gustav Jung saw the dichotomy between Aryans and Jews in terms of the vital, youthful, barbarian versus the over-refined and overcivilized (Pietikainen 1998).

There was however no necessary correlation between a belief in eugenics and anti-Semitism; nor had anti-Semitism been a universal theme of European racial anthropology. Many professional, intellectual and educated Jews shared the eugenic beliefs of their fellow citizens; Jews in Germany held a wide range of socio-political views, and were also active across the political spectrum, including in conservative or nationalist politics. Not all definitions of the *Volk* specifically excluded German Jews, though this 'liberal' view of the *Volk* typically required Jews to abandon all vestiges of difference in order to be accepted. For some Jewish intellectuals, racial anthropology was a vehicle for reflecting on or resisting the anti-Semitic discourse of late nineteenth- and early twentieth-century Europe (Efron 1994).

National Socialism: between racial nostalgia and modernity

Within Nazism, the emphasis on hierarchy and elitism was in tension with ultra-nationalist egalitarianism, in which that elite status was offered to the *Volk* as a whole. Many Nazi ideologues looked back with nostalgia to lost racial elites and caste hierarchies, whereas others emphasized a modern, meritocratic vision of *Volk*, in which educational and other opportunities were to be offered to all. Premodern, dynastic forms of governance, and systems where wealth was inherited, had at best an ambivalent status for radical, revivalist nationalism (Büchner 1894). Although a conservative-reactionary ideology of the *Volk* was promoted in Nazi Germany, with an emphasis on folkloric culture and the cultural revivalism of pure Germanic forms, this gradually lost ground to the technocratic vision of *völkisch* modernity. Walther Darré (1895–1953) saw it as the mission of Nazism to bring a new leadership caste (*Führerschicht*) or 'new nobility' (*Neuadel*) into being (Darré 1939: 13). As in other areas, a degree of ambiguity in terms such as *Adel* ('nobility') was politically and intellectually functional, but Darré's vision of a new agrarian order was not ultimately realized.

After 1939, Darré's plans for the resettlement of the east with a Nordified German peasant stock came into conflict with Heinrich Himmler's project of 'Germanization' (*Germanisierung*). Himmler had been given a high-profile role in the eastern territories by his appointment to the position of Reich Commissioner for the Strengthening of German Nationhood (*Reichskommissar für die Festigung deutschen Volkstums*). This project involved selecting those fit to be 're-Germanized' (*wiedereindeutschungsfähig*) from assimilated or lost Germanic elements within the eastern populations, including Poles, Czechs and Russians (Mai 2002: 311, 357; Heinemann 2003). Darré's influence also waned on the home front, in the so-called *Altreich*, where his emphasis on the rural population met opposition from Josef Bürckel (1895–1944), the *Gauleiter* of the Saarpfalz, who sought a settlement policy that would unite both rural and urban workers (Mai 2002: 223–87).

National Socialism was not in essence a reactionary or nostalgic political formation. Once in power in 1933, Hitler showed no interest in the restoration of Kaiser Wilhelm II and the monarchy, and viewed the institution with contempt (Overy 2004: 101). The Habsburg monarchy had after all presided over a hybrid polity which had separated the Austrian Germans from their rightful place within Greater Germany. Nazism reflected the anti-bourgeois sentiments of a whole range of radical ideologues of left and right. An ideology grounded in a 'socialism' of the *Volk* suggested an organic modernity rather than a return to the feudal past. Hitler viewed the urban worker as ideologically central, and the concept of the *Volk* as a single community without inner class divisions (*Volksgemeinschaft*) was fundamentally a forward-looking one (Overy 2004: 227–36).

The embrace of modern technology by leading Nazi ideologues and by the key elements of the state apparatus was seen as a means of overcoming the 'cultural crisis' of German conservatism, and creating what Goebbels termed 'a new romanticism in the results of modern inventions and technology' or 'steely Romanticism' (*stählernde Romantik*) (Herf 1984: 196–7). This fusion of avant-garde enthusiasm for the machine age with Romantic organicism envisioned National Socialist society as an organic machine. Combined with the drama of public spectacle and display, this reflected Nazism's roots in 'fascist modernism' (Hewitt 1993). The revolt against egalitarian, mediocre, bourgeois modernity and against the mongrelized *Massenmensch* (as opposed to the high-achieving *Leistungsmensch*,

Danzer 1937: 7) was most effectively pursued with the tools of modernity itself.

With its apparently revolutionary insights into human diversity, science offered the possibility not only of contributing a new dimension to a historical understanding, but also of bringing that analytic power to the policy agenda of bio-social renewal. With the prestige of the medical and biological sciences behind it, a science of race promised to be able to see through the confusion of surface social categories to lay bare the deep structures of bio-racial reality, both in their historical evolution and in their contemporary distribution. The more powerful the analytic model, the greater the likelihood of the project of renewal being successful, provided that the political will was there. On the brink of the total triumph of the raceless masses, amidst the fragmentation of an original categorical order – an order now being overtaken by the new, misshapen or bastardized groupings of modernity in which only the Jews seemed racially invulnerable – this represented the last hope for an important section of the European intelligentsia. It offered an apparently viable alternative to cultural and racial pessimism and nostalgia for a lost greatness suffused with *thanatos*.

Nazi ideology was an uneasy fusion of different strands of racial elitism and populism. The political rhetoric of Nazism was directed at the German *Volk*, and the fulfilment of its historical mission. In this sense, much of the political appeal of Nazism was grounded in racial egalitarianism. Within the true boundaries of the *Volk*, all were promised racial equality, provided they met the eugenic criteria of the state. This offered a promise of liberation from class barriers, and the possibility of social mobility in a new meritocratic social order (Aly 2003: 230). Every recruit could hope that he is carrying 'the field marshal's baton in his kitbag'. Whether he obtained high rank or not was determined to a considerable extent by his genetic make-up (*Erbveranlagung*), though a totally reliable prognosis could not be made in advance (Verschuer 1944: 20).

Conclusion

The idea that Nazism represented the fulfilment of humanism and the Enlightenment project would have been puzzling to those German-Jewish scholars who saw in the Enlightenment legacy the counterweight to chauvinist nationalism, to exile German scholars who saw in Nazism a betrayal of Germany's Enlightenment legacy, and not least to Nazi scholars and ideologues themselves, who poured scorn on the Enlightenment's promise of progress, rights and increasing equality under the reign of reason, and traced Germany's ills to the political and social emancipation of the Jews. The alienation of Jews from the 'natural' groupings of humankind and from the 'natural' relationships between peoples and territory fuelled an association between Jews, modernity and the Enlightenment. If the division of humanity into different *Völker* was ordained by God or by nature, then any group which threatened that ecology was striking at the fundamental order of things: 'Every race, every people is an idea of God's made flesh, which we must nurture. It is our task to protect their distinctive nature' (Ekkehart 1936: 2).

The equation of Nazism with Enlightenment humanism and rationality complements an understanding of Nazism as an attack on 'difference' or 'otherness'. But Nazism, while it shared conventional European racism directed at 'inferior' peoples (Reche 1943: 163), was fundamentally an attack on assimilation. That attack was carried out in the name of 'difference'. To view Nazism as a direct reflection of Enlightenment's perceived contempt for 'difference' is to stand history on its head. For it was Nazism that dreamed of an unlimited horizon for the unfolding of difference (NSLB 1933), of a perfect, authentic self-realization at the fullest extent of that difference, and which found in 'Jewish modernity' hybrid racial, political and conceptual forms, including the awful possibility of looking at the world authentically from more than one point of view.

Jews were not understood as conventionally inferior, but as radically unnatural. Humanity was held to vary geographically, linguistically and culturally according to a natural ecology of difference. Jews were an unnatural people, since, within modernity, they were simultaneously different and apparently the 'same'. The attack on assimilation fed on a paranoid hostility to the blurring of racial and cultural boundaries and to the uncanny *sameness* of the Jews. Bizarrely, the idea of Enlightenment modernity as 'Nazi' is the mirror image of the idea of Enlightenment as 'Jewish', with the Nazis, instead of the Jews, understood as destructive of racio-cultural difference within modernity.

3

Peoples, Races, Genes

Introduction

Racial ideology under National Socialism was derived from three basic understandings of the relationship between individual and collective. Firstly, the individual could be understood as a member of a people (*Volk*); secondly, the individual was defined by anthropological race (*Rasse*); thirdly, the individual was understood as the intersection of genetic lines of transmission (*Erblinien*) within a population defined as a reproductive community or 'stock' (*Vitalrasse*). Each of these understandings of individual identity had a political life in popular debate, as well as being the object of specialist disciplinary inquiry.

There were two basic theoretical oppositions. The first was between 'race' and 'people', *Rasse* and *Volk* (see below). The second was between 'system race' (*Systemrasse*) and 'vital race' (*Vitalrasse*). In racial anthropology, a 'system race' was a group or sub-category in the study of human racial diversity (the 'Nordic race', the 'Negro race'). In biological or eugenic discourse, *Rasse* was used in the sense of *Vitalrasse* to mean individual and collective genetically inherited fitness, understood in terms of physical and mental health, strength, intelligence, leadership qualities, etc.

The terminology of *Systemrasse* and *Vitalrasse* had been elaborated by Alfred Ploetz (1860–1940) (1895, 1911: 114), and the terms were theoretically quite distinct (Rittershaus 1936: 183–4). A 'vital race' was an actual living population taken as a whole, judged according to the quality of its genetic lines and its collective physical and mental health, strength, abilities and capacities down the generations.

The geneticist Hermann Siemens offered the following definition: 'the super-individual unit of ongoing existence which is represented by a circle of similar individuals living together as a reproductive community' (1937: 195). A second meaning of *Vitalrasse* gave the notion of *Volk* a biological basis: 'the ongoing living continuity of the body of the people' (*Volkskörper*). The equating of *Vitalrasse* with *Volk* (Viernstein 1935: 10) was however controversial, as *Volk* was understood in academic discourse primarily as a linguistic and cultural construct.

Two terms which took on a politically productive but imprecise range of associations were *Blut* and *Art*. One could evoke ties of 'blood' (*Blut*) and imply racial kinship without directly invoking the problematic concept of anthropological race. Thus we have *Bluteinheit* ('unity of blood', Schultze 1934: 21), the famous slogan *Blut und Boden* ('blood and soil'), *Blutbewusstsein* ('blood consciousness', 'racial consciousness'), *Blut(s)gemeinschaft* ('community bound together by blood ties'), etc. (Schmitz-Berning 1998: 109–24).

In natural scientific discourse, *Art* is a synonym for 'species' (Marle 1936: 71), but it was frequently used in a wide range of compounds as a synonym for 'race' or for a racially determined concept of human type (Schmitz-Berning 1998: 63–70). In the context of human racial variation, Otto Reche used *Art* to refer to what was effectively a subspecies, a higher-order racial grouping, for example the original, long-skulled European races. This *Art* consisted of the Nordic, the Phalian and the Mediterranean races (Köhn-Behrens 1934: 97). The term *artverwandt* ('related by racial type or blood') was used in the 1935 Nuremberg Laws. Academics who advocated a specifically German or Germanic approach to intellectual life termed this ideal an *artgemässe Wissenschaft* (Bieberbach 1940: 5). The term *Entartung* was used in the sense of the racial degeneration, loss of purity of type, the biological decay of the *Volk*; the opposite was *Aufartung*, the attempt to improve or purify the *Volk*. Similarly, 'Nordification' (*Aufnordung*) was an ideology or policy which aimed to increase the proportion of Nordic blood in the German people, and the decline or loss of that racial element was 'denordification' (*Entnordung*).

Volk

As members of a *Volk*, individuals were understood to be members of a historically united organic collective, a descent group with its own territory, language, culture and world-view. The origins of this concept can be found in the biblical notion of a people with its own language and territory as a lineage group descended from a single patriarch. The biblical theory of *Volk*, the idea that there was God-given order of human diversity, fused within modernity with the idea that the *Volk* was a natural entity defined by common descent.

The idealization of the German *Volk* evoked a historical entity with a collective trajectory and unique mission. The elaboration of the theory of the German *Volk* was carried out at the beginning of the nineteenth century, in the context of the Napoleonic Wars in Europe, with a strong focus on the German language, and an envisioned but politically 'virtual' homeland where that language was spoken. This concern with the virtual homeland was complicated by attempts in the spirit of biblical speculation and European Romanticism to link the present-day German *Volk* with prehistorical and early historical peoples and migrations, in particular an Aryan or Indogermanic *Volk*, postulated initially on the basis of linguistic reconstruction.

Depth of historical continuity, in a popularized reworking of notions of aristocratic lineage, was assumed to confer legitimacy and status. There were 'five thousand years of German history', with the first *Reich* of 'free Germanic tribes' founded around 2000 BC (Pastenaci 1933). But the German state in its modern form was not founded until 1871. The *Volk* was the fundamental expression of German collectivity, understood as a unity through historical time, across geographical space and independent of the contingencies of political boundaries. The concept was fundamental to academic disciplines like history (there was after all no German state with a clear linear history), linguistics (since language was one of its fundamental defining elements) and *Volkskunde* or folklore, which looked at the culture, customs and beliefs of the authentic members of the *Volk*. But it was also the central term in political rhetoric from a broad range of political standpoints, from the left to the radical *völkisch* groupings. *Volk* was the key politically mobilizing collective concept in Nazi Germany.

In Romantic identity theory, each *Volk* was assumed to have its own culture, folklore and customs, its own law and social institutions, and its own world-view. An individual was joined to the *Volk* by being born into it, and became a full member by absorbing from earliest childhood the patterns of thought and associations unique to it. These were expressed in its language and in the emotional bonds between family or clan, landscape and language. The 'mother tongue' was the most vital expression of the *Volk*, and could be used as a criterion to differentiate one people from another. The intellectual disciplines that elaborated and explored this concept included the academic study of language (historical and comparative philology, linguistics), folklore, history, law and archaeology.

While Germanophile ideologues celebrated the unity of the German *Volk*, Germany was in reality deeply divided. Germans lacked a shared political philosophy and a shared sense of destiny. There were deeply rooted confessional and regional loyalties, accompanied by mutually incomprehensible forms of vernacular speech. Germany had no single political, economic and cultural centre. Bismarck's creation of a German state under Prussian leadership in 1871, the so-called second German empire, did not resolve these tensions but brought them more clearly into focus. Unity had been achieved by military force. For Pan-German ideologues, there was the issue of the status of the Germans outside the new boundaries of the Reich, most importantly in the Austro-Hungarian Empire and then in the new state of Austria founded after the First World War. Not all members of the German *Volk* were citizens of the German *Reich*. In modern terminology, they had become 'minorities' (*Minderheiten*) (Bahr 1933) in states themselves largely defined as ethnic collectivities. If the German state was the political realization or manifestation of the German people, why did it not include all Germans? Why did it include many Danes, Poles and French? Even the 'proper' Germans themselves could be presented as a colourful mix of diverse racial and national origins ('ein Sammelgemisch aller möglichen Rassen- und Volksbestandteile', Wachler 1916/17: 48). Wirth presented the German *Volk* as made up originally of Celtic, Lithuanian, Germanic and Slavic blood, then Romans, Jews, Huguenots and Italians, with a smattering of Swedes, Scots, Croats, Irish, Hungarians, Spaniards and Turks (1914: 72). 'What a complicated people!' concluded Willy Hellpach (1877–1955) (1926: 138).

The possession of German citizenship and mastery of German as one's first language was not universally understood as sufficient to make someone 'German'. According to ultra-nationalist or *völkisch* ideologies, Germany needed to reassert its place as a great European power, regain lost territory and rid the body of the *Volk* of what was seen as a foreign and overly influential element, namely the Jews. While mother tongue was the most visible and dynamic sign of membership of the *Volk*, the increasing assimilation of Jews into German society, which gave rise to a substantial German-Jewish middle class, put a question mark against the definition of the *Volk* as the collective of mother-tongue speakers of German.

The most radical political expression of the politics of *Volk* was *völkisch* thought itself. Hitler himself, with his eyes on making a serious bid for power, complained in *Mein Kampf* of the 'conceptual boundlessness' of the term. It was unsuitable as the basis of a political movement, as anyone could use it for their own purposes ([1925–6] 1992: 328–9). The key to a politically operational conception was the recognition of the importance of race and 'the presence of the Aryan' (1992: 348). Hitler stressed in addition the creation of a disciplined party which could rival that of the Marxist in its unity, rather than present a 'hodge-podge of views'. This Party-supervised formulation of the 'folkish world-view' (*völkische Weltanschauung*) was the key to political victory (1992: 349; see Essner 2002: 21).

The theoretical question raised by the Nazi embrace of the concept of *Volk* was its relationship to the ideological central *Rasse*: could the unity and the boundaries of the *Volk* be expressed in racial terms?

Race and racial anthropology

The category 'race' has a complex prehistory. The scientific study of race had its origins in the mid-eighteenth century, and became a branch of scientific learning at the beginning of the nineteenth century with the application of morphological techniques from animal and human anatomy, botany and zoology to the study of humankind. Many physical or racial anthropologists had zoological or medical training, and in the history of the discipline anthropology was often practised as an offshoot of comparative anatomy. The basic premise of this discipline was that human beings could be divided into distinct races, and that their physical and mental characteristics were shaped by climate and geography.

The modern scientific understanding of the natural world as ordered in hierarchical systems of categorization was applied to human beings, and as the nineteenth century progressed increasingly complex taxonomies of human racial diversity were proposed. In the course of the nineteenth century, race science achieved recognition as an academic discipline, with a distinct methodology and with different criteria for classification from those applied by linguists or historians.

Racial anthropologists often had very different understandings of how race was actually to be defined. As with other areas, scholars employed various tactics to attract professional status. Terminological innovation offered ambitious scholars the chance to put their own stamp on the discipline. The classical methodology was based on an assessment of external bodily appearance. The primary measurement was the so-called 'cephalic index' (*Schädelindex*), also termed 'cranial index', 'length–breadth index'. This was obtained by multiplying the width of the head at its maximum point by a hundred and dividing that number by the length of the head. The key terms were dolichocephaly (*Dolichokephalie*), referring to a long or narrow skull, and brachycephaly (*Brachykephalie*), a short or round skull, round-headedness. Another extensively studied feature was the nose, notably by Paul Topinard (1885). The two views of the human head, from the front and the side, thus became characteristic for the photographic representation of racial types. For all the statistical sophistication of many approaches, racial anthropology belonged as much to the realm of the aesthetic, the intuitive and the metaphorical as to natural science. A racial aesthetic promoted in northern Europe claimed superiority for the long skull over the round skull. This aesthetic race theory, as well as the positivistic-statistical approach to the comparative measurement of the human body, faced a strong challenge from the new genetics in the early twentieth century.

The application of techniques of natural scientific observation to human variation implied that humankind was part of nature, not above it, and therefore subject to its laws. This was true of all human beings, from the most regal and aristocratic to the humblest peasant. In this sense, modern racial science not only blurred the distinction between animals and humankind, it also potentially struck at the notion that some human beings, in virtue of their aristocratic titles, were a 'race apart' from the rest of humanity, and from nature. A science of human measurement and racial evaluation was potentially meritocratic, since in theory it judged first and foremost the body itself, abstracted away from social status, education or fine manners. According to race science, clothes certainly did not 'make the man'. Although race science could be used to provide royal and aristocratic lineages with a scientific explanation of their superiority, it was equally a potential ideological tool for the advocate of the common people. The yeoman, the sturdy peasant living close to nature could be set against a corrupt and decadent – frequently 'foreign' – ruling class.

From the mid- to late nineteenth century, the concept of *Volk* as expressed in linguistic community seemed to be triumphing over regional, confessional divisions and the pre-existing boundaries of a shifting patchwork of imperial and dynastic states, kingdoms and principalities. This process culminated in the unification of Italy in 1870 and Germany in 1871, and the rise of pan-Slavism, pan-Arabism and other movements based on linguistic affinity. However, racial anthropologists pointed out that these communities were far from racially uniform. To racial anthropologists, it was evident that not all of those who spoke Arabic, indeed relatively few, were descendants of the original speakers, just as not all of those who spoke Aryan languages were descendants of Aryan stock (Wirth 1914: 61 ff.). The criterion of language-as-identity led to the inclusion of foreign elements in the *Volk*.

Thus the claim that the racial taxonomy of humanity captured the reality of human diversity, the deep structure of human variation, undermined the authenticity of 'natural' status of *Volk*. A racial analysis of the human species did not correspond in any simple way to the division of the world's population into *Völker*, which were linguistic, cultural or political rather than purely racial collectivities. As this developed, it became part of the disciplinary rhetoric of racial anthropology – and indeed that of the academic study of language – to distinguish racial or race-anthropological categories from linguistic ones, but the tension between these disciplines remained fundamental to the intellectual life of the Third Reich.

Racial anthropologists were however divided about the key issues in the study of race, e.g. the nature and definition of the concept 'race' itself and the number of human races. There was no consensus about which physical criteria could be used to identify racial identity, though generally the shape of head was favoured as the most salient and the most 'noble' feature of the body. There was also widespread disillusion with the 'cephalic-index' as a racial diagnostic (Wirth 1914: 35). However, racial anthropology was continually reinforced by the commonsense perception that human racial diversity was an observable fact: 'Everybody can recognize without further ado who is a Mongol, who is a black person, who is an Indian or a white person. No one will confuse a Chinese, even a naked one, with a Papuan' (Wirth 1914: 37–8). Racial anthropologists did not agree as to how to define the German *Volk* in positive terms. But there was consensus that the term 'Aryan' was primarily a linguistic term, and should not be used to designate a racial identity (Wirth 1914: 33–4). This was the position of both linguists and racial anthropologists in the late nineteenth century, and this distinction ultimately provided a scholarly justification for the Nazi regime to exclude Jews from the German *Volk*, even if many Jews were by all other criteria – namely citizenship, cultural affiliation, mother tongue, consciousness of self – Germans.

There was near universal agreement that each *Volk* was made up of elements drawn from more than one race. Thus the German *Volk* did not have a single racial identity; it was *racially mixed*, and in racial terms overlapped with the membership of other *Völker*. This view

remained academic orthodoxy in the racial anthropology of the Third
Reich. By the 1930s, the German *Volk* was held to be made up of
approximately six races, namely the Nordic (*nordisch*), Mediterranean (*westisch*), Dinaric (*dinarisch*), Alpine (*ostisch*), East Baltic
(*ostbaltisch*) and Phalian (*fälisch*) races (see chapter 4). One branch
of racial anthropology saw the Nordic race as superior, and sought to
promote the Nordic element in modern European societies. Racial
anthropologists debated readings of the racial composition of the
German *Volk* and of individuals, in particular celebrated Germans in
the military, political, artistic or intellectual spheres. For example,
Friedrich Nietzsche was judged by Walter Rauschenberger to be a
Nordic-Dinaric-East Baltic composite, and his life and thought read
against the different traits of these races (1939a: 10). Ludwig van
Beethoven was primarily Phalian-Nordic-Mediterranean (1939b:
119); Schiller was Nordic-Dinaric, like many of the great minds of
humanity such as Plato, Dante and Goethe (1941).

This Nordic race was characterized by a long skull, blue eyes, blond
hair and a set of noble virtues and characteristics. One extreme view
saw the Nordic race as responsible for all major achievements of
humankind; other racial anthropologists saw this as exaggerated and
unscientific. Racial anthropologists saw Jews, Africans and Gypsies
(Roma and Sinti) as racially 'other', that is as racially foreign elements
which should not be allowed to mix with the 'blood' of Europeans, in
particular the German *Volk* (Arlt 1938: 46). While there was a
'German people' (*deutsches Volk*), there was generally held to be no
'German race' (*deutsche Rasse*). It was the *Volk* that had a historical
trajectory and unity, and this sense of mission and destiny could not
be straightforwardly mapped onto anthropological race.

One aspect of the history of the race question that has been
neglected is the question of how white Europeans themselves were
ranked racially, and who among them was superior racially (Young
1997). This was a serious intellectual and political question, and
racism was not merely directed at outsider groups such as Jews, but
in many instances took on a regional or class character. Racial
elitists thus often looked with displeasure on the exploitation of
racial ideas for crude mass-nationalist purposes. Racial anthropology
was in this sense hostile to nationalism, or at least provided no simple
script for nationalists to follow, since nationalism celebrated and
heightened what in its terms was a racially hybrid political form. As
Madison Grant emphasized:

> Modern anthropology has demonstrated that racial lines are not only
> absolutely independent of both national and linguistic groupings, but

that in many cases these racial lines cut through them at sharp angles and correspond closely with the divisions of social cleavage. The great lesson of the science of race is the immutability of somatological or bodily characters, with which is closely associated the immutability of psychical predispositions and impulses. (1916: xv–xvi)

The clearest expression of race boundaries were not the dividing lines between nations but those within them, those of class as well as more obvious racial boundaries. The only area of the world in which the factors of race, language and nationality persisted 'in combination' was Scandinavia (Grant 1916: 4).

The study of race took place as a cross-disciplinary enterprise both within the humanities and social sciences and between these and the natural and medical sciences. Racial anthropology, while it had pretensions to scientific status in the various meanings of that term, was built on, and interacted with, popular understandings and stereotypes. Thus even the most politically liberal lines of racial anthropology were unable to distance themselves from the notion that the 'Negro' was essentially inferior. This assumption was built into the foundations of that academic science from the very beginning.

As physical anthropology evolved in the early twentieth century, the emphasis on exact measurement of the human body, in particular the 'anthropometrics' associated with Rudolf Martin, was increasingly challenged by biological and genetic understandings of human physical variation (Gessler 2000: 29, 31–2). The use of 'race' in polemical history and sociology as an equivalent to *Volk* also suggested that the concept was problematic. In the 1920s and 1930s there was increasing uncertainty about the status of anthropological features such as hair colour and skull shape. Paradoxically, the rise of evolutionary biology and genetics, as well as new developments in psychology, offered 'race' a second chance at scientific status. The attempt was made to appropriate Mendelian genetics to salvage the concept of anthropological race.

Darwin, genetics and eugenics

By the close of the nineteenth century, biology stood at the beginning of the genetic revolution. The genetic model of human identity was one in which each individual acquired aspects of their make-up from the interaction of the inherited characteristics of both parents. The science of genetics was an attempt to understand the basic units of heredity, the laws applying to the combination and transmission of those units, and the extent to which aspects of the human physical, psychological and intellectual make-up were determined by genetic inheritance as opposed to environment, upbringing and culture. Each individual existed as a point of intersection where lines of inheritance which stretched back though boundless time interacted and could be transmitted further. The collective associated with this concept of human heredity (a 'population') was not clearly bounded, but rather displayed degrees of network density.

Charles Darwin's theories of evolution and natural selection had been enormously influential both in science and politics, but, until the genetic revolution, the mechanisms of transition in heredity remained ill-understood, as were the causes of change. Gregor Mendel's experiments on common pea plants, which became widely known in the early twentieth century, showed that the mixing of two distinct but pure ('homozygous') lines in respect of the gene for the trait for pea-colour (green versus yellow) did not lead to a merger or blending of inherited traits. Although the offspring in the first generation (f1) were heterozygous (i.e. they had inherited two different alleles), they were not a blend of the two, but were all yellow. However, in the next generation (f2), some peas reappeared as green, in ratio of one green to three yellow. A trait that seemed to have disappeared reappeared after missing a generation. This suggested that genetic inheritance involved discrete units, which interacted in terms of dominance and recession and were transmitted independently rather than blending.

The impact of August Weismann (1834–1914) in Germany and Europe was fundamental. Weismann drew a clear distinction between the so-called 'germ line' (*Keimplasma*) and the 'somatic line' (*Soma*). There was no way to show a link between the germ line ('the sex cells in an organism's ovaries or gonads') and all the other cells of the body. Changes to the body during an organism's lifetime could not be transmitted to its off-spring (Weismann 1885; Dennett 1996: 321–2). The implication was that fundamental improvement in the quality of a population was only possible through selection, and this moved eugenic measures to the centre of the political agenda (Weiss 1990: 13–14). Education, training and other environmental influences could only be effective if the appropriate genetic potential was present. A further element in the developing understanding of evolutionary change was Hugo de Vries's (1848–1935) theory of mutation. Processes of selection were understood to act on spontaneous genetic discontinuities, which could be studied experimentally. Subsequently, debate in relation to mutation concerned the nature of change: whether it was sudden and discontinuous (as Mendel's theory seemed to suggest) or produced out of large numbers of minute incre-

mental variations. The argument was made that the theory of mutations could not explain the development of new species (Schneider
1934). The reconciliation of Mendelian genetics with mutation theory
within a theory of evolutionary change is normally termed the
Modern or Neo-Darwinian Synthesis.

The effect of this was to marginalize so-called 'neo-
Lamarckianism', i.e. the belief that characteristics acquired by the
organism in the course of its lifetime, for example in reaction to the
environment, could be transmitted to its offspring. A whole range of
theories associated with Lamarck became suspect in terms of their scientific status. Vitalism saw life as driven by an autonomous 'life-force',
towards a perfect or harmonious final stage, and from this perspective
the theory of evolution was often seen as materialist or philosophi-
cally impoverished. The theory of 'orthogenesis' associated with
Lamarck held that the evolution of an organism, species or culture
was not primarily determined by external factors, but followed an
inner drive involving a series of evolutionary stages which were latent
in the initial stage. Change was understood as progress towards a
greater degree of perfection, an inner harmony or a higher consciousness. In twentieth-century Germany, the vitalist notion of 'entelechy'
(*Entelechie*), derived from Aristotle, was applied to biology by
the 'neovitalist' Hans Driesch (1867–1941). According to Driesch,
cells and organisms had an innate tendency towards wholeness
or harmonious form, an inner drive towards self-realization or self-
fulfilment, the product of a vital force controlling the development of
the organism. (Driesch, a pacifist, was forced to retire in 1935, but
vitalist thinking was frequently used to underpin fascist ideologies).

Darwin's theory was purged of its Lamarckian traits, and modern
Darwinist thought is more accurately referred to as 'neo-Darwinism'.
Environmental factors were fundamental to neo-Darwinism, but not
as the direct cause of changes to the germ line. Darwinism and neo-
Darwinism provided a framework and a new vocabulary within which
to understand the place of human beings within nature, and the forces
that act upon them. Nature was constantly in motion, and acting with
the inevitability of scientific law to root out the maladapted. One
direct application of this vision was in modern eugenics (*Eugenik,
Rassenhygiene, Rassenpflege, Fortpflanzungshygiene*).

Eugenics sought to use the insights of science to improve the
'breeding stock' of families, nations or humanity as a whole. The
'insane', the 'feeble-minded', those with genetic illnesses, the alcoholic, the criminal, the vagrant, as well as racially inferior elements,
might have five, six or seven children (often supported by the state
or charity), whereas the elite groups had one or two per family.

Women from elite families were marrying later and having no – or fewer – children. Measures advocated by eugenicists included sterilization and legal-medical controls on marriage and social engineering (tax structures etc.) which would encourage the superior elements to have more children. Eugenicists argued that social reform and improved education were of no use unless accompanied by measures to control the quality of the population, since social engineering alone could not improve society.

The British statistician Francis Galton (1822–1911) is generally seen as the founder of eugenics. In the German context, Darwin was understood as the fundamental thinker, in particular as interpreted by Ernst Haeckel, with Alfred Ploetz and Wilhelm Schallmayer formulating eugenics as a social and political programme. Galton's intellectual successor, Karl Pearson (1857–1936), approached human heredity through the statistics of 'biometrics'. Pearson was a critic of Mendel, and engaged in a polemic with William Bateson (1861–1926) over the status of statistical studies of the human body (Pearson 1903). From the point of view of Mendelian genetics, these measurements were largely meaningless; however, Mendelians were accused of simplifying the relationship of heredity to 'feeblemindedness' and intelligence (Spencer and Paul 1998). Pearson's 'law of ancestral heredity' was 'the very antithesis of pristine Mendelism' (Froggatt and Nevin 1971: 1). One German scholar who cited Galton frequently was the Catholic eugenicist Hermann Muckermann. Muckermann credited Galton with the key synthesis of evolution, heredity and selection as it applied to human culture (1932: 77–83, 1933: 7–9, 1934a, b) and even read Galton as sympathetic to a link between religion and eugenics (1934a).

Evolutionary theory was central to political-ideological developments in Germany, and to Nazism as an intellectual phenomenon. For Darwin seemed to offer a scientific framework for understanding the rise and fall of individuals, races and species, and hence salvation, from the doom to which the German *Volk*, like all great civilizations before it, seemed condemned, and which racial pessimists such as Gobineau foresaw. Darwin's theory captured the paradoxical position of human beings as animals subject to natural laws, and yet able to understand those laws and manipulate their response to them. Science could offer a path to the salvation of the *Volk* and the white races in general. The neo-Lamarckian notion of 'the inheritance of acquired characteristics' was rejected by academic and political orthodoxy in Nazi Germany.

One effect of this Darwinian shift in the understanding of the relationship between human beings and animals was to clarify the status of humankind (especially the so-called civilized peoples or *Kulturvölker*) as a domesticated species. Humanity had paradoxically been domesticated by itself, since humankind's socio-biological environment, and its mating practices, were regulated by culture and politics. The determination that humankind was part of nature and governed by natural laws was accompanied by the realization that humankind was, like domesticated animals, sheltered from the 'pure' operation of those laws. In Darwinian terms, in the case of domesticated animals, where particular variants were bred for, and others selected against, variation was not 'random', but the product of human intervention.

Domestication (*Domestikation* or *Haustierwerdung*) came to have three related meanings: the 'transformation of wild animals into domestic animals', 'the breeding of wild plants as useful plants [*Nutzpflanzen*]' and 'the transition of humans from the natural state to civilization' (Marle 1936: 256). Darwin's insight had begun with the observation of artificial selection, and this had led him to the theory of natural selection (von Frisch 1936: 350–1). The dramatic effects of the human breeding of animals and plants contributed to the discrediting of Lamarckianism, since no one had yet observed that environmental influences alone could lead to changes in inherited characteristics and to 'an improvement of the races' (*Verbesserung der Rassen*).

A further paradox was that the purpose of political intervention within self-domestication was to mimic the effects of true natural selection, understood as the 'survival of the fittest'. The objective scientific approach was here essential, as this required potentially harsh political and legal intervention. In this way, radical human intervention in the individual and cultural mating practices of human beings was justified as restoring a pre-civilization natural order, as revealed by science. This also involved political and ideological control of human sexuality, not just of women but also of men. For example, the sexual autonomy of males in the colonial situation was a threat to racial and eugenic health (Grosse 2000). Culture would have to mimic nature, and since in the domesticated species this did not happen naturally, it had to be imposed by a determined application of the will, expressed as an absolute political force. As Earnest A. Hooton, Professor of Physical Anthropology at Harvard University, declared: 'We need a biological new deal which will segregate and sterilize the antisocial and the mentally unfit. Intelligent artificial selection must replace natural selection' (1935: 31).

What kinds of policies were required to stem the tide of degeneration? At the intersection of racial anthropology and eugenics, there existed a range of views about the kinds of racial engineering that were most desirable. Alfred Ploetz, for example, while he shared the general view that the Nordic race represented the best of the white races, envisaged the overall engineering of the racial diversity of humankind on eugenic lines as involving a degree of racial hybridity. It would be a mistake to base a future ideal humanity and an ideal 'superman' (*Übermensch*) solely on the Nordic race, as the Nordic race also had some weakness. This ideal humanity would take on elements from other races. From the coloured races one might get adaptability to the tropics; from the Jews, strength of will and a strong sense of family (Ploetz 1927: 252).

This kind of eugenic view of the benefits of racial mixing, though it was grounded in the standard critique of modernity and did not presume racial equality within the human species, was highly suspect in the eyes of many racial anthropologists, and was particularly offensive to Nordicist ideologues. This explains the strong reaction to theorists who were perceived to favour racial mixing in the early months of Nazi rule. Many Nordicist ideologues, as it turned out wrongly, equated 'the Nordic idea' with Nazi ideology.

Under the impact of modern genetics, many scientists came to conceive of human identity primarily in terms of a genetically transmitted biological inheritance. As with the relationship of *Volk* to *Rasse*, the new paradigm raised the question of how the categories of race science stood up to the scrutiny of genetic science. Just as the concept of race threatened the intellectual integrity of the concept of *Volk*, so the rise of human genetics offered a serious intellectual challenge to traditional racial anthropology.

Like racial anthropology, eugenics was on one reading hostile or indifferent to nationalism (and even racism), and was far from consistently anti-Semitic. One could be an advocate of eugenics or 'race hygiene' without subscribing at all to the existence of anthropological races. Given this ambiguity, the tendency to translate *Rassenhygiene* as 'race hygiene' is potentially misleading. This term was used primarily to suggest a specifically German or Germanic approach to eugenics, but this did not imply a rejection of international standards in science. Although eugenic theorizing was not in practice absolutely distinct from racial anthropology, there was a widespread consensus that these were different theoretical frameworks. Eugenicists generally assumed the general superiority of the 'white race' over the 'yellow' or the 'black', while at the same time showing concern for the biological development of humankind as a whole (Goldstein 1913: 93–6). But there was scepticism about many of the specific claims of racial anthropology, e.g. the idealization of the long-skulled north European type (Goldstein 1913: 17).

Eugenicists were also ambivalent about modern warfare, since it killed off the youngest and fittest members of society before they could breed and protected the unfit (Nicolai 1917; von Frisch 1936: 359). Opposition to war in Europe was compatible with belief in the inevitable decline of inferior non-European races and the desirability of their eventual extinction. Alternatively, war could be presented as a process of selection, whereby healthy and dynamic populations triumphed over inferior ones, as an expression of the natural instinct for warfare, which was part of a natural biological selection process.

As the twentieth century progressed, many racial anthropologists were involved in a complex attempt to adapt their taxonomic work to the rapidly developing biological and genetic sciences, and this process continued within Nazi Germany. The implications of this were far-reaching. This became evident with the formulation of the distinction between the observed physical body of an individual, the 'phenotype' (*Erscheinungsbild* or *Phänotypus*), and the totality of that individual's inherited genetic make-up, the 'genotype' (the *Erbbild* or *Genotypus*), by Wilhelm Johannsen (1857–1927). In a so-called 'pure' population of genetically identical organisms, Johannsen had shown that artificial selection among beans could not create a new population with a higher average size. He concluded that the observed fluctuations were due to the environment, and coined the terms 'genotype' (the genetic constitution of the organism) and 'phenotype' (the product of the interaction between the organism and the environment) to express this (Johannsen 1909). In the case of a mixed population, selective breeding could however produce such an effect. It was thus both very important and extremely difficult to distinguish environmental factors from inherited variation in any mixed population.

If these advances in understanding heredity were accepted, then merely measuring and comparing human bodies was insufficient to ground a scientific understanding of race. A purely descriptive racial anthropology appeared out of step with advances in science, since one could not directly observe the distinction between phenotype and genotype. This also triggered a potentially radical redefinition of the concept of race. Racial identity was increasingly understood as a composite of inherited Mendelian characteristics. Only those features which were inherited in discrete Mendelian fashion could be considered as properly racial. But since such inheritance involved the independent transmission of racial characteristics (the shuffling of the genetic deck of cards), no single modern individual could be said to be the member of a race, where race was understood as a collective or grouping of individuals. The genotype of the individual was not treated in an integrated fashion, as was the case with Galton's concept (Mai 1997: 29–30). The observed phenotypical similarities and differences in populations as they varied over time and space did not mark the boundaries between races, but rather between areas where the original congruence of genotype and phenotype was partially preserved (the Nordic race in Scandinavia) and areas of greater mixing. A race was a set of hereditary features, and consequently did not strictly have any social or political identity. It was not possible to create new races out of the mixing of pre-existing racial elements. Thus the idea that the German *Volk* could interact dialectically with its component racial elements and evolve into a new German race was academic heresy. Indeed, the charge that Nazism promoted the idea of a German race was later identified by the Nazi ideologue Bolko Freiherr von Richthofen with Soviet propaganda (1942: 324).

Conclusion

The concept of race as defined within racial anthropology was profoundly decentring for the nationalist vision of a united *Volk*. However, the challenge to racial anthropology from the developing science of genetics was clear, and the extent to which racial anthropologists accepted the full logic of this challenge varied considerably. But this new paradigm also offered an opportunity for racial anthropology to escape the trap of data-oriented positivism. Mendelian genetics suggested that an inventory of discrete features was shuffled in hereditary transmission, and that these features, though they were subject to random mutation, would not vary much over time. The effects of natural selection would impact only on the distribution of these features within a particular population. But the Darwinian view of the natural world was also one of constant dynamism and change, and this seemed to stand in stark contradiction to the idea of races as fixed in nature in prehistoric time. Those racial anthropologists who opposed Mendelian genetics and stressed the dynamic nature of race often paid more attention to environmental factors, and this opened up their work to the charge of neo-Lamarckianism, which was associated with Marxist materialism and Soviet genetics.

The interaction and partial synthesis between genetics, eugenics and racial anthropology strengthened the case for a eugenic understanding of social and political problems, as well as for a rejection of reforms based purely on changes in socialization and education. For if the key elements of the individual were laid down at the moment of conception, it was pointless to rely on social engineering alone to deal with the crisis facing the *Volk*. Education and reform could be understood as bringing the best out of the potential that existed (Lenz 1925), but the crucial determinants of an individual's 'quality' were genetic and racial, not social and environmental.

As a result of the interaction between these strands, a complex set of meanings had become attached to the term 'race'. The ambiguity inherent in the term race proved politically and rhetorically useful, and the flexibility of the concept gave it 'strong integrative power' across a wide range of research agendas (Schmuhl 2003a: 26–7). But it also masked real intellectual tensions, in particular in relation to the anthropological concept of race. The physical stereotypes of the 'Jew' and the 'Nordic' in popular imaginary could not be sustained by science, though they might exist in parallel with it. The Nordic race was sometimes imagined as a living reality with actual 'members'. But in strict scientific terms there was no contemporary reality to races. They were not reproductive or biological communities. Peoples or *Völker* could be understood as biological collectives, in that they represented an actual lived reality existing through social networks, kinship ties, as well as a shared language and culture. It was *Völker* rather than races that were 'self-conscious' or 'self-aware' (Wirth 1914: 71; Ruttke 1939: 9). While it was possible to understand a *Volk* as a *Vitalrasse*, these two terms belonged to different intellectual traditions, and many opposed any conflation of the two (Rittershaus 1936: 184).

One branch of racial thinking accepted the basic lessons of the new sciences of race and genetics, and rejected the notion that the engineering of the physical, social and cultural environment, for example through education, could eradicate inherited, biological ('natural') inequalities. These inequalities existed between individuals, as well as between human races, and were part of the natural ordering of the human species. Only a political programme of action based on the appreciation of this fundamental scientific truth, and led by a leadership with the will to carry through that programme to its logical conclusion, could save Germany and the German *Volk* from destruction.

There was a strong ideological rationale for the priority of modern science over all other ideological considerations. The geneticist Erwin Baur (1922: 12) had argued that there were no grounds for despair, in that it was not a general law of nature that all civilized peoples

(*Kulturvölker*) were destined to decline and disappear, and that the West would repeat the fate of Greece and Rome. But decisive action had to be taken if this fate was to be avoided. The need to overcome this pessimistic model of the life-cycle of advanced peoples led to an emphasis on natural science. For science and science alone, in its neo-Darwinian formulation, could show why this pessimism was unfounded.

We need to look closely at the tensions between the three basic trends discussed in this chapter, as they were involved in a complex and evolving set of relationships during the Nazi period. The category of *Volk*, with its biblical roots, had made a successful transition from pre-modernity to modernity, but when viewed from the point of view of race, the unity of the *Volk* was shown to be illusory. There was no one-to-one correspondence between *Volk* and *Rasse*. *Volk* was however central to the political rhetoric of Nazism, much more so than any racial category. Further, the categories of racial anthropology were themselves intellectually vulnerable to the much more sophisticated understanding of heredity offered by genetics.

It will be argued that there was a dynamic quality to the interaction between ideology and science of race in the Third Reich that led to the gradual neutralization or marginalization of trends that were openly anti-scientific or of unclear scientific status. In characterizing Nazi ideology, it is not enough to take a static view and point to the writings of key individuals or particular policies; we must look for an underlying process or dialectic. Racial anthropology was politically and ideologically problematic on a number of levels. It ultimately failed to offer a convincing definition of the nature of the German *Volk*, and there was increasing pressure for it to adopt a lower public profile. Having served a useful purpose in justifying the exclusion of Jews, Blacks and Roma and Sinti from the body of the *Volk*, and by clarifying that not all native speakers of German were 'true' Germans, racial anthropologists were relegated to a secondary role, useful primarily for the production of certificates of racial identity.

4

Hans Günther and Racial Anthropology

Introduction

Racial anthropology offered a range of methodologies and approaches. For example, the 'anthropometric' method involved a positivistic and inductive approach to physical and medical anthropology. The body was studied standing, at rest, and treated as a static, symmetrical object, with its bodily measurements understood relationally. This approach was associated with Rudolf Martin (1914). By contrast, the 'race psychologist' Ludwig Ferdinand Clauss (1892–1974) was concerned with the human body as a dynamic object, with a relationship to landscape. For Clauss, 'race' was studied in the expressivity of the human body through an act of intuition or insight on the part of the investigator. Most racial anthropologists operated somewhere between these two methodological extremes. This was true of Hans F. K. Günther (1891–1968), though he was widely regarded by other racial anthropologists (particularly those with medical or natural scientific backgrounds) as primarily a successful and well-connected popular author. Other racial anthropologists were not generally ideologically opposed to his racial anthropology; but they frequently saw themselves as offering an intellectually more rigorous alternative.

In Günther's presentation, each race has a set of bodily characteristics, combined with a set of psychological or mental attributes (*seelische Eigenschaften*). There is at least a partial link between these two dimensions, that is the descriptive language as applied to the body is to an extent a metaphorical index of the racial psychology. The male is generally seen as the anthropological norm. Günther's understanding of race occupies a middle ground between an aesthetics or stylistics, in which the body is a metaphor for temperament and value, and a science of anthropology, in which there is an arbitrary link between body and mind and the body is seen as a set of comparative measurements. This also placed Günther between a discourse of popular racial and cultural stereotypes and a would-be science of human diversity, which rejected this popular or folk image of human races.

According to Günther, six basic races made up the German *Volk*: the Nordic (*nordisch*), the Mediterranean (*westisch*), the Dinaric (*dinarisch*), the Alpine (*ostisch*), the East Baltic (*ostbaltisch)* and the Phalian (*fälisch*). The existence of a Sudetan (*sudetisch*) race had also been proposed, but Günther gave few details, beyond a brief sketch of the bodily type. In addition, the German-speaking population had undergone influence from non-European races, such as the Negro (*negerisch*) race (in particular via southern Europe), the Mongolian (*innerasiatisch*) race, the Near Eastern (*vorderasiatisch*) race, which is related to the Dinaric race, and the Oriental (*orientalisch*) race.

Günther's highly influential model is introduced below. This account follows Günther's concise introduction to the racial anthropology of the German people (in the 1933 edition), but not all details in his descriptions are given. It should be borne in mind that the taxonomy below represents the tip of a massive scholarly iceberg, and every racial term and every characteristic attributed had a complex history of scholarly and popular discussion.

The Nordic (*nordisch*) race

The Nordic type is tall, slender but strong, long-skulled, thin-faced, with the back of head prominent in relation to the neck, has a narrow, pronounced (*hochgebaut*) nose and narrow jaw with a strong chin (figure 1). The average height of the man is 1.74 meters; the cephalic index is around 75, facial index over 90. The features are unusually bold and forceful, at least in the case of the males; in women the features are less pronounced. The skin is a light rosy colour, as the blood shimmers beneath it, and in the young and females up to middle age it is often like 'milk and blood'. The hair is straight or wavy, in some children curly; the hair colour is blond, which can range from the common reddish undertone through golden blond to dark blond. Blond hair also often gets darker with age. The eyes are blue, blue-grey or grey; often they have a luminous quality. In certain states of

Figure 1   Nordic type (Günther 1933: 23)

excitement, the Nordic has a terrifying gaze, as had been noted by the Romans in relation to the mainly Nordic Germanic tribes. In terms of sport and physique, Nordic types are suited to middle-distance running and to the throwing and jumping disciplines.

The psychological make-up can be summed up in terms of ideals such as bravery, single-mindedness, determination, nobility, heroism; the Nordic displays a clear-minded strength of will, discriminating powers of judgement matched by a keen awareness of the real, a pre-disposition to a chivalrous sense of justice. In a few cases these traits can rise to the heights of visionary leadership of a state or creativity in technology, science or artistic expression. A relatively high pro-portion of the outstanding individuals produced in the West have Nordic or predominantly Nordic racial traits, and comparatively few of the important and successful individuals have been without any noticeable Nordic influence. In dealings with others, the Nordic is restrained in word and action and moderate in the expression of feelings, even sometimes cool, and perceived by other non-Nordic people as cold and stiff and less than personable. Nordic people often lack the inclination to penetrate the inner life of foreign races.

Though Nordic people never entirely lose their chivalrous approach, they can act with toughness or even ruthlessness towards their human surroundings. Other characteristics include a mischievous gift for storytelling; an inclination towards technology and the natural sciences rather than the humanities; an understated self-confidence, a sense of competition and an effusive power of imagination, which is seldom revealed to outsiders and which, after taking flight, nonetheless returns to reality. This Nordic boldness can in some cases lead to irresponsibility and extravagance; Nordic coolness can become cold calculation.

The leading statesmen of Europe have all been predominantly Nordic, and this drive to leadership has seen many such figures rise up through society. This social rise is often at the price of having small families, and this provides a clue to the gradual decline of the Nordic race. The Nordic person reaches maturity late, and thus enjoys a longer, more carefree youth, and this goes with an enjoyment of exercise, sport and hiking. A very lively feel for nature might also play a role there. Nordic types are also found in proportionally large numbers in open-air professions. The Nordic person has relatively high standards in bodily hygiene, but a characteristic disposition in favour of a well-groomed appearance is usually found only in the middle and upper strata of the people.

The Mediterranean (*westisch, mediterran, mittelländisch*) race

The Mediterranean is generally small in stature, not thick-set but slender. The men are on average 1.6 meters, and the physique overall is a smaller version of the Nordic, although the height of the legs is somewhat more pronounced. Even the broad hips of the women do little to diminish the impression of a slender form. The head shape is the same as the Nordic race, although the brow is somewhat lower, and more rounded at the sides and the back, that is more domed than sloping back. The nose is relatively short and seldom as sharply defined as in the case of the Nordic race, mostly straight or slightly

Figure 2   Mediterranean, from South France (Günther 1933: 26)

curving outwards, in rare cases inwards. The chin is less definite and more rounded (figure 2).

The facial features are in general softer, or, one might say, more feminine than the Nordic race, and the fleshy parts of the body also play a part in this. The skin is brownish, and has a warm-smooth appearance; rosy cheeks are seldom seen, and the red of the lips shades off into a bluish tinge. The hair is sometimes straight and shiny, more often curly; the individual hair is thin and soft. It is brown, black-brown or black in colour. The eyebrows are thicker than is the case with the Nordic race, the eyelashes seem to be longer. The beard is brown or black; beard growth is quite thick. The eyes are brown to black-brown, with a warm hue. Mediterranean individuals and also

Nordic-Mediterranean individuals often display a particular gift for fencing.

The Mediterranean race is hardly represented in the German population by pure racial types, and thus their psychological make-up does not need close attention. It is a lively and passionate race, easily aroused to anger and quick to be reconciled, open and receptive to external impressions, with hearty but at the same time tense and inquisitive relations with others, elegant in appearance and in language, eloquent and inclined to crafty calculation. The Mediterranean likes to enjoy life and work as little as possible, and has a strong sense of personal honour in relation to reputation in the eyes of others. Wit and verbal skill open up particularly in relation to sexuality. There is an inclination towards cruelty, the mistreatment of animals and sadism among predominantly Mediterranean populations.

The Mediterranean person displays a lively love of children, but in the running of states reveals the lack of a strong sense of order and careful planning, as well as a fickle temperament. There are higher levels of criminality and murder in regions with predominantly Mediterranean populations, in particular in Sicily and Sardinia, but also in parts of Germany such as the Pfalz, the Mosel region, the Rheingau.

The Dinaric (*dinarisch*) race

The Dinaric type (figure 3) is generally tall, long-boned and thin without being frail (*derb-schlank*). The arms are relatively short compared to the Nordic and the Mediterranean, the limbs less finely shaped, the neck slightly thicker or shorter. The form of the head is round but combined with a narrow face (cephalic index of around 85–7). The length of the head exceeds that of the width by only a small margin, as the back of the head barely protrudes beyond the neck, and in most cases the head appears chopped off (*abgehackt*) at the back. The narrowness of the face is determined by the relatively long nose, and the high, coarse chin; the forehead is in general broader than the Nordic or the Mediterranean. The nose is fleshy at the tip; the lips are fuller, or at least broader than with the Nordic race. Dinaric individuals often have fairly large, fleshy ears. The skin is brownish; the hair mostly curly, rarely straight. Individual hairs are thin and fairly soft, but hair on the head, as a beard and on the body is fairly strong. Beard hair is brown to black. The eyes are brownish black.

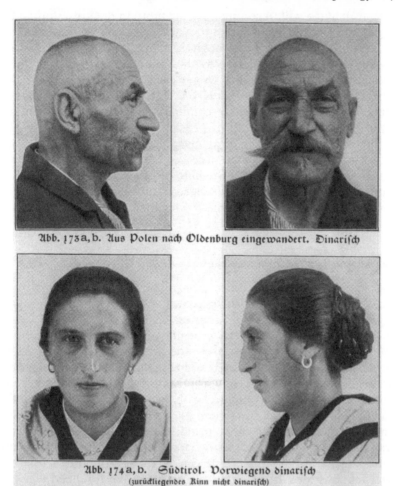

Abb. 173a,b. Aus Polen nach Oldenburg eingewandert. Dinarisch

Abb. 174a,b. Südtirol. Vorwiegend dinarisch
(zurückliegendes Kinn nicht dinarisch)

Figure 3   Dinaric and predominantly Dinaric types (Günther [1922] 1936: 101)

In character the Dinaric race is epitomized by the Alpine freedom fighter, as seen in those involved in the struggle against Napoleon or in the mountain warriors of southern and southeastern Europe. The Dinaric individual has raw strength and is of upright character, has a strong sense of honour, shows a great love of native region and land-scape (*Heimatliebe*) and has a lively connection with nature, bringing a sense of order to home and landscape. However, the Dinaric indi-vidual, though physically courageous, lacks strong forward-looking dynamism and a will to conquer. Living more in the present than the Nordic, the Dinaric is not suited to planning long-term undertakings. A certain conviviality and rough joviality goes together with a tendency to physical violence, as the crime statistics for southeast Germany suggest. The ability to get carried away, to become passionate, violent or vehement is also connected with a disposition to acting. Showing great insight into human character, the Dinaric is also inclined to exhibit a degree of peasant cunning. The Dinaric also exhibits ability for music, in particular song, and Dinaric-Nordic individuals are often the greatest musical talents. The Dinaric race is related to the Near Eastern race, in that they both descend from the same original race, and have diverged in different directions from it by a process of natural selection.

The Alpine (*ostisch, alpin*) race

The Alpine type is short, thick, heavy-set and, even though of average height, gives quite a different impression from the slender form of the Mediterranean. The average height of the male is around 1.63 meters; the entire body expresses stockiness, with short legs, heavy calves, short, wide feet, broad, round hands, which often appear padded, and short fingers. However, the pelvis of the women seems relatively narrow when compared with the other European races. The head is wide and round, and sits on a short, thick-set neck, with a tendency to a bull-neck. The cephalic index is on average around 88, the facial index under 83. The cephalic index is high because of the width of the head, and the Alpine type can be called 'round-headed'. The facial features look blunt, due to a steeply rising forehead which is curved back and to the sides; the root of the nose lies flat. The nose is short, low-built, with a blunt tip above the lip; the chin lacks prominence and is widely rounded. The soft parts of the body give a stout impression due to stores of fat and perhaps a thicker skin. The skin is yellow-brown and appears dull. The hair colour is brown to black; beard and body hair are apparently thinner than in the Nordic, Mediterranean and Dinaric races. The eye colour ranges from brown to blackish brown, without the warm hue of the Mediterranean.

A painter who wishes to portray a complacent, respectable, conventional type, perhaps a small businessman or trader, would tend to give the figures the rotund, heavy-set characteristics of the Alpine race. Alpine individuals can be sullen and mistrustful in dealings with outsiders. They are patient, practically minded, and often achieve a position of respect and standing, in particular in those areas where this practical sense can be applied, rather than where boldness or decisive actions are required. The Alpine type is a person of moderation, who wishes to combine pleasure with utility, and who seeks to avoid direct competition. In the contemporary world they are sympathetic to the idea of equality and democracy, and can be resentful and jealous of the outstanding.

The Alpine type is oriented towards the familiar and the near, and rejects what is distant, 'pushy', disliking frivolity and waste. In religious life they display an intimate, warm and contemplative piety, with a tendency to self-righteousness. Although not naturally inclined to display martial qualities, the Alpine can be as effective in defence as the Nordic and the Dinaric are in attack. They are quiet, malleable underlings. Within a given people, the Alpine type is represented at all social levels, but less so as we go up the social scale. A proportion, though, can work their way up in society by hard work, acquisitiveness, frugality and moderation, through their personal warmth and their practical ability to understand other people.

The East Baltic (*ostbaltisch*) race

Heavy-set like the Alpine race, the East Baltic individual is on average somewhat taller, noticeably thick-boned, and broad at the shoulders (figure 4). The head is likewise broad and thick-boned. The area of the face looks particularly solidly built when compared with the skull covering the brain. One factor in this is the broad, stubby, solidly built and bony lower jaw. The cephalic index is somewhat lower than in the case of the Alpine race; heads of the two races with apparently the same width differ in that the East Baltic race has a domed back of the head than with the Alpine race. The facial features appear blunt; the root of the nose is less prominent than with the Alpine race. The soft parts have a lower degree of fatty deposits than the Alpine race, and thus do not conceal the large boned structure of the face. The skin is light, but without a rose tint; it generally has a grey undertone. The beard hair is thin with hair that can grow long and stiff. The hair colour is light, but tends more to the ash-blond rather than gold-blond. In contrast to the golden or reddish tinge in the hair of the Nordic, the East Baltic has an underlying grey colour. The eye colour is grey, grey-blue, whitish-blue or blue, but rarely true blue, generally tending to the grey or the whitish-blue.

Abb. 204 a, b. Schweden. Oftbaltifch

Abb. 205. Danzig. Schichau, 1814—1890, Be-
gründer der Werft. Oftbaltifch-nordifch

Abb. 206. Pommern. Oftbaltifch mit nor-
difchem Einfchlag

Abb. 207 a, b. Finnland. Vorwiegend oftbaltifch

Figure 4   East Baltic and predominantly East Baltic types (Günther [1922]
1936: 136)

The strong physique of the East Baltic race, combined with their tough and doggedly determined character, makes the East Baltics excellent long-distance and endurance runners. Artists who seek to depict deceitful, vengeful, servile or grim figures often reproduce the bodily characteristics of the East Baltic race, likewise in the representation of gloomy or rapacious, hate-filled people, or those in a state of unbridled excitation. East Baltic individuals appear to strangers to be withdrawn, brooding, ponderous, mistrustful or shifty, apparently content with little, and also a dully or grimly determined worker. But on closer inspection the East Baltic type exhibits more complicated traits. They can become quite talkative in the presence of intimates, and cannot quite conceal a never-to-be-alleviated discontent, an imagination marked by a boundlessly wandering, soaring fantasy, turning the conversation towards wild ideas and plans, which, given the East Baltic's poor grasp of practical reality and the inability to see things to completion, are never realized.

In spite of all his talk of plans, the East Baltic is no friend of innovation, and lets everything continue in the old way, leaving things 'in God's hands', falling victim again and again to a gloomy belief in fate. However, the East Baltic can put up with a great deal of deprivation, oppression and pain. The East Baltic displays a mass mentality and can be easily led, and, given that they generally have a lively sense of patriotism, can be a willing follower under the right leadership. This can lead to a dependence on the leader that sometimes borders on servility. With family and friends the East Baltic is helpful and hospitable, often accommodating in the extreme, and tender towards close family. In dealings with outsiders the East Baltic inclines towards dishonesty and on occasion also to calculating vengefulness. A tendency to brutality and underhandedness is unmistakable, and this most likely explains the high levels of criminality in East Prussia, Posen and Silesia, especially in regard to crimes involving grievous bodily injuries and serious robberies.

One striking contrast with other European races is the rapidity of the East Baltic's mood swings, so that they can move rapidly from violent anger against someone to tearful self-indulgent remorse, from being downcast to wild exuberance, from dull indifference to fanaticism, from humility to arrogant superiority, from weeks of drudgery and frugal penny-pinching to carefree extravagance, which can end in mindless vandalism. Nihilism is an East Baltic state of mind. The East Baltic has a good understanding of human nature and can portray others in a forceful way, even though these portrayals are often somewhat incoherent and nebulous; their narratives have a tendency toward a grimly hopeless mood. We often find individuals with a gift for acting or music, combined with the tendency to the ethereal and the nebulous. Bodily cleanliness and cleanliness in the dwelling are in general somewhat lacking.

The Phalian (*fälisch, dalisch*) race

The Phalian is tall in stature, on average taller than the Nordic, at least in the case of the male; not slender, but solidly or squarely built, a bulky, burly figure. This bulkiness is reflected in different facets of the body, in the form of the head and the stocky neck, in the substantial width of the shoulders and, even in the case of the men, of the hips and the thick joints. The Phalian race is broad in the face and has a long to medium skull shape (figure 5). The Phalian head, as is the case with the Nordic and the Mediterranean, is extended well out over the neck, but in general in a more angular, heavier form. The facial features differ from the Nordic or the Dinaric races in having a lower forehead, which rises more steeply than the Nordic forehead. The lower jaw appears thick and heavy, in part due to the emphatic angle of the jaw.

The fleshy body parts underlie the impression of stockiness, with a well-defined philtrum, even in early youth, a crease from the corner of the mouth to the chin and a rather wide mouth, with thin, compressed-looking lips. The horizontal is emphasized by the ridge of the upper eye sockets, the rather wide, hard-looking opening of the mouth and the emphatic, often prominent lower jaw. The skin is light rosy, in the face tending to the light reddish, though without the distinct red cheeks of the Nordic race. The skin of the whole body looks thicker and coarser than in the case of the Nordic and the Mediterranean. The hair is coarser than with the narrow-faced European races, apparently rarely straight, frequently more wavy or curly than is the case with the Nordic race. The hair on the head is very thick and apparently very robust, even in old age. Its colour is similar to the Nordic race, but perhaps inclined more to reddish. The eye colour is light, perhaps tending to the grey or the blue.

The Phalian race is mixed throughout the populations of central and western Europe, but rarely to the extent that pure or predominantly Phalian types can be discerned or are able to influence the unconscious racial awareness of painters and sculptors. None the less where an artist wishes to depict someone whose bodily features suggest a certain solid strength of spirit or a defiant steadfastness

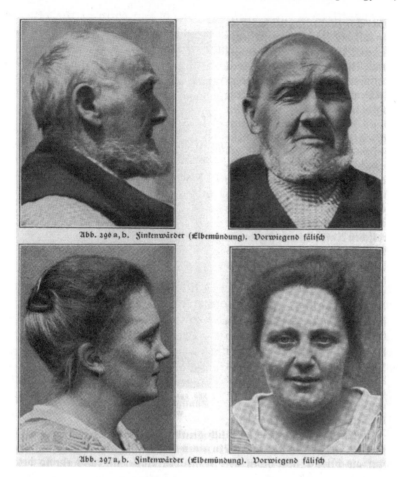

Abb. 296 a, b. Finkenwärder (Elbemündung). Vorwiegend fälisch

Abb. 297 a, b. Finkenwärder (Elbemündung). Vorwiegend fälisch

Figure 5   Predominantly Phalian types (Günther [1922] 1936: 148)

or honest reliability, then they will also give the figure Phalian characteristics.

The Phalian is as heavy and ponderous psychologically as physically. They can be characterized as steadfast, resolute in carrying out calmly considered decisions, with a drive to conscientiousness and probity, indeed a certain need to show themselves to be loyal. The worthy reliability of many Phalian individuals radiates a really rather comforting feeling, in particular given that, for all their gruffness and a less than engaging self-contained character, they have a quality of warm-heartedness and sensitivity, which also suffuses the religious life of Phalian people. A tendency to brood and to take life very seriously (never or seldom expressed) is also characteristic of the Phalian. In contrast to the pioneering, driving determination of the Nordic, the Phalian is more dogged and persevering, and is capable of iron-willed resistance, which can also develop into stubbornheadedness. Phalian influence can be seen in the portraits of many important figures, and this speaks to the influence of the Phalian race in the life of the *Volk*. For Lenz, the combination of Nordic daring and Phalian forcefulness has shaped men such as Bismarck and Hindenburg. One can also discern a Phalian racial influence in Martin Luther.

The Jews

According to Günther, there was no Jewish or Semitic race, in the same way that there was no German race; Jews, like Germans, varied as to their racial make-up. The southern Jews or Sephardim, about one-tenth of the Jewish people, were a mixture of Oriental, Near Eastern, Mediterranean, Hamitic (*hamitisch*), Nordic, Negro, in which the Oriental race was the predominant influence; the eastern European Jews (*Ostjuden*) were made up of Near Eastern, Oriental, East Baltic, Mongolian, Nordic, Hamitic, Negro elements, with the Near Eastern race as the dominant factor. The Near Eastern race was related to the Dinaric race, that is they both arose from the same root race (*Stammrasse*), and developed by means of selection in different directions.

For Günther, the racial quality of the Jewish people as a whole was primarily determined by the Near Eastern race, in the same way that the German *Volk* was essentially determined by the Nordic race. The Jewish question was not a religious one, nor primarily an economic one, although the main representatives of hegemonic international money-lending capital were Jews. The Jews were on average better off than their fellow citizens, but the Jewish question was not the same as the question of capitalism. What was at issue was the psychological or mental influence that this financial dominance had allowed the Jews, who were predominantly of non-European racial origin, to obtain within Europe. This was the 'Jewish question', and it was an ethnological and race-anthropological one (1933: 57).

Günther devoted a substantial appendix of his *Rassenkunde des deutschen Volkes* ([1922] 1926: 419–91) to the Jews. This was subsequently published as a separate work (Günther 1930), as well as providing the basis of a section of the anti-Semitic *Handbuch der Judenfrage* (Fritsch 1933: 18ff.). Günther estimated that there were approximately 620,000 registered Jews in Germany, and at least the same number again of unregistered German citizens of Jewish blood. In addition, there were a certain number of eastern European Jews, often in transit to Britain or America ([1922] 1926: 419).

The number of Jewish-German *Mischlinge* was impossible to estimate, but it was likely that the number was greater in the ranks of the aristocracy. The Jews were an exceptional case. They maintained their identity as a people in spite of the fact that they were spread over the entire globe and lacked a homeland and a state. They were not united by a common spoken language, as was the case with the Gypsies ([1922] 1926: 422); nor were they united by a religious faith, and the 'Mosaic core' was gradually shrinking under the impact of western freedoms. What Jews had in common was a consciousness of shared blood, and this was expressed in a highly developed sense of separate identity. This had only been slightly loosened in the course of the nineteenth century. The idea that there existed a 'Jewish race' was incorrect, but not necessarily harmful in a non-scientific context. As a particular fusion of races with a strong tradition of intermarriage, it had taken on a certain racial unity, and could be called a secondary racial grouping ('eine Einheit zweiter Ordnung', [1922] 1926: 422).

That the Jewish people was not a race was evident from the range of racial types, in addition to cases of conversion. In racial type, the Jews overlapped to a greater extent with southern Europeans, and in particular with the Greeks. Attempts had been made by Francis Galton (1822–1911) and Joseph Jacobs (1854–1916) to create a composite portrait of what was distinctive about the Jewish type. (On Jacobs, see Efron 1994: 58–90). Günther quoted at length from the *Jewish Encyclopaedia*'s description of these studies, including a composite analysis of the ten portraits of schoolboys ([1922] 1926: 423–6), but his conclusion was that this composite portrait was not very informative, and instead he offered a racial description of his own, drawing nonetheless on Jewish sources ([1922] 1926: 426–30). Below is a summary of Günther's discussion.

In terms of stature, the Jews are short, on average 1.63 meters, and even shorter in Poland. Jews mature physically relatively early, especially when compared with the northern European races. There is an unusually great disparity between the male and the female in terms of weight; the female is often especially fat, though Jews as a whole are heavy-set. Many are short-legged. Other characteristics include narrow-chestedness, rather short legs minimal calves, often crooked legs and flat feet. Most Jews are round-skulled, which is itself an indication that the Jews are not of original 'Semitic' blood, i.e. of the Oriental race. Bedouin Arabs are long-skulled. Ripley has observed that Jews have relatively spaced-out teeth. One could observe that Jews have strangely recessive chins.

The 'Jewish nose', i.e. the hooked nose, is rarer among the Jews than is generally assumed; it often is not so much the shape as the fleshy quality of the nostrils that is a Jewish trait (figure 6). Jacobs has argued that the characteristic Jewish nose viewed from the side resembled a 6. The lips are thicker than with the European races, with the lower lip often prominent. The eyelids are often heavy or thick; often the ears stick out, a trait that is particularly common among Jewish children. The ears are often located higher on the head than with other races; in Austria these are called 'Moritz-ears'. Jews, in particular the females, have a substantial layering of fat on the neck. The skin is generally darker than with peoples of predominantly northern race; often Jews and mixed-race individuals with Jewish blood have dull-yellowish skin. The skin is usually characterized as sweet-smelling. The body hair is often thick, as is the beard; often men have noticeable blue-black stubble which points to particularly thick, dark beard growth. One might find greater Negroid (tight-curled) beard growth if fashion were not against mutton-chop whiskers. Eyebrows are often thick and grow together above the bridge of the nose. An American survey has shown that 67 per cent of Jews have straight hair, 20 per cent wavy, 6 per cent curly and 1 per cent frizzy hair. However, it is likely that among those with straight hair, many have tough, stiff hair. In the central European environment, Jews with Negroid, very curly hair-weave are quite noticeable, and even blond Jews or Jewesses have tightly curled hair. Anthropologically this is most interesting, as it shows a mixing of Nordic with Negro blood.

The hair is mainly dark, either brown or black. There are a remarkable number of red-headed Jews, and blond hair is so well represented among the Jews that in some areas of Europe they are blonder than the non-Jews. According to the anthropological survey of the population of Germany undertaken by Rudolf Virchow (1821–1902), among German schoolchildren 31.8 per cent could be labelled blond, 14.5 per cent brown; among Jewish children 11 per cent are blond and 42 per cent brown-haired. The blondness among Jewish children is more often the East Baltic rather than the Nordic blondness. Mixed or intermediate forms are more common among the Germans than the Jews. Günther quotes the anthropologist Johannes Ranke (1836–1916) as follows: 'The purer the race, the lower the number of mixed forms. In this respect it is certainly an important fact that we meet among the Jews the lowest number of mixed-raced individuals.

Figure 6   Jewish porter from Kurdistan (Clauss 1939: 152)

From this we can recognize quite clearly the decisive racial separation of the Jews from the Germanics among whom they live.'

Dark eyes predominate but there are common cases of light-coloured eyes, due to East Baltic or Nordic influence. The dark-eyed

Jews are often characterized by their strangely shining, sometimes moistly shining, eyes. The expression of the eyes has a somewhat unsteady quality. The body language of the Jews is hard to describe, perhaps easier to imitate. The head movements sometimes have a rocking motion, the movements of the whole body are often soft, so that Jews often appears to themselves and to non-Jews as unsoldierly. The Jewish gait is often indicative of flat-footedness; the feet are often barely pointed outwards, indeed often point inwards (This trait is also found among people with Negro blood; is its presence among Jews related to a Negro racial influence?). Jewish body language is often perceived by non-Jews in Europe as having something of the Oriental. The influence of the European style is however often so strong that many Jews can now barely be distinguished from non-Jews, but in many cases there is something forced, self-conscious in their manner. The Jews have preserved their own folk-character best in eastern Europe.

The phenomenon of 'Mauscheln' [a stereotype of Jewish speech, used in stage caricatures of Jewish characters] must be a racially influenced trait, whereby Jews lend their own stress and intonation to different languages. This is not only seen among German-speaking Jews, but among Jews of all nations. One can explain this as an attempt by Jews to give a racially foreign (*artfremd*) language at least their own native (*arteigen*) quality. Among many western European Jews this phenomenon is hardly present and has even disappeared in some cases.

According to the physiologist Robert Stigler (1878–1968), there is a blurring of the distinction between the sexes with regard to secondary sexual characteristics, both psychological and physical (*sexuelle Applanation*). There are relatively frequent cases of women with broad shoulders and narrow hips, and of men with wide hips and narrow shoulders. It has been pointed out that Jewish women showed high degrees of 'hirsutism', combined with disruption of menstruation and a funnel-shaped pelvis. The psychiatrist Alexander Pilcz (1871–1954) confirmed that in his experience homosexuality was relatively common among Jews. Among Jewish women there is high frequency of unfeminine psychological characteristics, with a loss of passivity, which means that normal psychological inhibitions, such as in relation to appearing in public, are set aside. This explains the large number of women in Jewish public life, and the general disregard of, and loss of the normal instinctive sense for, the traditional social and vocational division between the sexes.

Among Jewish men there is often an inability to recognize the blurring of this psychological boundary between the sexes, whereas among normal men this is present, even in cases of much lower intelligence. Indeed it is often unfeminine women who were regarded among Jews as particularly desirable. This seems to be the transition point to the infantilism so common among Jews. There is frequently strong support among the Jewish intelligentsia for feminist causes. A highly strung sense of existential despair among Jewish men can be contrasted with the unfeminine qualities and unrestrained ambition for personal status and success in public life among Jewish women. This is apparently the result of a pervasive inhibition of instinctive, unconscious processes in the cerebral cortex and the sub-cortical centres through purely conscious processes.

Jewish emancipation has led to increased rates of suicide, paralysis, alcoholism, syphilis, judicial punishments, moral delinquency, mixed marriages and mortality. The suicide rate has risen particularly dramatically in Germany, whereas it is remarkably low among the Orthodox Jews of eastern Europe. It should be noted in addition that there are relatively large numbers of the blind and the deaf-and-dumb among the Jews. Jews are often lispers, and this might be a racially determined characteristic. In terms of criminality, Jews are associated with economic crimes and crimes of financial corruption rather than with crimes of violence and drunkenness. Jews are less likely to commit crimes of rape, incest and child abuse, but are involved in the distribution of indecent materials, and the trafficking of women is almost exclusively under Jewish control. There are links between Jews and vagabonds and swindlers, as the large number of Hebrew words in the language of the underworld, *Rotwelsch*, indicates. Jews are in general more refined criminals than the cruder, perhaps more violent, non-Jew. The sense of family is strong, and rates of illegitimate birth are lower than among the non-Jews. Jews are well adapted to city life, where their rapidity of thought and piercing intelligence in the observation of events and phenomena is bringing them increasing success.

Günther quoted figures from Fritz Lenz (1923b) in order to illustrate the predominance of Jews in trade and business. According to Lenz, Jews were in professions which required mental ability, especially where there was a requirement that the behaviour of others be influenced. These included the clothing business, art dealerships, the theatre and cinema, department stores, the stock exchange, journalism, acting, music, the law, medicine.

Günther ([1922] 1926: 437) noted that the materials he had presented were in themselves perhaps no more informative than those of the *Jewish Encyclopaedia*, or than a general description of a German type. The diversity of the Jewish people in terms of both bodily and psychological characteristics was obvious once one listed the variety of qualities that were ascribed to them. What was required to make sense of the Jewish racial character was a reconstruction of its history (Günther [1922] 1926: 437ff.).

Günther's discussion of the Jews can be usefully compared to that of Otmar Freiherr von Verschuer on the race biology of the Jews (1938a). Verschuer dealt with the problem of characterizing the racial difference between non-Jews and Jews by defining the two groups in terms of the distribution of features which overlap (1938a: 138). Much of the discussion follows the same course as Günther's, but the anti-Semitic rhetoric is sharper. According to Verschuer, the Jews are and always have been distinct in racial character. The central anomaly of the Jew is stressed: that they are a community which has survived without a state in spite of 2,000 years of dispersal. Jews are committed to denying the links between race and culture and attributing their difference to milieu and upbringing. But it is a fact beyond dispute that both the psychological and bodily characteristics of the Jews are genetically transmitted. Research into twins has shown this, and also that the differences between Jews and Germans lie in their distinct racial origins. The Jews are not a race in the sense of anthropological race (*Systemrasse*).

The Jews are a people who have 'bred themselves' (Verschuer 1938a: 149). All the central features of the Jews have operated as factors in biological selection: the Jews' lack of a natural relationship to territory and the instinctual sources of life and nature, their urbanism, their trading disposition, their adeptness at formal-logical Talmudic thinking, the sense of being a chosen people. The race-psychological character of the Jews has become more uniform through this process of selection, whereas the bodily characteristics are less uniform. The medical resistance to tuberculosis is evidence of their biological adaptation to the city, as also is the preservation of certain physical pathologies such as blindness and deaf-and-dumbness, which are normally selected against in a more natural environment. As part of this process, Jews are also prone to psychological and neurological complaints. Their alienation from nature leaves the world emptied of spiritual meaning. There is no room for true religiosity, for genuine, selfless love and for true reverence. Are not urbanites of other races not also felt to be in some sense 'Jewish'? It is no coincidence that it is predominantly urbanites who enter into mixed marriages with Jews (Verschuer 1938a: 150). For Verschuer, Jews posed a double danger for the German *Volk*: firstly, that of racial alienation, so that a complete and unconditional separation of Jews from the Germans was required; secondly, the spiritual alienation associated with Jews sought to introduce fundamentals of life and principles of selection which were propitious for the Jews, but which meant destruction for the German *Volk*. Thus, while the Jews were not a race, they were a descent group with a particular biological history and inherited characteristics which set them apart from the European 'guest peoples'.

Metaphors of race

Günther's model was grounded in a well-established discourse of regional and national character. It involved an implicit metaphorical hierarchy or set of hierarchies. The restraint and moral purity of the Nordic type was contrasted with the passionate, feminized Mediterranean. The Nordic race is the male, adult; the Mediterranean is the more feminized or childlike. The German *Volk* contains a multi-dimensional set of contrasts, where the constitutional or bodily type is to a degree reflected in the psychological make-up. A race which is physically 'heavy' is also psychologically 'heavy' or ponderous. Günther's discourse straddles the scientific (facts or revelations unknown to the general public) and popular racial and regional stereotypes. It is not an attack on racial commonsense, but rather the refinement of it, a superior form of the common 'insight'. It attempts an alliance of science with commonsense and subjective, metaphorical intuition.

The eugenicist Hermann Muckermann (1877–1962), conceptualized the racial composition of the German *Volk* as a composite of races with different 'genders' (1935). The Alpine race as a whole showed childlike or primitive character in terms of its development, but less so in the case of the men. Women, regardless of race, were less advanced in their racial development and as individuals. On Muckermann's model, the Alpine race as a whole was feminized or infantilized in relation to other more advanced races, and in that sense one can conceptualize the German *Volk* as a 'marriage' of the male and the female, the racially advanced and the racially primitive (1935: 91–2). The Dinaric race was presented by Muckermann as the opposite of the Alpine. Although the Dinaric type also has a short head, it was a different shape, and the total impression made by the male face was one of extraordinary daring. The Dinaric race (found mainly in the south and southeast) was the racially most advanced, and this was true also of the females, although they were slightly less advanced than the males (1935: 95). The Mediterranean race, which for Muckermann had made the least impact on the German *Volk*, was also described, in somewhat feminized terms, as being the smallest and the most delicate (*zierlich*). In the case of the men, the body was thin and 'well proportioned'. The women had strongly developed hips, and, compared to the strong chin of the male, the chin was more softly rounded in the case of the females; a light moustache for women was regarded among the women as part of an ideal beauty, and this might have been artificially cultivated, particularly in Spain (1935: 97–8).

An alternative line of thought was concerned with the relationship between body type (build) and personality (Kretschmer 1931). Kretschmer's work and constitutional psychology offered one approach to the study of character within psychology, and stood in uncertain relationship to the psychological types postulated by race psychology. Kretschmer identified three basic constitutional or 'psychosomatic' types ('somatotypes'): 'leptosome' (tall and thin), 'athletic' (muscular), 'pyknic' (squat, short and heavy-set). Different personality types, criminal behaviours and mental illnesses were associated with each body type.

Rittershaus (1936) sought to reconcile these two approaches by elaborating a complex system of racial types, which reflected the interaction between an original set of 'constitutional types' (*Konstitutionstypen*) and racial types. These original constitutional types became racial characteristics (*Rassenmerkmale*) once races developed (1936: 183). The problem with this was that to make the system work Rittershaus had to introduce a much higher number of racial types and subtypes (1936: 182–3). However, many studies of character made no significant reference to race-anthropological categories (Heiss 1936; Künkel 1944). One discipline that became increasingly significant was hereditary psychology (*Erbpsychologie*), in which the attempt was made to distinguish between hereditary and environmental aspects of human abilities, behaviour and personality on the basis of advances in genetics.

One racial anthropologist whose work echoed both Günther and Kretschmer, but whose understanding of race as style or as a mode of being represented a more fundamental break with systematic anthropology, was Ludwig Ferdinand Clauss. Clauss's approach to the study of human diversity was controversial within the field of racial anthropology, but he had many admirers among the reading public, and even those who disagreed with his methods were often impressed by the skill with which he had elaborated his model. He made use of the categories of racial anthropology, and contrasted for example the achievement-driven Nordic type (*Leistungsmensch*), who treats the external world as a separate, resistant entity to be operated on and overcome, with the accommodating Alpine type, (*Enthebungsmensch*) who seeks a comfortable niche within the world, and seeks to be left undisturbed rather than challenge reality (1936: 17–19). The Phalian was characterized by determination and persistence (*Verharrungsmensch*); the Mediterranean type (figure 7) aims to please, to make offerings, to sacrifice for others, often as a way to find God (1939: 99ff.). The goal of the Desert (*wüstenländisch*) or Oriental type was revelation (*Offenbarungsmensch*); the Near Eastern type sought spiritual redemption (*Erlösungsmensch*) (Clauss 1939).

For Clauss, a race 'was not an agglomeration of features or traits, but a mode of experiencing which permeates the totality of a living form' (1936: 17). Clauss's method thus involved the marginalizing of physicalist or biological theories of race in favour of what he termed the 'mimetic method' (*mimische Methode*), in which the investigator strove to 'live with' (*mitleben*) the group he was studying. This began with the imitation of externals, such as dress and food, and progressed until the true self of the investigator was set aside or locked away inside a new self which performed or became the 'other'. This process was the internalization of a form of life through a process of acting or 'playing along' (*mitspielen*). This implied a more profound form of integration into the life of the community being studied than mere participant observation. This is not to say that Clauss regarded the body as irrelevant; Clauss did make comments about bodily type, and understood the human type as a totality formed in relation to a particular landscape: 'It is the meaning of the body to be the manifestation of the soul' (1939: 94).

Clauss's formative experience had been his fieldwork with the Bedouin in Palestine in the period from 1927 to 1931, where he had explored the problems of 'living with' or 'living as' a Bedouin at the same time as he studied their culture and took photographs (figure 8). This required a simultaneous and paradoxical self-awareness and forgetting of self. As part of his adoption of the Bedouin role, Clauss had presented himself as a 'German Bedouin', indeed the 'pasha of the German Bedouin on the other side of the Arabian desert', a performance that he completed by sending his research assistant, Margarete Landé, to join the women's tent as his wife. Landé was an Arabic speaker and of Jewish origin (Clauss 1933).

Clauss's understanding of the Bedouin world was shaped by hostility to the effects of modernity and western individualism, and a sense that their racial or cultural essence was to be found in collective movement and rhythm, a rejection of 'work' in the modern sense and the strategic and ritual use of violence. Racial research was a

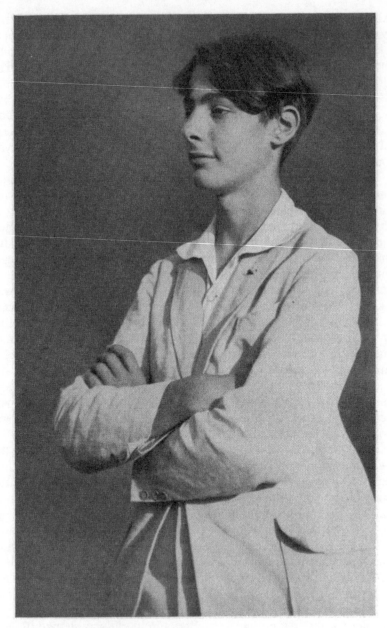

Figure 7   Mediterranean type (Clauss 1939: 93)

Figure 8   Semi-nomadic girl from Palestine: 'Fear and hate in desert style'
(Clauss 1939: 124)

process which involved reading the human body against its natural
landscape and environment; generalizing tendencies about race,
world-view and belief were set against close readings of individuals.
Each race was understood as having its own set of self-validating
ways of being, this being expressed in the body as a dynamic or
expressive entity. 'Nordic', the dominant mode of being of the

German people, 'represents a value for us, not a value in and of itself' (1939: 48). While Clauss belonged to the broad trend of Nordicism, he set himself against populist and academic Nordic chauvinism, noting that the label 'Nordic' implied a mode of experience, but that the content of this experience might be morally good or bad: 'One can be a dissipated or criminal person in a Nordic way – we can say without qualms: one can also be a real swine in a Nordic way.' Clauss rejected the notion that races had 'characters'; the properties that defined a race were on a more abstract – and elusive – level (1939: 48–9).

Conclusion

Central to Günther's (highly eclectic) view of the Jews were the pathologies of modernity. Not only were the Jews themselves falling prey to the ills of modernity, but they embodied many of its most striking features, notably the blurring of the lines between male and female. The Orthodox Jews of eastern Europe were in this sense unproblematic. But once the Jew crossed into modernity, the radical breach with the natural racial order begins. The Jew was both disrupted as a type, and disruptive. Jews had no common spoken language, no territory and no shared state. Paradoxically, the Jews were a people whose sole unifying force is consciousness of blood, yet they did not form a single, unified race.

Science and politics interacted in complex ways in relation to the question of the definition of *Volk*. For, as Günther's model illustrates, racial anthropology did not offer a straightforward model of German unity; indeed, it stressed that *Volk* was a hybrid collective of different races and psychological types. In addition, analysis of the German *Volk* made clear that there was no clear racial boundary between the German people and its neighbours. Thus, rivals and potential or actual enemies of Germany on the political, economic, military, cultural and linguistic level (that of *Volk*) actually overlapped with the internal divisions of the Germans on the level of race (*Rasse*). There was also a curious, half-repressed racial link between the German *Volk* and the Jewish *Volk*. Both shared a partial origin in the Near Eastern race.

If the Nordic race was given too much prominence, then the other races were at best diluting, and at worst contradictory or harmful, racial elements. The Nordic Scandinavian was a better potential member of the German *Volk* than an East Baltic type. But if the other

(European) races also brought positive virtues to the *Volk*, then this seemed to suggest that racial mixing (at least among European races) was a positive phenomenon. This view also downgraded the importance of the boundary of the *Volk*, or at least left the status of that boundary fundamentally unclear.

From the point of view of a scientifically trained racial anthropologist or geneticist, even of a committed *völkisch* or Nordicist ideologue, many of Günther's ideas and formulations were unscientific, or at best represented an earlier, humanities-based stage of the study of race which was rapidly being superseded. However, Günther accepted that Weismann and Mendel were fundamental to the study of human heredity (1927: 273), and criticism of his work was often as much a reflection of his lack of scientific training as of any particular intellectual faults.

The faults of Günther's model from a hard scientific point of view, i.e. its subjectivity, the reliance on a particular aesthetic, the caricaturing of group character, were shared by his more respectable medically and biologically trained colleagues. In his study of the reception of the Baur-Fischer-Lenz volume (editions from 1921 onwards), Fangerau notes that Eugen Fischer's (1874–1967) presentation of a racial taxonomy of the Europeans was not subject to a single serious criticism (2000: 86). But the assumptions that underlay Fischer's and Lenz's racial anthropology were not fundamentally different from those of Günther. It was Fischer who had declared confidently:

> The brains of the different races are organized in different ways; their total psychological make-up [*Psyche*] is extraordinarily different; and extraordinarily different are their intellectual achievements, their cultural creativity. (Fischer 1910: 19)

Fischer's elaboration of the basic taxonomy of the races that made up the German people included praise for the long-skulled, blond-haired Nordic race as the origin of all the creative energy in the history of Europe (1910: 19). Günther's model followed Fischer in most essential details, in particular in the parallel between the hybridity of the Jewish and German peoples.

One Nordicist who was mildly critical of Günther was Fritz Lenz. Lenz objected to the artificiality of the contrasts between the different racial characters in Günther's model, but praised him for having demonstrated that the Nordic race was the creator and carrier of the Indogermanic cultures. However, he considered Günther's postulation of the Alpine and Dinaric races superfluous. The term 'Alpine' had had its origins in Carl Linneus' (1707–1778) taxonomy of the human races as one of the categories of racial 'monstrosities' (*Monstrositäten*), and had been taken over by Ludwig Wilser (1850–1923) and Lapouge to describe a geographical race. There was insufficient evidence to set up a separate racial category; the same was true for the East Baltic race (Lenz 1936: 726–7). In the case of the Dinaric race, the observed facts could be accounted for by traits from the Nordic, Mediterranean and Near Eastern races (1936: 731). The Mediterranean race was however better attested.

Lenz further objected to talk of 'the races of the German people', which seemed to imply that there were clearly defined separate races present in the German *Volk*. What could be observed was the clustering of particular physical and psychological traits. But these did not amount to autonomous races. There was a general correlation between physical and psychological traits, so that the areas with less Nordic populations in physical terms were also less psychologically or temperamentally Nordic (Lenz 1936: 727).

Günther's scientifically trained colleagues were themselves far from reluctant to engage in racial stereotyping. Fischer saw the east in terms of an undifferentiated mass with indeterminate degrees of Mongoloid blood (Fischer 1936b: 192–3). For Lenz, the gap left by the deconstruction of the Alpine and East Baltic races was filled by a vast fatalistic Mongoloid race element mixed in with other races in the east. Populations with a strong Mongoloid element lacked mental agility; they were a fertile ground for mass suggestion (*Massensuggestion*) and rule by a Mandarin class (*Mandarinentum*); they clung to superstition, lacking both a sense for nature and for modern technology (Lenz 1936: 725).

One pragmatic line to take was that Günther, like Gobineau, had played an important role in identifying and promoting the racial question in the public domain, even if the implication was that his intellectual framework was defunct (Keiter 1941: 127; Verschuer 1941: 9–10, 92; Weingart et al. 1992: 453). Keiter's rhetorical question as to why Gobineau's work was still controversial, whereas Darwin and Mendel were recognized as authoritative, was answered by pointing to their status as biologists. While questions of race and culture might seem to waver between science and the humanities, they actually fell under the heading of biology and the natural sciences (Keiter 1938–40, I: 2). There was a clear parallel in this between Gobineau and Günther.

Günther's account of race could at moments be read as implying that there were actual living individuals who could be described as racially 'Nordic'. But the academic consensus was that the original racial collectives had broken down and mixed into *Völker*. Günther hedged on this point by speaking of individuals whose racial identity was 'predominantly' Nordic. There was a clear tension between the political promotion of the Nordic race and the recognition that races no longer existed in their pure form. This was particularly the case once the mainstream concept of race had shifted from a generalization about a body type, in combination with particular character or psychological dispositions, to a Mendelian or genetic understanding of racial characteristics. In the evolving intellectual landscape, the fundamental problem with Günther's model was that, contrary to his overt rhetoric, he effectively blurred the distinction between *Rasse* and *Volk*, or at least downgraded the value of *Volk* as a lived community in favour of nostalgia for lost racial community.

Günther did have some success in reorienting his work in a more scientifically acceptable direction (Weingart et al. 1992: 453), and it was in any case not politic to attack Günther directly. For example, Günther's work, with its static concept of race, was attacked by the proponents of a dynamic theory of race – Karl Saller and Friedrich Merkenschlager – with their concept of continua between racial 'zones'. However, the dynamic concept of race itself ran into political problems in the early years of Nazi rule (see chapter 10), when the Nordic ideal with which Günther was associated was at the height of its political influence.

Günther was a highly significant figure in the academic and ideological profile of the Third Reich. His appointment by the Minister for the Interior and Education for Thuringia Wilhelm Frick (1877–1946) to a professorship in Jena in 1930 was an early Nazi attack on the autonomy of the universities. It would however be a serious mistake to identify Nazi ideology with his work (Breuer 2001: 70). Official recognition did not translate into genuine political influence (Lutzhöft 1971: 162). The effect of the strong opposition to Günther's appointment was however to cement the association of Günther's work with Nazism (Weingart et al. 1992: 453).

5

Racial Mixing or 'Bastardization'

Introduction

The question of racial mixing (known variously as 'miscegenation', 'racial crossing', 'hybridization', 'bastardization', 'mongrelization') is fundamental to the Third Reich. The National Socialist regime is widely associated with a political doctrine of racial purity expressed in virulent polemics against racial mixing. The racially mixed individual (*Mischling*) was frequently described as pathological. The phenomenon of racial mixing lay at the intersection of sociology and criminology, psychology, racial anthropology and genetics, where a wide range of social and medical pathologies were identified (Herling and Hildebrandt 1935). The question of racial purity, which is a cliché of popular presentations of Nazi thought, was however far from straightforward in academic and political reality.

After the Nazi seizure of power in 1933, the regime came under strong pressure from its radical supporters to enact stringent legislation against racial mixing, particularly between members of the German *Volk* (known popularly as 'Aryans') and groups perceived as 'racially foreign', in particular Jews. Within the regime, there was widespread uncertainty about the best course of action, with civil servants and legal experts concerned about the vagueness of the categories involved, especially the legal definition of the category 'Jew'. The overall architecture of the law did not, for example, easily allow for compulsory divorce. On the level of political pro-paganda and mass education the authorities wished to drum home the message that racial mixing was harmful to the *Volk*, with the Jew and the 'Negro' presented as racially foreign (*fremdrassig*). But on the administrative and academic level the situation was much more confused.

This chapter looks at the background to theories of miscegenation in the Third Reich by focusing on Eugen Fischer's *Die Rehobother Bastards und das Bastardisierungsproblem beim Menschen* (1913). This was the study of a racially mixed population of the descendants of male white settlers (Boer farmers) and so-called 'Hottentot' (Nama) women from South Africa who had migrated to German Southwest Africa (today Namibia). It established Fischer's reputation as one of Germany's leading experts on the biology of race, setting him on the path to academic eminence and a successful career in the Weimar Republic and the Third Reich.

Fischer's work was widely accepted as representing an advance on traditional theories of racial mixing. Fischer established that racial mixing gave rise to biologically and socially viable populations. However, he argued that there was a distinction to be drawn between the mixing of closely related races (e.g. white Europeans) and between distant races (i.e. between Europeans and Africans). Fischer was credited with a successful synthesis of classical taxonomic racial anthropology and modern genetics, in particular Mendelian genetics. Further, his work contributed to the popularization of the fundamental distinction between genotype (*Erbbild*) and phenotype (*Erscheinungsbild*). The genotype was the totality of the genetic inheritance of an individual, whereas the phenotype was the actual constitution or make-up of the individual. The lesson of modern genetics was that one could not arrive at an understanding of the inherited racial make-up of an individual merely by observation of their observed racial characteristics. It followed from Fischer's interpretation of Mendel that racial mixing did not and could not give rise to new races. It was not possible, for example, for the various races that interacted in the German *Volk* to fuse together into a single race.

Miscegenation and purity in European thought

Racial anthropologists in the early nineteenth century were centrally concerned with monogenesis versus polygenesis, with the relationship of climate and landscape to human racial diversity, and with the fundamental nature of the human species. The European intellectual tradition lacked an agreed definition of the term 'human' and 'race' and hence of 'racial purity'. Scholarly discourse on the question was a mixture of observation and second-hand anecdotes. Wrestling with the terms 'species' and 'race', Charles Darwin (1809–1882) gave a mixed report in the *Descent of Man*, noting that Paul Broca (1824–1880) had found 'good evidence that some races were quite fertile together, but evidence of an opposite nature in regard to other races' (Darwin 1871: 171).

For much of the history of European colonization there was no fundamental anxiety about sexual relations and reproduction across race lines. The pre-modern view was often that interbreeding or miscegenation was a means of elevating indigenous populations, and thus a key policy element in maintaining settler colonialism (Anderson 1991: 13–14; Livingstone 1987). But as the nineteenth century progressed, there was an increasing horror of miscegenation with 'lesser breeds' (Hyam 1990). This was clearly related to the dissemination of ideas from racial anthropology, which had a dramatic impact on the world-view of educated Europeans. The later empire remained however a place of sexual opportunity, in which there existed 'a compulsive libidinal attraction disavowed by an equal insistence on repulsion' in relation to the non-white colonial subjects (Young 1995: 149).

Within European nationalism, particular forms of racial hybridity were often celebrated. The British nation was sometimes conceived of as drawing strength and vigour from its mixing of Celtic, Norman, Anglo-Saxon and Danish elements. Broca, rejecting Gobineau's pessimistic propositions about racial hybridity and national decline as 'far too general', pointed to the rise of the United States, 'where the Anglo-Saxon race is still predominant, but which is overrun by immigrants of various other races'. Nonetheless, 'the prosperity and power' of the United States was growing with 'unexampled rapidity'. However, other intermixtures were 'notably inferior to those of eugenesic hybridity', and 'Mulattoes of the first degree, issued from the union of the Germanic (Anglo-Saxon) race with the African Negroes, appear inferior in fecundity and longevity to individuals of the pure races' (Broca 1864: 21–2).

At the turn of the century, the intellectual situation remained confused. Houston Stewart Chamberlain (1855–1927) offered an anti-Semitic re-reading of Gobineau's model of racial decline. He described a Jewish racial conspiracy which exploited racial mixing as a strategy of domination. This consisted in retaining a core stock of pure-blooded Jews while other Jews mixed with the Indo-Europeans. These would be reduced to 'a herd of pseudohebraic mestizos'. By polluting the blood of Europeans, Jews would become the only pure-blooded people ([1899] 1932: 383). The American geographer and neo-Lamarckian Nathaniel Shaler (1841–1906), a student of Louis Agassiz (1807–1873) claimed 'the offspring of a union between pure black and white parents is, on the average, much shorter lived and much less fertile than the race of either parent'. The 'mulatto' was inferior to both parental racial stocks. Intermixture of closely related European races, by contrast, might result in an equally valuable or even more valuable racial product (Shaler 1904: 252; Livingstone 1984: 183–4, 193). But, from a scientific standpoint, both Chamberlain and Agassiz's frameworks looked increasingly dated, as monogenesis and neo-Darwinism became orthodoxy.

There was no general agreement as to how to evaluate racial mixing. For Albrecht Wirth, racial mixing was the dynamic force behind human history ('without it, no world history'), but an excess was damaging (1914: 83). It was after all racially hybrid peoples rather than pure races which acted as historical agents. But the modern, mongrelized city, with its 'raceless masses' (*Grossstadtpöbel*) was a vision of horror (Wirth 1914: 1, 95).

The German debate about colonialism

British colonialism in India, and the resulting scholarly and intellectual excitement, played a fundamental part in shaping German thought, in philosophy, literature and philology. In addition, the European empires offered access for German scholars, in particular archaeologists, anthropologists and linguists, to an ever-widening horizon of investigation. In the late nineteenth century, the newly formed German state began to acquire colonies of its own. In 1884 and 1885, Germany acquired substantial territories in Africa, i.e. Togo, Cameroon, German Southwest Africa and German East Africa, as well as territories in the Pacific. In 1898, it acquired Kiautschou (Jiaozhou, including the port of Qingdao) in China, and in 1899 a number of South Sea territories, including Samoa. In 1911, Germany acquired territory in French Equatorial Africa (Grosse 2000: 20).

In Germany, there was deep anxiety that racial miscegenation in the colonies would have repercussions at home (Rodenwaldt 1938). While it was felt that Germany as a great power was no less entitled to colonies than the other European powers, there was uncertainty about the exact nature of such a colonial project. Empires were intrinsically projects of political and racial hybridization. It was unclear whether colonies were primarily to be sources of raw materials (Berger 1938: 146–51) or whether their role was military, including the raising of a colonial – and therefore multiracial – army. Was there to be dense settlement by whites, so that the colonies would be centres of emigration, or was the white presence to be restricted to a small administration? There was a question mark hanging over the long-term viability of white settlement in hostile climates (the so-called *Akklimatisationsfrage* or 'acclimatization question', Livingstone 1987), and confusion and fear in relation to the racial mixing that inevitably followed. Settler colonialism in the east in what were seen as ancestral territories of the *Volk* was seen by many *völkisch* ideologues as a more viable option. These territories fell within the natural sphere of influence (*Grossraum*) or 'living space' (*Lebensraum*) of the German *Volk* at its widest and healthiest extension. Germany was the heartland, the centre of Europe (*Land der Mitte*) (Keiter 1936:89).

Thus, the former colonial official Georg Fritz was to argue for the priority of National Socialist settlement policy in the territories to the east of Germany over colonial settlements overseas, on the grounds that the Nordic and Phalian races (*Nordrasse*) were not suited to warm climates, and the effect of the different environment, given natural selection and the additional threat of racial mixing, would be to create a new racial type distinct from the home population (*Heimatvolk*) (Fritz 1934, 1935; Aschenbrenner c.1935).

One strand of anthropology, although perhaps racist by contemporary standards, was critical of crude racism, and of colonial policy in relation to the indigenous peoples. This liberal-colonial tendency was exemplified by the Protestant missionary and anthropologist Diedrich Westermann (1875–1956). Westermann took part in efforts to protect the Ewe and other coastal peoples of Togo from land expropriation (Smith 1991:172). By contrast, the physician and racial anthropologist Philalethes Kuhn (1870–1937) participated in the 1904 campaign against the Herero and Nama uprisings in German Southwest Africa. These were brutally suppressed (Eckart 1997:255–90).

Germany's colonies were lost under the Treaty of Versailles (1919). There were however ideologues and politicians who saw their return as indispensable to Germany in its rivalry with the other European powers, though the multiracial nature of the British and the French armed forces was a cause of great distaste, mixed with envy. Fritz Lenz complained that the French had put their 'coloured hordes' into battle against the Germans (1927a: 267).

Eugen Fischer and the 'Rehobother Bastards'

Historical background

Fischer's attention had been drawn to the racially mixed Rehobother population (figure 9) by the publication of a study by a colonial offi-

Figure 9   Rehobother women (Fischer 1913: 273)

cial, Maximilian Bayer (1905). The number of the Rehobother was put at between 2500 and 3000. Fischer saw his study as representing an important departure from more sociologically oriented, in Fischer's view, unscientific studies, such as those carried out by Georges Hervé (Fischer 1913: 137; Hervé 1912). Fischer's reflections on interracial breeding involved an acute awareness of wider socio-political questions both in the colonies and in Europe, as is evident from a lecture Fischer gave in 1913, in which the question of mixed marriages both in the colonies and between 'Germanics' and 'Semites' were described as raising important policy questions (Fischer 1914: 3–4).

Fischer saw the Rehobother as victims of an unjust land grab by the Boers. Following this, the Rehobother had crossed the River Orange to Rehoboth and founded the so-called 'Nation of Bastards' in 1870 (1913: 29), though they were caught in the middle between the warring Hottentots (Nama) and the Herero. The Rehobother had come under German administration in 1884, but did not find peace until 1892. According to Fischer, the population had undergone a rapid transformation from a loosely associated group of related families under a single pastor to one that had shared suffering and hardship. They had struggled with the harshness of the natural environment, and this had led to the preservation of many of their Hottentot traits. They had also benefited in terms of cultural level from the impact of the missionaries. This had led to the formation of a sense of identity, and marked out the group as distinct from the indigenous people. Under German administration, once order had been established in 1892, this group had then been able to flourish, becoming identified with, and allies of, the colonial administration, and distinguishing themselves as soldiers fighting alongside German troops in putting down Hottentot rebellion (1913: 36).

Racial mixing and the status of the 'Bastard'

In his introduction, Fischer noted that the phenomenon of race mixing had been neglected in favour of attempts to study 'pure' racial groups. All kinds of views about race mixing were to be found in the anthropological literature, but no detailed study of these processes had been carried out, and the Rehobother case was perhaps a unique opportunity (1913: 1). One key issue was the rise and fall of races ('Rassenentstehung und Rassentod', 1913: 1).

Fischer contended that the Rehobothers' intelligence was not low, and that many of them were equal in intelligence to the Boers (1913: 294). However, intelligence taken in isolation was less important than normally believed in assessing the potential of the dark-skinned races. Their relatively high level of intelligence had been erroneously used to argue that it was only culture that separated them from the whites. Fischer's argument was that for all their achievements the Rehobother were inferior to the pure whites in terms of cultural level and in mental ability and performance (1913: 296). What differentiated the Rehobother from the Europeans was that the masses in the urban centers of Europe regularly produced individuals of exceptional ability. The superiority of these exceptional individuals was not purely intellectual; it lay in energy, imagination, in planning, in making associations, in creative production and in qualities of character, such as self-assurance and consistency and loyalty to self (1913: 296). This quality of bringing forth remarkable individuals was a distinctive racial characteristic, and one that was completely lacking in the dark-skinned races.

The effect of Fischer's work was to highlight the term *Bastard* in the context of European-African racial mixing, though Fischer did also note that the population of central Europe was 'a completely unstable bastard mixture' (1913: 190). This implied, though Fischer did not spell this out, that the German *Volk* was composed of 'racial bastards'. Fischer stressed however that the Hottentots and the Europeans were distinguished by 'very many anthropological characteristics' and were 'very strongly distinct from each other' (1913: 140). There was a greater gap between a Hottentot and a European than between two Europeans. It was the existence of this gap which justified the use of the label *Bastardvolk*.

Fischer was unable to determine precisely the racial nature of the European component of the population, but he assumed that the Nordic race predominated (1913: 45). As regards the non-European elements, they were made up of Hottentot rather than from the slave elements which had been brought in from a variety of areas. In general, the Rehobothers' very strong 'racial pride' (*Rassestolz*) prevented marriages with the indigenous people. In such cases, especially where the man was from the *Bastardvolk*, the child would remain with the mother rather than become part of the *Bastard* population (1913: 45).

Fischer was in no doubt that all mixed European-African populations were inferior to Europeans, and this included the Rehobother population. For this reason, the Rehobother required leadership by whites, as in free social competition they would be unable to survive. They were however superior to the dark-skinned races from which they were partially descended. Fischer rejected the generalization that all mixed offspring were inferior, especially morally inferior, to their parent races. However, it might happen that the mixing of two highly distinct racial groups gave rise to disharmony in certain cases. The most serious examples of this were the large urban centres, in ports and mining towns, in which deracinated mixed-race populations lived a degraded existence. However, 'where a person of mixed descent is born from two races of high value, and is in a recognized position in society, that is he is free from these negative environmental influences, then he will certainly be of equal value, or has the potential to be so' (1913: 298).

The observed phenomenon that persons of mixed race were of inferior quality to their parental races was thus to be attributed largely to environmental factors, and in a small number of cases to the combination of totally disharmonious characteristics. The notion that degeneration was the inevitable by-product of this process was erroneous, as could be shown by the superiority of the Rehobother population to the indigenous peoples. While the Rehobother had useful qualities from both races, there were negative aspects to their character, deriving from a sense of superiority to the indigenous people, and a consequent laziness and desire to play the master. They had the consciousness of being the master without the concomitant sense of duty. This was attributable by Fischer to mishandling by the Europeans. Fischer's final verdict was that the Rehobother offered a multifaceted picture, but not a totally displeasing one. They were 'a capable little people', so long as they were restrained from their two frailties, pride and alcohol (1913: 299).

Fischer thus did not contend that mixed populations were unviable. The struggle for survival of the Rehobother in the countryside had hardened them into a compact group with a strong sense of identity, thereby preventing their assimilation into the racially promiscuous milieu of the urban areas. Racial mixing could not be seen as directly harmful, since there was no degeneration of racial inheritance. The application of Mendelian genetics implied that the racial characteristics themselves were transmitted intact; they were not merged into a new racial genotype in each individual. The crucial determinate of the social usefulness of the mixed racial population was the social structures within which the group found itself. The only exception to this was a small minority of cases in which the racial characteristics combined in a particular disharmonious way. While such a group as the Rehobother could not take on a leadership role in colonial society, it could perform useful social roles in an intermediate position between the whites and the indigenous peoples.

Fundamentally, this was a work of colonialist paternalism. The political position implied in Fischer's text was the need for authoritarian social control, in which the nature and effects of different forms of interbreeding were monitored, and eugenic intervention was used as necessary to promote the welfare of the population. In the case of the German or other European peoples, it was clear that the admixture of non-European blood would lower the overall level. Fischer made this very clear, stating that any European people that admitted the blood of inferior races had paid for this with a mental-spiritual and cultural decline: 'But if then there is only a probability, or merely a possibility, that Bastard blood would damage our race, without there being against this a good chance that it would improve us, *then any reception of this blood must be prevented* (1913: 303). Ethical and legal norms needed to take account of this absolute biological truth (1913: 203).

Fischer's relative observational objectivity was potentially more explosive than the traditional prejudice that racially mixed populations had low fertility rates and were subject to decay. The conclusion was there was no biological mechanism for preventing the spread of mixed-race populations; their viability was a function of the kind of socio-political order under which they lived. The key to the question then became social and political, and the paradoxical consequence of a finding that racial mixing was not biologically pathological was an increased awareness for the need for eugenic social engineering.

Reception and critique

An example of the initial positive reception in the international scholarly community was a notice in *Nature*, in which Fischer's key finding was summarized as follows:

> His observations have convinced him that a new and permanent human race cannot be formed by the amalgamation of two diverse forms of man – not from any want of fertility – for amongst the Bastards there is an average of 7.4 children to each family – but because certain characters are recessive, others are dominant, and the original types tend to re-assert themselves in the course of generations, according to Mendel's law. Although the mean head-form of the Bastards is intermediate to those of the two parent races – Hottentot and Boer – yet in each generation a definite number of the Bastards tend to assume the head-form of the one or the other of the parent races. There are certain facts relating to head-form known to English anthropologists which can be explained only on a Mendelian basis and are in harmony with Dr. Fischer's observations. Between three and four thousand years ago England was invaded by a race with peculiarly formed, short and high heads. During those thousands of years the Bronze age invaders have been mingling their blood with that of the older and newer residents of England. Yet in every gathering of modern Englishmen – especially of the middle classes – one can see a number of pure examples of the Bronze Age head-form. On the Mendelian hypothesis the persistence of such a head-form is explicable. (Anon 1913: 162)

Fischer's study was also welcomed by Theodor Mollinson (1913/14), who had done research in German East Africa (Kater 1989: 230–1), and in general terms by Franz Boas in the United States ([1922] 1982: 51, 52). Fischer's study continued to be cited favourably in North America (Hooton 1935: 28), and has retained a vague aura of scientific respectability down to the present. The Austrian sociologist Friedrich Hertz (1878–1964), a Catholic (but later, dismissed from his post at the University of Halle on account of his Jewish background), noted that Fischer had shown the falsity of many ideas about racial mixing, but rejected Fischer's conclusions about the negative impact on European peoples of racial mixing (Hertz 1925: 168–71). Fischer's presentation of his research at an International Congress for Population Research was praised by Eric Voegelin (1901–1985) as 'a modern arrangement of races of a high methodological quality' ([1933] 1998: 78 fn.).

In an effusive tribute to the work published in 1938, Otmar von Verschuer stressed that the work had achieved the crucial step from traditional anthropology, with its emphasis on skull-measurements and exotic races, to 'racial biology' (*Rassenbiologie*). This new discipline had been elevated under National Socialism to become the foundation of the new state (1938b: 138). Without National Socialism, racial biology would not have reached its present level; without racial biology, the eugenic laws could not have been enacted so effectively (1938b: 139).

More recently, it has been persuasively argued that Fischer's general social and cultural commentary on the Rehobother was entirely unsupported by his own anthropological investigation. In an interview with Fischer's daughter, Gertrud Fischer, the geneticist Müller-Hill commented that it was strange that Fischer 'didn't once explain Mendelian segregation of physical characteristics, let alone mental traits, in that book' (1988: 107). In any case, Mendel was able to isolate homozygote (genetically uniform) populations before beginning his experiment, whereas Fischer was confronted with the offspring of populations which he knew to be racially mixed, as neither the European population nor the 'Hottentot' population was racially pure. This did not merely introduce a further level of complexity into the study, as Fischer implied, but invalidated it as an application of Mendel's method.

One can sense a fundamental ambivalence. Within his own firmly held views on the hierarchy of races, Fischer rhetorically situated himself as the paternalistic defender of the Rehobother. Though he did conclusively deny the negative effects of racial mixing, his study was much more positive in tone than contemporary academic and popular race theory. Fischer seemed to suggest that this 'little people' could maintain a useful existence if the social frame were correctly managed. Their culture was a harmonious fusion of the different elements that made it up, but was now threatened by the arrival of the railway and mining concerns (Fischer 1913: 230).

The evolution of Fischer's views

In his contribution to the 1923 volume, *Anthropologie*, Fischer argued that racial crossing (*Rassenkreuzung*) was the historical norm for both primitive (*Naturvölker*) and civilized (*Kulturvölker*) peoples

(1923: 136–7). Observation had shown that almost all the traditional ways of thinking about racial crossing or *Bastardisierung* were false. Fischer stressed that only laws governing the inheritance of racial and other individual characteristics were Mendelian. In that sense, a characteristic or feature could not be a racial characteristic unless it was inherited according to Mendel's laws. Importantly, skull shape was also inherited in this way, and thus could be determined to be a genuinely inherited racial trait. Thus, any change in bodily characteristics which was not transmitted according to Mendel's laws was *ipso facto* not a racial trait, though not all hereditary characteristics were racial (1923: 138).

Fischer reiterated that in the case of racial crossing, no one side was preponderant (*präpotent*), contrary to popular belief. There was no evidence that one race predominated over the other in the transmission of racial characteristics. This belief had become widespread in part because of the psychological salience of the 'foreign' part of the inheritance, leading the observer to miss the true proportion between the two sides of the inheritance. This explained the erroneous perception that the Jewish racial type was dominant over the European (1923: 139). Fischer noted that there was a great deal to learn about the inheritance of racial traits, but it was clear that these were inherited independently of one another, i.e. that there was no correlation between different racial characteristics.

Fischer's firm conclusion remained that no new races could be created by racial crossing, except in the case of selective breeding, so that in mixed populations where the original hair colours were blond and dark, pure types could still be found after many generations. This needed to be distinguished from cases of alleged 'demixing' (*Entmischung*), where a conquering race which mixed with an indigenous population, as with the Nordic race in southern Europe or the Near East, were subject to the effects of selection (*Auslesewirkungen*) because the incoming race was unsuited to the environment. Fischer stressed that there was no such thing as the natural death of a race. Races could only be destroyed or wiped out. This was what happened when migrant members of the Nordic race in the warmer climates of the south disappeared after a relatively short time, or, in reverse, when South Sea peoples disappeared in the face of European contact (1923: 141–2).

Fischer noted a tendency for crosses to exceed their parents in height and strength, a phenomenon known as *Luxurieren* (now termed 'heterosis' or 'hybrid vigour'), for example among European-American Indian and the European-Hottentot crosses. On the subject of their psychological attributes, Fischer again stressed the importance of environmental factors in the fate of cross-breeds in urban centres, mining towns and ports, and he rejected the generalization that *Mischlinge* were intrinsically morally inferior. However, there might be a greater frequency of disharmonious offspring in terms of the totality of their predispositions (*Gesamtbeanlagung*), for example in the case of Laplander *Mischlinge* in Norway, though they might be fortuitous or favourable cases where a foreign element brought some advantage (1923: 140).

In terms of the debate within racial anthropology up to the 1930s, Fischer's position was an intermediate one: between the view 'that a people of racially mixed ancestry is inferior to unmixed stock' and the view that 'crossing tends to better the population in which it occurs' (Herskovits 1934: 401). In relation to the lurid denunciations of many of his contemporaries of the evils of racial hybridity (for example in the works of Madison Grant), Fischer's position was complex, since he stressed the role of environmental and political factors in determining the viability of mixed populations. Thus while Fischer evoked the race chaos of modernity, that chaos was not the direct and sole result of race mixing.

Wider implications of the study

Throughout his career, Fischer stressed the importance of racial crossing not only as a field in its own right but for racial anthropology as whole:

> A systematic understanding of the human races can only be attained when we possess sufficient knowledge of the hereditary nature of different characteristics, and this can only be obtained from a study of as far as possible all types of racial crossing. (Fischer 1940: 22)

The impact of Fischer's study of the Rehobother on racial anthropology was dramatic. If Mendelian genetics were fundamental to understanding the transmission of racial characteristics, then the measurement of the human body as an object of study, so-called 'somatic' anthropology, could not on its own yield decisive insights into the scientific study of race. It also impacted on the basic definition of race. In general, races were defined as human groups which shared physical and psychological characteristics. But the logic of Fischer's position was that, while at the point of origin a race may have been a collective of 'pure types', in historical time there was a process of mixing of the features which could be separately transmitted.

The conclusion was that a race was not a human group or collective with members. It was fundamentally distinct from a category like *Volk*. A race was a set of hereditary features, which could be realized independently in different individuals. While it was possible to find regions where there was a preponderance of somatic types which approximated the original race, these tended to be geographically or culturally marginal (for example, the Nordic type in Scandinavia). Racial characteristics were not subject to change under the impact of the environment, and with the exception of chance mutations they did not lose their essential character. Thus a race could not disappear, unless all the individuals carrying its racial characteristics were wiped out without heir.

This offered a scientific answer to the pessimism of Gobineau and Spengler, who argued that human races or peoples had a natural life-cycle. It offered to some the possibility of recreating the original race, by breeding out the original pure types, but this possibility was rejected even by scientists sympathetic to Nordicism on the grounds that one could at best achieve only a superficially 'Nordic' appearance (Baur 1936). This understanding that the true Nordic nature was primarily temperamental, spiritual and psychological posed difficult questions to racial anthropologists. The ultimate effect of this paradigm shift was to marginalize racial anthropology as a whole, since the physical appearance of an individual was not conclusive as to their true racial nature. This was particularly important if psychological or mental attributes were included as racial characteristics, since one might have a Nordic mind in an Alpine body. But if this was the case, what was the point of focusing on the measurement and analysis of the individual body?

Scholars in twentieth-century Germany were almost without exception monogenists, and recognized the biological and genetic unity of the human species (Rüsche 1937: 73ff.; Fischer 1940: 4–5). If the human race was biologically one, then there was no natural barrier to the collapse of the world's racial ecology: 'All races display an unrestricted and undiminished fertility among each other. This fact can be seen as proof of the unitary descent of humanity. It contradicts the hypothesis which is sometimes put forward that the human races have multiple origins from different animal roots' (Verschuer 1941: 92). The assertion of this 'zoological humanism' fed the racial anxieties of European intellectuals, and lay behind laws against miscegenation passed in the United States and Nazi Germany.

There is a direct parallel between the recognition of the mutual fertility of the human races and Sir William Jones's assertion (1786) of the original unity of European and Indian languages, in particular Sanskrit (see chapter 6). Far from being grounded in God-given order or in biology, human difference was subject to erasure or confusion, by conquest, migration and assimilation. The fall of humankind into historical time began this process, and in modernity it was accelerating at a frightening rate. There were no natural boundaries to racial mixing, nor to the spread of languages across racial boundaries. Modernity was a second Babel.

One possible conclusion to be drawn from Fischer's analysis was that the mixing of races that had given rise to the German *Volk* was a positive fusion of different traits and abilities, whereas the mixing of Africans and Jews with European races was pathological. But this view of the nature of the German *Volk* was rejected by those who saw the Nordic race as superior to all other European races, and the *Volk* as involving the fall of the Nordic into racial hybridity. In this sense, the case of the African colonies or India was directly analogous to the early history of Europe, in which a superior conquering people had fallen into hybridity through sexual relations with an inferior servant or slave class. Most Germans would not have thought of themselves as being of mixed race. But in effect, according to racial anthropology, all Germans were *Mischlinge*:

> Racial anthropology is above all in the disagreeable position of having to pronounce the overwhelming majority of Europeans to be of mixed race, to be bastards. This renders it an awkward, disturbing science, making it something discomforting in the manner of that exhortation to 'know thyself'. (Günther [1922] 1934: 16)

Academic orthodoxy required recognition that the German *Volk*, no less than the Rehobother, was composed of 'bastards'.

Mendelian racial anthropology was nostalgic for lost purity, but in a different sense than classical anthropology and popular Nordicism. The Mendelian framework offered scientific reassurance that the Nordic race was not biologically doomed to destruction, but in the present it remained tantalizingly out of reach, its traits scattered in diverse combinations throughout the current German *Volk*.

Conclusion

Fischer's framework offered no clear answer to the general problem of racial mixing in the German *Volk* on a policy level. However, the case of the 'Rhineland bastards' – the offspring of black, North African and Asian French troops and German women illegally sterilized during the Third Reich – was theoretically unproblematic for

Fischer and his fellow experts, since they had the immediate family history before them, and were able to use their intellectual authority to stress the undesirable effects of mixing between 'distant' races (Pommerin 1979; Burleigh and Wippermann 1991: 128ff.). As Verschuer acknowledged, there was a direct line between Fischer's study and the investigations of Wolfgang Abel (1905–1977) into this population in the mid-1930s (Verschuer 1938b: 138), commissioned from the Kaiser Wilhelm Institute by the Prussian Ministry of the Interior. Abel identified a number of pathological physical and mental conditions among the mixed offspring (Abel 1937: 311; Kranz 1940: 7).

However, the extent and nature of Jewish racial assimilation into the German *Volk* was not defined clearly in academic terms. Nor was there a consensus about the extent of mixing between Slavs and Germans and the nature of the racial border between these two peoples, if any. On the question of racial mixing between Jews and non-Jews, Fischer acted as academic assessor (*Referent*), along with Günther, for a doctoral dissertation on the mixing of 'Jewish' and 'German' blood (Paul 1940). This thesis explicitly welcomed the anti-Jewish policies of the National Socialists. After the collapse of 1918 there had seemed to be no racial dividing line, and, while the removal of Jews from the territory of the German people would prevent the production of further *Mischlinge*, there remained the problem of those already in existence. What would take many decades was the revival of the shattered racial instinct of the German people (Paul 1940: 7–8).

A combination of scientific respectability and racist ideology was to serve Fischer well in his career in the Third Reich. By the 1920s Fischer's reputation as an objective scientist was established, and his leading position in the German academic establishment was confirmed by his move to Berlin. In a talk held before the senate of the Kaiser Wilhelm Society he criticized aspects of Günther's work as 'tendentious', while praising Franz Boas's work on the environmental factors in the evolution of skull shape (Fischer 1926a: 749). He argued that mixing between suitable races was more advantageous than racial purity (1926a: 754), a position which could be read as anti-Nordicist, or at least contrary to popular or vulgar Nordicism. But the raceless chaos of the proletarian masses reflected the effects of promiscuous racial mixing (Fischer 1927a; Gessler 2000: 100). Fischer praised the legacy of Gobineau and Chamberlain and the contributions of Günther and Ludwig Schemann (Fischer 1926b, 1927b: 137; Massin 2003: 191–4). While their work did not conform to the latest scientific standards, there was a core of truth which should be recognized.

6

The Myth of an Aryan Race

Introduction

The notion that Nazi race theorists promoted the notion of a superior Aryan race is deeply embedded in academic and popular perceptions of Nazism. The term 'Aryan' was widely used in Nazi Germany, and 'non-Aryan' became in many contexts a synonym for 'Jewish'. However, Nazi race theorists opposed the promotion of 'Aryan' as a racial concept. By 1935, the National Socialist regime had accepted that this use of the term was unscientific. Almost every academic commentary – outside specialist writings on race science in the Third Reich - fundamentally misrepresents the intellectual history of this question. The notion that the Nazis 'confused language with race' or *Volk* with *Rasse* in relation to the Aryan question is completely false.

The biblical paradigm

An explanation of Aryanism as an ideology requires a brief discussion of the 'biblical paradigm', which dominated the understanding of human linguistic and national history in early modern Europe. The biblical model of human identity was founded on the notion of a lineage traced forwards through time from an original male ancestor. Lineages were distinguished by language and territory. For humanity taken as a whole, the language of the Garden of Eden was the original or 'primitive' language' (Webb 1669); the identity of the original 'Adamic' language of the Garden of Eden was the subject of intense theorizing (Olender 1992: 1ff.).

The search for links between the lineages of 'kings and princes' and biblical figures (Anderson 1732) was gradually transformed into the search for the lineages of nations or peoples. Proto-nationalist scholars began to use this framework to make the case for the antiquity and ancient purity of particular European peoples and languages. The sons of Noah, i.e. Shem, Ham and Japhet, were seen as the progenitors of three branches of humankind, the Semites, the Africans and the Europeans: 'every one after his tongue, after their families, in their nations' (Genesis 10). The closer the language to the speech of these ancestors, the more 'original' it was. These models however increasingly involved working backwards, from the observed language communities of contemporary Europe back through history to the biblical story.

In his *Elements of Universal History*, J. A. L. Montriou had painted this picture of the origins of human diversity:

> Noah's descendants multiplied greatly, and attempted to build the stupendous tower of Babel as a monument of their power, and a safe retreat in case of any new inundation, 2247 BC. God punished their presumption by producing divers languages amongst them: they spoke, yet no longer understood each other; whereupon they parted, and dispersed over the whole earth: Japhet settled in Europe, Shem in Asia, and Ham in Africa, about 2287 BC. (Montriou c.1787: 4)

The methodology for establishing such claims was that of comparative linguistics. Paul Pezron (1639–1706), in his influential *The Antiquities of Nations* ([1703] 1706), applied the technique of linguistic comparison to the reconstruction of the history of nations (1706: 136): 'But seeing the language of these Two People were like one another, the Reason is, because both of them came from the same Stock.' Pezron assumed that the linguistic unity of humankind was preserved up to the time of the Tower of Babel, i.e. that 'this first Language was preserved by Mankind, not only till the time of the Universal deluge, but even to the Building of the Famous Tower of *Babel*, since called *Babylon*' (1706: 141–2).

Pezron located the origins of human diversity in the descendants of the sons of Noah. The process of gradual diversification followed from the fact that 'the Heads of Families or Tribes having at that time different Languages, began to form different Peoples or nations' (1706: 142). The question became that of identifying the historical evolution and contemporary disposition of what he termed 'original languages' (1706: 221, 233): 'The *Celtick* or *Gaulish* Tongue, which We call the *British*, is [. . .] therefore an Original Language.' Other languages were the result of the mixture of these primary speech forms.

In the dedication to his *Remains of Japhet*, James Parsons (1705–1770) spoke of using his leisure hours 'employed in considering the striking affinity in the languages of *Europe*' (1767: iii). For Parsons, only the descendants of Ham were at Babel ('I, for my own part, cannot help exculpating the whole descendents of *Japhet* and *Shem* from having any hand in the attempt', 1767: 24), and the languages of Japhet and Shem formed a link to the antediluvian world. The descendants of Ham, starting with his son Canaan, were cursed by Noah and condemned to be 'a servant of servants unto his brethren' (Genesis 9: 24–5).

The adoption of this biblical framework for understanding human affinities led to the discounting of the descendants of Ham, and the juxtaposition of the Japhetic and the Semitic. The biblical account was gradually hollowed out from within by the framework of linguistic comparativism. The biblical story was interpreted and in effect reconstructed retrospectively in the light of the linguistic affinities revealed by the study of contemporary linguistic diversity. This represented a radical re-reading of biblical history, and shifted the evidential power from the biblical text itself to the linguistic affinities observed by the philologist.

Japhetic affinities

What emerged from the Japhetic tradition was a concept of linguistic affinity that set the European 'us' against two forms of 'others': there was the opposite, the dual other, the Semite, the Jew (Shem), who likewise could trace back a lineage to the very beginnings. The descendents of Ham, whose language was confounded at the Tower of Babel, had fallen into a thousand rootless histories.

From a search for the location of the original homeland of humankind, the Garden of Eden, attention moved to the original homelands of particular divisions of humankind. The postulation of ideal ancestors in remote mountain ranges also increasingly stood in ideological tension with a nineteenth-century Romantic emphasis on continuity of occupation of land, on rootedness and on the relationship of language and culture to landscape. Discussion had broken free of the debate about the location of Eden – the universal homeland of humankind – to locate specific moments in the historical formation of ancestral nations or peoples. European exploration and expansionism brought scholars into contact with a potentially bewildering variety of peoples and languages. This, together with the development of the modern geological and archaeological understanding of time, posed profound intellectual problems for the developing human sciences.

The key metaphor remained the genealogical tree (Bouquet 1994), which started at a single point or origin (an ideal ancestry) and then divided into branches and sub-branches. The radical effect of this model for human history and diversity was that human unity was present at the point of origin only, there was no means within the metaphor whereby the branches and sub-branches could be rejoined. The emphasis was on reconstructing a basic set of national, regional or racial origins, though there remained a theologically inspired universal linguistics. In these nationalist reconstructions, the original language was restored through all the vicissitudes of 'Mixture and Change' (Pezron 1706: 150). The stricter the philological method, i.e. the more the method was dominated by methodological purism and caution in the face of superficial resemblance, the more difficult it became to offer chronologically 'deep' reconstructions of history.

The power of the philological method was in part the power of writing systems themselves. For once words were written down, they were decontextualized in a fundamental way and could be compared. The resulting observed affinities were then presented as independent truths which could be brought to bear on matters 'which have hitherto lain in Obscurity' (Pezron 1706: 34).

Linguistic speculation created an extremely unstable horizon of identification, since the resemblance between a few words in geographically and culturally distant languages might lead to the postulation of complex migrations in order to make the link between the present diversity and past affinities. Claims of antiquity for particular vernacular languages entered the idiom of modern European linguistic nationalism. Eventually, questions of the antiquity, lineage and original homeland of languages took on real political resonance. As the modern sciences of language emerged, they were critical of the speculative etymology of eighteenth- and early nineteenth-century scholars, which on the basis of perceived similarity between word forms led to what seemed in retrospect outlandish claims about prehistoric affinities and migrations.

The Aryan hypothesis

The origin of the Aryan question is usually, though somewhat simplistically, traced to Sir William Jones's address to the Royal Asiatic

Society in 1786. Jones argued on the basis of linguistic resemblances for a historical 'affinity' between the ancient language of India, Sanskrit, and European languages such as Greek and Latin. This affinity was so strong that 'no philologer could examine them all three, without believing them to have sprung from some common source'. Applying the biblical model, Jones, in identifying a linguistic connection between European languages and Sanskrit, had also suggested a historical affinity between the speakers of those languages. This statement, canonized in the context of a rising comparative and historical science of language, posed a profound set of questions for European intellectuals, concerning the nature of linguistic affinity and the original homeland of the Aryan people. The debate about the Aryans became a debate about the original locus and essence of the Europeans, and their relation to other peoples and territories.

Japhet was effectively the first Aryan: the term 'Japhetic' was used in the late eighteenth and early nineteenth centuries for a language family made up of European and Asian languages, that is, in the terms preferred by the new science of historical and comparative linguistics (comparative philology), 'Indogermanic' (*indogermanisch*), Indo-European (Siegert 1941/42: 73–7) or Aryan. The third son of Noah, Japhet, became the idealized ancestor of the European; in this sense he became a transitional figure between the biblical account of history and the secular, philological story which looked back to a set of ideal ancestors known as Aryans. Secular versions of this history sought to locate the Aryans in an original homeland, a point of origin which was in effect an Aryan Garden of Eden (Olender 1992).

In the context of British colonialism in India, the impact of 'Aryanism' was dramatic. For some, the existence of a linguistic affinity was a justification for a benign paternalism. Canon Farrar, in contemplating the branches of the Indo-European language family, concluded that it was proof of the affinity between Europeans, Persians and Indians; British colonialism was a coming home 'with splendid gifts to visit a member of one common family' (1878: 306–7). Samuel Laing gave a public lecture in Calcutta in 1862 'on the virtues of Aryan brotherhood', though the Indian Aryans were understood as the older brother who 'once far out-stripped us' but now had 'fallen behind in the race' (Laing 1895; Leopold 1974; Maw 1990: 36–7).

Under the influence of European Romanticism, national movements based on the linguistic affinity played an increasingly important role in the transformation of the European dynastic order. However, the gradual rise of a scientific discipline devoted to the study of race, the discipline of racial anthropology, drew attention to what appeared in retrospect as the ill-defined and confusing concept of *Volk*. This led to the replacement of the biblical concept of a people defined as a descent group or lineage sharing a common language with two independent indices of affinity: the linguistic and the racial. The weight of scholarly or 'scientific' opinion eventually accepted the distinction between racial and linguistic identity. However, the assumption was generally made that, at the point of origin, racial and linguistic identity had been congruent, that *Volk* and *Rasse* had been one.

In the case of the Aryans, the original Aryan *Volk* was made up of 'true' Aryans (i.e. racially pure Aryans) speaking the Aryan language. The distinction provided a potential index of historical change by providing an ideal 'pure' origin, since the greater the disjunction between language and race, the greater the distance from that origin. There was room for debate about how far these original relationships had been disrupted in particular contexts, and many linguists argued that linguistic affinity did have a role in reconstructing the past.

This model had two important consequences. The first was that the linguistic affinity between Europeans and Indians was held to say nothing definitive about their racial relationship. The determination of racial affinity was the disciplinary task of racial anthropology. The second was that the presence of an Aryan language in India was evidence that a once great civilization had been destroyed by racial miscegenation, since the original speakers of that language had been lost to history. Archibald Henry Sayce (1845–1933), Professor of Assyriology at Oxford, made this clear when he noted: 'When scholars had discovered that the Sanskrit of India belonged to the same linguistic family as the European languages, they jumped to the same conclusion that the dark-skinned Hindu and the light-skinned Scandinavian must also belong to one and the same race.' (1888: 167) The logic of this position also applied to contemporary linguistic communities. The blood that ran in the veins of the English, who were bound together by a common language, was derived from 'a very various ancestry' (Sayce 1888: 168): 'The Cornishman now speaks English; is he on that account less of a Kelt than the Welshman or the Breton?'

The insistence on the distinction between linguistic and racial identity became the foundation of a racial critique of modern nationalism. The French race theorist Georges Vacher de Lapouge (1854–1936), whose work *L'Aryen* was an important text of 'Aryanism', wrote that Aryan 'was far from being a satisfactory term' (1899: 330), as it fed the impression that 'all the Indo-European peoples . . . descended from the Aryan stock, which is supposed to have swarmed all over Europe and a part of Asia'. Lapouge was troubled by the indiscriminate use of 'Aryan' as a racial term since it included many modern individuals who were not of the original type, that is the long-skulled blond-haired type he referred to as *Homo Europaeus*, the dominant element of the original Aryans (1899: 341). To call all the speakers of Aryan languages 'Aryan' was to confuse the part with the whole. For the racial aristocrat, the use of the term 'Aryan' for the 'brachycephalic' (short-headed) masses flattered racially those of inferior type, who were destined to be followers and never leaders. Lapouge's discourse was intrinsically problematic for European nationalism: 'In countries inhabited jointly by Homo Europaeus and Homo Alpinus, the former element possesses more than its proportionate share of wealth' (1897: 61).

Houston Stewart Chamberlain, in the preface to his *Arische Anschauung* ([1905] 1938: 9), noted the problems with the term, accepting a phrase like 'Aryan world-view', but preferring to reserve it for that people [*Volk*], which descended several thousand years ago from the Central Asian high plateau into the valleys of the Indus and the Ganges and which, claimed Chamberlain, by means of strict caste laws had kept itself pure from mixing with foreign races. In his influential work *Die Grundlagen des neunzehnten Jahrhunderts*, first published in 1899, Chamberlain concluded that we can perhaps only say of individuals rather than whole nations that they are Aryans: 'Linguistic affinity does not provide an absolute proof of a communality of blood.' Theories about the migration of the Aryans from east to west or west to east are based on only meagre evidence, and the evidence is strong that the 'European Aryans' have been settled in Europe since time immemorial ([1899] 1932: 314–15).

The separation of linguistic identity from racial identity offered reassurance that dark-skinned Indians were not of the same blood as Europeans, yet it was also problematic for the new linguistic nationalisms of Europe, since it brought into focus the racial diversity of the European nation states. It suggested that communities based on language were inauthentic, in relation to the deep structure of race: 'The distinctions of race must be older than the distinctions of language' (Sayce 1888: 168).

The scientific recognition of the distinction between racial and linguistic identity was therefore fundamental to anxiety about racial miscegenation and cultural decline. This fed a virulent racism and a horror of the assimilation of the superior by the inferior. The contemporary relevance of Aryan invasion theory was outlined by Madison Grant (1916: 64–5), who made a direct parallel between ancient India and the south of the United States: 'In Hindustan the blond Nordic invaders forced their Aryan language on the aborigines, but their blood was quickly and utterly absorbed in the darker strains of the original owners of the land. [. . .] In our Southern States Jim Crow cars and social discriminations have exactly the same purpose and justification.' The modern-day Indian spoke 'a very ancient form of Aryan language', but no trace was left of the blood of the 'white conquerors':

> The boast of the modern Indian that he is of the same race as his English ruler, is entirely without basis in fact, and the little dark native lives amid the monuments of a departed grandeur, professing the religion and speaking the tongue of his long forgotten Nordic conquerors, without the slightest claim to blood kinship. [. . .] No ethnic conquests can be complete unless the natives are exterminated and the invaders bring their own women with them. (Grant 1916: 64–5)

From the second half of the nineteenth century onwards there had arisen a series of political movements based on communality of language, but within the assumptions of affinity within the biblical paradigm. These were Pan-Germanism, Pan-Italianism, Pan-Slavism, Pan-Arabism and the pan-Turkic movement known as the Turanian movement. But if language was not an accurate guide to blood kinship, then these movements, if understood as grounded in a historically real descent group or lineage, were based on intellectual fictions, and the collectivity of language covered or masked an underlying miscellaneous assortment of races. In successive waves, linguistic and then racial concepts of 'natural' or 'authentic' offered a continual challenge to the socio-political order, with the notion of linguistic nationalism challenged almost immediately by racial anthropology. The new collective ideologies that were transforming the political map of Europe defined dynastic states and colonial empires as 'inauthentic' in relation to the natural ecology of human diversity.

Aryan versus Semite

The term 'Aryan' and its equivalents (Indogermanic, Indo-European) had an extremely complex and diverse development in the course of the nineteenth century. In Gobineau's *Essai* (1853–5), there had been no historical or polemical contrast between Aryans and Semites, but Gobineau's work contributed to the spread of the term 'Aryan' in intellectual circles and popular science. Its most public, politicized usage was in the opposition between Aryan and Semite. While many pan-German ideologues argued that participation by Jews in the life

of the German *Volk* was possible if they relinquished all particularity of belief, Wilhelm Marr (1819–1904) rejected the idea of Jewish
assimilation, and saw Germans and Jews locked in a life-and-death
struggle (Marr 1879). The philologist Friedrich Max Müller
(1823–1900) viewed this opposition as fundamental:

> As the language of the Veda, the Sanskrit is the most ancient type of
> the English of the present day (Sanskrit and English are but varieties
> of one and the same language), so its thoughts and feelings contain in
> reality the first roots and germs of that intellectual growth which by
> an unbroken chain connects our own generation with the ancestors of
> the Aryan race – with those very people who at the rising and setting
> of the sun listened with trembling hearts to the songs of the Veda, that
> told them of bright powers above, and of a life to come after the sun
> of their own lives had set in the clouds of the evening. Those men were
> the true ancestors of our race; and the Veda is the oldest book we have
> in which to study the first beginnings of our language, and of all that
> is embodied in language. We are by nature Aryan, Indo-European, not
> Semitic: our spiritual kith and kin are to be found in India, Persia,
> Greece, Italy, Germany; not in Mesopotamia, Egypt, or Palestine.
> (Müller 1871: 4)

In many anti-Semitic ideologies, a Manichaean struggle was
evoked between two cosmic forces fighting for the soul of western
civilization, and at the centre of this struggle was a debate about the
nature of Christianity. Was Christianity a 'Semitic' religion, and if so,
how could it play a central role in the European identity? If Jesus
was a Jew, did not the conversion of Europe to Christianity represent
a form of Semitization? One solution to this problem, offered by
Theodor Fritsch (1852–1933), was to emphasize the role of Jesus as
a radical critic of Judaism, defined as corrupt and priest-ridden, with
its mechanical rituals, its legalism and logocentricism ('Gesetzes- und
Buchstabenreligion'), its rationalism and worship of Mammon, and
its messianic yearning for a world dominion of the priesthood (Fritsch
1933: 64–5). Academic theorists located an alternative origin in the
lost Aryans, a people which erupted into history by sweeping down
from the mountains or high plateaus of Asia onto the lowlands below.
It was this opposition between Aryan and Semite that shaped the
use of the term 'Aryan' in various strands of anti-Semitic and anti-
Catholic thought prevalent in the south of Germany and Austria. The
opposition between Aryan and the non-Aryan as the Jew was popularized by Ludwig Schemann, the German translator of Gobineau,
through the Wagner circle at Bayreuth (Schmitz-Berning 1998: 55).
This usage was institutionalized through the term *Arierparagraph* or

'Aryan clause'. Such clauses excluding Jews were introduced by Austrian sporting associations and student societies in the late nineteenth century. The term was used in this oppositional sense in Hitler's *Mein Kampf*, and through these sources entered the public language of the Third Reich.

However, the developments in the scholarly world discussed above, in particular the rise of a self-consciously scientific discipline of racial anthropology, had led to a widespread academic consensus that 'Aryan' referred to a family of languages, not to a discrete human racial group. This was recognized by Max Müller himself, who realized that, according to the latest developments in science, this was a strictly inaccurate phrase: 'Aryan, in scientific language, is utterly inapplicable to race' (Müller [1888] 1912: 90). Scholars increasingly devoted a great deal of energy to disambiguating racial, linguistic, national and political categories (Steinthal 1896; Helm 1923), which they saw as being constantly muddled up by ordinary citizens and nationalist ideologues. Max Müller offered this much-quoted conclusion: 'To me an ethnologist who speaks of an Aryan race, Aryan blood, Aryan eyes and hair, is as great a sinner as a linguist who speaks of a dolicocephalic dictionary or brachycephalic grammar' ([1888] 1912: 120).

In his *Biographies of Words*, Müller noted that sites for the Aryan homeland had been proposed in the east and the north (but not in the south or the west), but the 'actual site of the Aryan paradise will probably never be discovered'. The site itself was not a matter of great importance: 'Most of the Aryan nations in later times were proud to call themselves children of the soil, children of their mother earth, autochthones' ([1888] 1912: 127). However, 'patriotic scholars' were now smitten with the idea of a 'German, Scandinavian, or Siberian cradle of Aryan life'. Müller himself was still convinced that the origin of the Aryans lay 'somewhere in Asia' ([1888] 1912: 127). A range of methodological and ideological factors were converging to promote the case of northern Europe as the cradle of the Europeans. The east was increasingly seen not as an exotic origin but as a source of racial menace.

Nazism and the term 'Aryan'

Nazism inherited the ambiguities of this political and intellectual scene. It was committed to creating congruity between the political and the natural boundaries of the *Volk* – this judged primarily by the (idealized) extent of its geographical speech community. Yet language alone was not a true guide to the boundaries of the *Volk*. There was no racial or biological barrier to linguistic assimilation. Nazi theorists pointed to the fact that Negroes in the United States spoke English rather than African languages. Jews were the very embodiment of the split between language and race in modernity (von Leers 1938: 400). German Jews spoke an 'Aryan language', i.e. German, as their mother tongue. The application of racial categories was, however, likewise problematic. For example, the Nordic race was not congruent with the boundaries of the German *Volk*; there were Nordic elements in all the populations of northern Europe. Racial anthropology was thus a disruptive discourse in relation to linguistic nationalism, which had been seen for much of the nineteenth century as the foundational principle of German unity.

In the early years of Nazi rule, there was a collision between this populist-political term and the basic tenets of racial anthropology. From the point of view of the National Socialist regime, there were a number of fundamental problems with the term 'Aryan'. Firstly, if used in a positive sense ('of Aryan descent'), it failed to distinguish Germans from non-Germans, since the concept 'Aryan' was much wider than 'German'. Used in the negative, the term also caused problems in relation to the status of foreign nationals resident in Germany (Gansmüller 1987: 82). Though it was primarily targeted at Jews, it actually failed to pick them out in any precise or legally defined way, even if everyone knew what 'non-Aryan' was intended to mean. There was the question of long-standing European populations such as the Finns and the Hungarians who did not speak an Indo-European or Aryan language. Furthermore, it had been long argued by scholars that the term 'Aryan' referred to a language family and connoted a linguistic not a racial identity. In short, the term 'Aryan' was unable to make the required racial distinctions (Feldscher 1943: 20), though one suggestion was to reject use of 'non-Aryan' for Jewish but retain 'Aryan' for peoples which consisted of predominantly Nordic racial elements (Mollison 1934: 47–8).

The term 'Aryan race' (*arische Rasse*) was not favoured in official documents in Nazi Germany, and instances of this phrase are extremely rare, though it is used in reporting the views of earlier race theorists (e.g. Lothar Tirala on Gobineau, 1935: 84ff.). Laws passed in the early years of the Nazi regime used the notion of 'Aryan descent', but exclusively in its negative form, so that those 'of non-Aryan descent' were excluded from different aspects of public life (Essner 2002: 135, n. 108). In the Law for the Restoration of the Civil Service (Gesetz zur Wiederherstellung des Berufsbeamtentumes, 7 April

1933, Reichsgesetzblatt I s. 175), civil servants who were 'of non-Aryan descent' ('Beamte, die nicht arischer Abstammung sind') were to be compulsorily retired (with exceptions made for those who were appointed before 1 August 1914, or who had served at the front in the First World War, or whose father or son had been killed in the war). Non-Aryan descent was defined so as to include those with one (or more) Jewish grandparent(s). The Minister of the Interior also had discretionary powers to make recommendations in other cases (ss. 3.1, 3.2). The Editors Law (Schriftleitergesetz, 4 October 1933, Reichsgesetzblatt I s. 713) excluded from editorial positions anyone of non-Aryan descent or married to someone of non-Aryan descent (s. 5.3). Similarly, the Defence Law (Wehrgesetz, 21 May 1935, Reichsgesetzblatt I s. 609) made Aryan descent a prerequisite for active military service, and for the taking of positions of authority (ss. 15.1, 15.3). But the racial use of the term 'Aryan' was politically and legally problematic (Schulle 2001: 75–6).

The question of how a non-Aryan was to be defined in relation to this and subsequent laws was controversial. There was concern from some of the bureaucrats responsible for policy that valuable and hitherto loyal racial elements were being alienated from the *Volk*. Someone who was a quarter Jewish was also three-quarters 'Aryan' (Gruchmann 1990: 168). For Party radicals such as Julius Streicher this was much too lenient; there were calls for the compulsory sterilization of *Mischlinge*. The expert on Jewish affairs in the Ministry of the Interior, Bernhard Lösener, wrote an account of the behind-the-scenes debates about how official anti-Semitism was to be translated into legal form (see Weingart et al. 1992: 505–13). Lösener subsequently defined his role as that of trying to moderate policy with regard to *Mischlinge*, since in this regard there was room for flexibility that was absent with the 'full-blooded' Jews (*Volljuden*) (Schleunes 2001). What is clear is the fundamental confusion about the nature of the racial hybridity involved (Koonz 2003: 171ff.). In contrast to the 1933 law, the 1935 laws defined any individual with three Jewish grandparents as a Jew. In the case of the *Mischlinge* with one Jewish grandparent (*Mischling 2. Grades*) or two (*Mischling 1. Grades*), the definition of who counted as a Jew merged the ostensibly 'race-biological' and cultural criteria, including membership of the Jewish community and marriage to a Jew.

In late 1935, a terminological shift took place in the language of the law, and the term 'Aryan' ceased to be used. The Citizenship Law (Reichsbürgergesetz, 15 September 1935, Reichsgesetzblatt I s. 1146) restricted citizenship to those 'of German or cognate blood' ('deutschen or artverwandten Blutes', s. 2.1), and the Law for the

Protection of German Blood and German Honour (Gesetz zum Schutz des deutschen Blutes und der deutschen Ehre, 15 September 15 1935, Reichsgesetzblatt I s. 1146) forbade marriage and sexual intercourse between Jews and those 'of German or cognate blood' (ss. 1.1, 1.2). These laws did not speak of a 'Jewish race', but of Jews defined 'according to race' ('der Rasse nach'), as opposed to converts to Judaism (Erste Verordnung zum Reichsbürgergesetz, 14 November 1935, Reichsgesetzblatt I s. 1333). This law also evoked the concept of 'the purity of the blood' ('die Reinheit des Blutes', ss. 6. 1, 6.2). The phrase 'of German or cognate blood' was used in the later Civil Service Law (Beamtengesetz, 26 January 1937, Reichsgesetzblatt I s. 41, ss. 25.1, 72.1).

The official solution was to replace the problematic term 'Aryan' with the notion of 'German blood ties'. Setting out the argument for a *Sippenamt* (Genealogical Office), Achim Gercke (1934) argued that such an office would 'watch over the purity of the blood' (*Blutsreinheit*) of the *Volk*. Its task would be to awaken the 'racial will of the people', and those who worked in the office should represent the best 'German blood' (*deutsches Blut*). Dr Ernst Brandis, a senior legal bureaucrat, in his commentary on the Law for the Protection of German Blood and German Honour and the Law for the Protection of the Hereditary Health of the German people (Gesetz zum Schutze der Erbgesundheit des deutschen Volkes or Ehegesundheitsgesetz, 18 October 1935), defined 'German blood' in the following terms:

> The German people is no unitary race, rather it is composed of members of different races (of the Nordic, Phalian, Dinaric, Alpine, Mediterranean, East-Elbian race) and mixtures between these. The blood of all these races and their mixtures, which thus is found in the German people, represents 'German blood'. (Brandis 1936: 33)

At the 1936 conference of the International Federation of Eugenic Organizations (IFEO) held in the Netherlands, Falk Ruttke, in presenting the German government's new eugenic policies, affirmed that *Volk* was the fundamental concept for the National Socialist worldview. The *Volk* was a self-aware composite of families related by blood, within which individual members represented racial mixtures out of the closely related races. The *Volk* as a whole was united by a single race that bound all its members (a reference to the Nordic or Nordic-Phalian race) and had developed its own moral and ethical system (*Gesittung*) and its own language (Ruttke 1937a: 25). There is no mention of an 'Aryan' race, and this notion of the racially hybrid German *Volk* followed academic orthodoxy (with variations in the detail, i.e. the designation, number, nature of the different races), not only that of German racial anthropologists, but also that of racial anthropologists internationally.

Feldscher (1943: 20–1) explained that to be 'of German blood' one had to be formed out of the racial mix of the German *Volk* as it had existed for millennia. This was a community with a shared biological inheritance. Each German shared a large number of ancestors with their fellow Germans, and that community was well-defined and distinct. Thus it *did* make sense to speak of 'German blood', in the sense of belonging to the German *Volk*. This designation did not give any information about the specifics of the individual's identity in terms of the races that made up the German people.

The expression 'of cognate blood' referred to members of peoples which were made up of the same races that were combined in the German *Volk*. The difference between the Germans and members of these other peoples was the contrasting proportions (*Anteilsgrad*) of the racial mixture (Feldscher 1943: 21). 'Racially foreign' (*fremdrassig*) were those peoples who consisted of races which were not components of the German *Volk*, such as Negroes, Gypsies and Jews (1943: 22). Racial mixing between related races usually led to harmonious results, whereas that between distant races was pathological (1943: 23)

A circular issued by the Ministry of the Interior on 26 November 1935 advised that the designation 'German-blooded' (*deutschblütig*) was to be used in preference to both 'Aryan' and what was perceived as the linguistically awkward 'of German or cognate blood' (Feldscher 1943: 20). Bureaucratic language required a single adjectival term to replace the original 'Aryan' (Schmitz-Berning 1998: 149–50). The term *deutschblütig* was prescribed for use in the context of the Registry Office (Feldscher 1943: 20). Feldscher however noted that the changed national-political circumstances meant that the use of the term ought to be restricted. This was – possibly – a reference to the fact that Germany was at war with the United States, which had a large population of German origin.

It was accepted in official publications that the notion of 'Aryan' was derived from linguistics, and was only properly to be used in relation to a language family, the Indogermanic or Aryan languages. It had no current racial basis (Ulmenstein 1941: 11–13; Feldscher 1943: 20). A prominent encyclopedia, in the briefest of entries, classified the term as belonging to race-political (*rassenpolitisch*) discourse, and its use was to contrast with 'Jewish' (ML, I 1936: 556). While some Nazi activists were not interested in definitional technicalities, these were a central concern for administrators and policy makers. Falk Ruttke

(1939: 7) argued that conceptual clarity (*Begriffsklarheit*) in matters of race and nationality was fundamental.

Critics of Nazism and the Aryan hypothesis

Critics of National Socialist ideology, both then and now, have failed to grasp this narrative. They have been misled by use of the term 'Aryan' in the early laws and in many public contexts in the Third Reich. The term 'Aryanization' (*Arisierung*) was used for the state-authorized seizure of Jewish property, and the popular terms for the genealogical certificate required to prove an individual's racial identity (the *Abstammungsnachweis*) were *Ariernachweis* or *Arierpass*. It has been assumed that this terminology reflected the ideologically distorted views of scholars and academics about the relationship of language to race.

Günther consistently rejected the racial use of the term 'Aryan', fearing that it would lead to the misleading classification of non-Nordic racial elements (1930: 13–14). Günther argued against its use in any scholarly context, including linguistics, ethnography and racial anthropology. The juxtaposition of 'Aryan' with 'Semitic' confused linguistic with racial identity. The use of 'Aryan' in linguistics instead of Indogermanic was also ill-advised, as the term would be again used to designate anthropological race in a confusing way (1934: 13–44).

The British bio-statistician Karl Pearson (1857–1936), who shared many of the eugenic and racist beliefs of National Socialist ideology (Semmel 1958), saw the Nazis as interrupting a natural process of assimilation by the Jews in Germany. This process of intermarriage had led to a change in the cephalic index of Jews, rather than to any environmental adaptation. On the label 'Aryan', he commented as follows:

> Of course the German-speaking peoples are far from forming a single race. They cover a wide range of racial groups still very imperfectly mixed, and no one pure German type really exists; they, the Germans, are far from a pure Nordic community. Under the circumstances, they have taken the term 'Aryan' to describe their commixture – a word stolen from linguistics – and covering a vast variety of racial groups other than German. (Pearson 1936: 33)

But by the time Pearson's piece was published, the label had been dropped.

Confusion about the actual situation in Nazi identity theorizing can be traced right through the critical literature on Nazi Germany.

The American social psychologist Knight Dunlap (1875–1949) stated that the Aryan myth was 'completely discredited': 'Ethnologists (outside Germany) do not speak of an Aryan race any more than they speak of a Jewish race. Linguists no longer speak of an Aryan family of languages, preferring the less succinct but more accurately descriptive term 'Indo-European' (1944: 206).

The historian Saul K. Padover, in a discussion of how the Japanese, now dubbed 'yellow Aryans', had assimilated 'the explosive potency of "race" as a propaganda instrument', argued that 'the dogma of race is an ugly weapon in the hands of the Axis powers precisely because it has no scientific validity' (1943: 191). Japanese propaganda had pointed to the hypocrisy of attacks on Nazi racial policy from the United States, given the low status of the Negro, and made use of anti-colonial rhetoric in appealing for Asian solidarity. Padover saw the danger of this propaganda in its accurate diagnosis of injustice and racial inequality among the western democracies. It needed to be countered by offering increased freedom to 'non-privileged peoples'. Padover saw the use of Aryan as a racial term as fundamental to Nazi ideology (1943: 191).

However, Morris Edward Opler (1907–1996), an American anthropologist and opponent of racism, criticized 'a smug and self-righteous tendency . . . to exculpate ourselves from responsibility for the "thinking with blood" that has made the world a shambles' (1944: 451). Opler stressed the international nature of these ideas, and the hypocrisy of criticizing German theorists for 'building the theoretical foundations of organicism and racism', giving a long list of apologists from the United States 'who have stood fast for biology against culture' (1944: 451).

This misleading line of criticism of the term 'Aryan' continued after the war and the defeat of Nazism. In his *Human Types* (1956), the British anthropologist Raymond Firth summed up the Nazi error as follows:

> The term Aryan much used in Hitlerite Germany is kept by scientists as a name for types of language only. To what original race or races the speakers of the ancient Aryan languages belonged we are not yet certain. But we are sure that the peoples of Europe who claim to be Aryan in physical type are using the term in quite a different sense from the scientific one; it must be regarded as a wish-fulfilment rather than a statement of fact. (Firth [1938] 1956: 20)

Firth also attacked the notion of racial purity, noting that 'all modern populations must be supposed to be very mixed from a racial point of view' ([1938] 1956: 21). But no Nazi racial anthropologist would have pretended otherwise.

One of the most significant discussions of language and race in Nazi ideology is that of Léon Poliakov (1974). Noting a contrast with other developing European nationalisms, Poliakov documents in detail a long history of deriving a German collective identity from the German (or Germanic) language. This history is unusual in the European context, he contends – following the twentieth-century German linguist Johann Leo Weisgerber, (1899–1985) – because the order of inference was from language to people rather than the reverse (Poliakov 1974: 73). Poliakov describes a tradition of 'Germanomania' down to the Romantic era with the historical speculations and idealizations found in the work of Johann Gottfried von Herder, Johann Gottlieb Fichte (1762–1814) and Friedrich Schlegel (1772–1829) (Poliakov 1974: 71–105). Speaking of these Romantic writings, Poliakov observes 'how little distinction these writers make between the criteria of *language* and *race*' (1974: 100). But this is an entirely anachronistic criticism, akin to accusing them of ignoring the findings of modern genetics. Poliakov is intent on locating the origins of the Nazi heresy in a confusion of language and race. There seem to be two contradictory ideas at work: firstly, the notion that the confusion between linguistics and race theory was set in motion by linguists; secondly, the notion that the idea of racial supremacy is the key idea behind Nazism. The problem is that there is no necessary relationship between these two positions. One might confuse language and race and believe in the equal worth of all human beings. Alternatively, one might rigidly separate linguistic and racial criteria, and be convinced of the superiority of some races over others. This was indeed the Nazi position.

More recently, James Mallory (1989: 269) argues that 'one hardly need emphasize that the implementation of Aryan supremacy by the Nazis was wholly inconsistent with Aryan as a linguistic term', since 'the myth of Aryan supremacy was neither a direct nor necessary consequence of the philological discoveries of the nineteenth century'. Nazism involved 'the misappropriation of a linguistic concept and its subsequent grafting onto an already existing framework of prejudices, speculations and political aspirations'. Mallory concludes that the Indo-Europeans 'leave more than the legacy of Aryan supremacy'. Yet one can see contemporary controversies in India concerning the rift between 'Aryan' and 'Dravidian' as a direct legacy of western linguistic theorizing (Chaudhuri 1974: 312).

Max Müller has acquired a quite unjustified reputation as the opponent of race theory and the ideological abuses of Aryanism. His argument was a methodological one, not an attack on Aryanism as an ideology: 'We [linguists or philologists] have made our own terminology for the classification of languages; let ethnologists make their own for the classification of skulls, and hair, and blood' ([1888] 1912: 120–1). No Nazi race theorist would have disagreed.

The proposition that terms like 'Aryan', 'Indogermanic', 'Celtic', 'Semitic', etc. properly refer to linguistic identities is highly misleading. These terms tended to be defined and elaborated by scholars of language, but historically they expressed the notion of *Volk* as a lineage group defined by its linguistic distinctiveness and territorial origin. This notion of identity operated until racial anthropologists began to promote their own claims to plot scientifically human affinities, and to argue that terms like 'Aryan' and 'Semite' should be used only to refer to linguistic unities.

There never has been a purely linguistically based theory of identity in European thought; rather, language has been used as an index of descent, affinity and shared identity. Developments in racial anthropology, interacting with the increasing sense of the blurring of boundaries in modernity, created a scientific framework and a meta-language in which one could separate racial lineage from linguistic affinity. The dramatic nature of this separation, the diagnosis of which was only possible once scientific concepts of identity had been developed, fed the anxiety that the original congruencies of human 'ecological' diversity were disappearing. While notions of linguistic affinity and homeland remained, the pre-modern notion of lineage could not withstand scrutiny from racial anthropologists.

Given the consensus that academics under the National Socialists abused the term 'Aryan', it is deeply ironic that one of the few serious historical analyses of this term has been written by a Nazi scholar, Hans Siegert, of Munich University (1941/2: 73). Siegert was a student and colleague of Professor Walter Wüst, the academic head of Himmler's scholarly organization within the SS, Ancestral Heritage or Ahnenerbe. This study remains arguably the single most authoritative discussion (Pollock 1993: 120). In addition to tracing the complex and confusing history of the use of the term, Siegert pointed to the current state of terminological confusion. Every German was familiar with the use of the term to mean 'non-Jewish', but even students of philology had little idea what to understand by a Seminar in Aryan Culture and Linguistics (Seminar für Arische Kultur- und Sprachwissenschaft) (Siegert 1941/42: 73 fn.).

At the close of his discussion, Siegert concluded that it was doubtful whether the usage of 'Aryan' as equivalent to 'of German or cognate blood', which had gained popular currency so quickly, could be eradicated. It might be possible to use a neologism, or adopt a form such as *teutisch*, meaning 'belonging to one's own people', but he noted that common usage could not be easily overthrown ('usus tyrannus!'). On the racial use of the term, Siegert commented as follows (1941/2: 99 fn.): 'For racial anthropology, the term "Aryan" is no longer usable in the first place because we have today a quite different understanding of race than earlier anthropologists'. For this reason, it was all the more important that precision be maintained in scholarly discourse, and that it be used only in the well-defined compound term 'Indoaryan' (*indoarisch*) or the equivalent, but that otherwise it be avoided.

Conclusion

In the Third Reich, the term 'Aryan' became embedded in popular discourse with a racial meaning; in addition, it was used in academic discourse when discussing the historical phenomenon of the Aryan people, and Aryan civilization, which might be argued to underlie contemporary German culture in opposition to the 'Semite'. However, any ambiguity about the contemporary status of the term 'Aryan' threatened to suggest that Jews were Aryans because they spoke an Aryan language. The disambiguation of this required reaffirming the scholarly consensus that 'Aryan' was a linguistic, but not a racial, term.

Taken in isolation, the status of the term 'Aryan' was not a serious problem for the racial anthropologists and linguists of the Third Reich, since they were agreed that there was a clear disciplinary and methodological boundary to be maintained. Its most vexing aspect was the rapidity with which the racial use of this term had taken root in popular discourse, leading to a degree of confusion and uncertainty. Its use in this erroneous way, however, allowed scholars to observe popular usage from a distance, and offered them a potential role in educating the political authorities and the general public on the latest state of scientific knowledge. The lesson for the political authorities was the importance of keeping a strict control of public discussion about race and identity, and of keeping the basic message simple in the public domain.

The consensus that racial and linguistic categories were distinct reflected a sense that an original congruence had been lost (Reche 1921; Günther 1936: 340). This fed the perception that the natural order of things was being broken down. This order was not protected by the operation of nature, since the link between language and race was fixed only at the point of origin, and could be disrupted by factors such as migration, conquest, miscegenation and assimilation. What the new scientific position on this question made clear was that only the operation of individual and collective will could prevent further disruption, and it was political action as an expression of collective will which offered the possibility of restoring or recreating that original congruence.

The idea that language and race were originally congruent in some sense also gave linguistics and racial anthropology the potential to cooperate in tracing the histories of peoples and languages (Günther 1936: 317). This original congruence model also dramatized the urgent need to halt the blurring of identity in modernity, and the fact that language was not a natural sign of race implied that the decisive operation of political will was required to prevent further slippage and to restore that original congruence (Günther 1936: 340).

There remained however intellectual questions about the extent to which that congruence had been disturbed, and how it might be restored, and the relative importance of the various disciplines that studied the notion of *Volk*. The use of terms like 'of German blood' in place of 'Aryan' displaced the problem from one category to another, and raised a much more fundamental problem, the scientific status of the concept of the German *Volk*. The notion of 'German blood' involved a profound evasion in respect of the nature of the racial mixture which formed the *Volk*, and the interaction between its different racial elements. For if the term 'Aryan' was primarily a linguistic one, then so was 'German' (*Deutsch*). The rejection of the category 'Aryan' logically put a question mark over the category 'German'.

While it was no doubt useful in a propagandistic sense to be able to point to Jews and Africans as a racially foreign element of the German people, there remained a much more politically sensitive issue, namely that of variation of the German people by region and by class. Lapouge's comments about the class structure of France potentially applied no less to Germany. Were some Germans more racially equal than others? Racial anthropologists and eugenicists were obsessed with mapping the relationships between race, class and inherited talent, and in analysing processes of social selection (*soziale Auslese*) (Lenz 1925: 21ff.). For example, as part of a detailed survey of the population of Upper Silesia carried out in the late 1930s, Ilse Schwidetzky (1907–1997) traced connections between racial origin and choice of profession and social mobility in Upper Silesia (Schwidetzky 1938).

The notion that Nazism involved a confusion of language and race is an extended historical red herring, as is the notion that the evils of Nazism can be traced back primarily to modern theories of anthropological race. What needs to be understood is the interaction between the categories of linguists, the discipline of racial anthropology and modern biological and genetic science.

7

Aryan, Nordic and Jew

The Nordic race

The image of the tall, bond, blue-eyed, clean-limbed Nordic is a familiar one in fantasies of physical perfection. This image is associated with the fascist cult of the body in the European tradition. The idealization of the Nordic race or 'Nordicism' (*der nordische Gedanke*) can be seen in the context of wider socio-cultural and political developments in northern Europe, such as the rise of Romantic 'folk' nationalism with liberal-bourgeois characteristics, a growing self-consciousness in relation to landscape and geography, and a new aesthetics of bodily beauty, in particular the idealized naked body set within a natural landscape (figure 10), coupled with anti-urbanism, ecological awareness and the aesthetics of purity (Surén 1936; Krüger 1991). Nordic beauty was held to be superior to, and removed from, mere sexual attractiveness (Hau 2003: 83). The north was the source of 'light', i.e. the creativity and dynamism of the northern European peoples (Pastenaci 1935: 94–5).

Nordicism covered a wide range of ideological and intellectual positions. As with the *völkisch* movement with which it overlapped, there was a wide range of Nordicist attitudes to Christianity. One tendency involved a neo-Pagan rejection of the other-worldliness and the mind-above-body dualism of Christianity, in particular Roman Catholicism, and Judaism. But mainstream bourgeois Nordicism was compatible with Christianity, especially its national, Protestant forms. In this discussion, we are concerned primarily with the impact of the idealization of a Nordic race on attempts to define or create a racially

Figure 10   The idealization of the Nordic race (Hans Surén 1936: 109)

purified German *Volk*, rather than with the wider cultural movement
in Scandinavia and Germany.

The rise of Nordicism as an explicitly racial ideology took place in
the late nineteenth century. The Nordic was associated with the purity
of nature, and had the vulnerability and innocence that was associated with the unworldly. But the underside of racial narcissism was
self-hatred and fear. This was expressed in feelings of inadequacy
in relation to the Jew, who was understood as antithetical to nature.
Jews were a counter-race (*Gegenrasse*). They had a more powerful
race instinct than the Nordic race or Germanic peoples (Driesmans
1912/13: 149; Jakesch 1909: 29), and could thrive in cities and within
the materialism of modernity. The Nordic could also be set against
the Celtic, in a contrast of light versus dark, 'a vision of huge, clear

spaces hanging above the Atlantic in the endless twilight of the northern summer, remoteness, severity' versus the 'Celtic, or sylvan, or terrestrial twilight' (Lewis [1955] 2002: 74; Bramwell 1985: 40).

Racial anthropology, and its political offshoot Nordicism, implied a re-reading of conventional history to bring out the lost 'deep structure' of racial conflict. For example, according to Lothar Stengel von Rutkowski (1908–1992) the Nordic element of France had been reduced by the expulsion of Huguenots. The French Revolution was read as an attack on the Nordic element by the racially inferior masses; it was enough during the French Revolution to have blond hair to be taken to the scaffold (Stengel von Rutkowski 1936: 45). Jens Paulsen saw the struggle between the Nordic and the Mediterranean races as the key to European history (1937). World history was part of racial history (Fischer 1927b: 137). Nordicism could mean admiration for the achievements of Britain or, more frequently, those of the United States: 'The best Europeans are today resident in America' (Lenz 1927a: 266).

The category 'Nordic' predated its appropriation within racial anthropology, and continued to have both parallel cultural-historical and racial meanings (Herpel *c*.1933: 9). Its popularization as a racial category is usually ascribed to the French racial anthropologist, Joseph Deniker (1852–1918), specifically his work *Les races et les peuples de la terre* (Deniker [1900] 1926; Günther [1922] 1930: 22). The immediate intellectual background to this work was a debate about the racial composition of the French nation, seen as divided geographically by the Germanic elements in the north and the Gallo-Roman elements in the south (von See 1994: 213).

Deniker argued on the basis of selected physical traits (cephalic index, hair and eye colour, stature) that there were six basic European races. But this scheme, like all racial taxonomies, was controversial. Ripley complained about Deniker's invention of new terminology, a 'seemingly unnecessary rejection of time-honoured names'. Deniker's Nordic type corresponded well to Ripley's 'Teutonic' (Ripley 1899: 168). Deniker's methodology, according to Ripley, was not a classification of races, but 'a classification of existing varieties' (Ripley 1899: 169–70; Deniker 1904). The Nordic race benefited in this methodological confusion from the apparent salience of its key characteristics. It in effect stood out as a clear case against the mixing and confusion of categories applied to the remainder of Europe. Günther also regarded Deniker's system as in many respects outdated (1933: 99).

Gessler (2000: 84) suggests that Fischer was most probably the first to use *nordisch* as a racial term in German. It was popularized by Günther and Clauss, with strong support from the Nordicist publisher

J. F. Lehmann (1864–1935). In Germany, the origins and pre-history of the Nordic race were a matter of controversy and debate. One question was the relationship of the Nordic race to other racial categories established on the basis of archaeological finds. Günther assumed that the Nordic race had taken on its modern form by 7000 BC, along with the other two foundational European races, the Phalian and the Mediterranean ([1922] 1934:339). One popular hypothesis was that the Nordic race was the result of a transformation of the Cro-Magnon race. The Nordic race had emerged, it was argued, from a small group which had undergone a highly rigorous process of selection and in-breeding during the ice age. However, the exact details were unclear. Fischer argued that the Cro-Magnon type continued to exist alongside the Nordic race in the form of the Phalian (*fälisch* or *dalisch*) race (Günther [1922] 1934: 320). There was debate about the exact nature, number and interrelation of the blond races in northern Europe, and the interrelationship between the Nordic and Phalian races, sometimes known collectively as the 'northern race' (*Nordrasse*).

The Nordic ideal was a fusion of two lines of thought. The first was the tradition of Romantic anti-urbanism. This involved the idealization of the German peasantry or *Bauerntum* (Mai 2002). Münkel (1996: 95–7) traces the origins of the National Socialist idealization of the relationship between 'blood' and 'soil' (*Blut und Boden*) to Wilhelm Heinrich Riehl (1823–1897), generally regarded as the founder of German folklore studies (*Volkskunde*). A sense of crisis was engendered by migration from the country to the city (*Landflucht*). Given that the peasantry was seen as the biological 'motor' which drove society, it was the duty of government to protect and nurture it; the city was a place of degeneration (*Entartung*). This tradition emphasized 'rootedness', organic connection to landscape, and had anti-Christian tendencies, as exemplified in the work of one of the leading folklorists under National Socialism, Eugen Fehrle (Assion 1994).

The second was a complex composite of martial qualities and mobility, associated with the Goths and the Germanic tribes. There was nostalgia for a lost heroic ancestry, as represented by a warrior race which had swept down from the mountains of Asia to conquer Europe. Gobineau had argued that all great achievements in world history were attributable to these lost heroic forebears. Nietzsche's Zarathustra, the symbol of 'the vitalism of ancient Aryan religion', had returned from ten years of mountain solitude to announce the death of God' (Herman 1997: 103). This was the Nordic as a 'warrior' or 'martial race' (*Kriegerrasse*).

There was a desire to evoke a glorious martial past; yet modern ideologies of *Volk* required a continuous history of occupation of the national homeland. This was necessary to clarify the distinction between Germans on the one hand and Jews and Gypsies on the other (Wirth 1914: 137). Both Günther and Walther Darré rejected the idea that the Nordic race should be seen solely as marauding invader, arguing that the history of the Nordic race showed the qualities both of peaceful agricultural settlement and of warlike heroism (Darré 1934: 12). It was important to stress that the Indo-Europeans had not been a 'nomadic' people, and this created an ideological preference for an original homeland within Europe (Reche 1936a: 119).

A further problematic opposition was that between the 'barbarian' prehistory of the Germanic tribes and the classical civilization of Greece and Rome. One strategy was to reject the historiographic tradition that defined the northern tribes as primitive savages and affirm a Germanocentric view of history in which the Germanic peoples were viewed as having their own institutions and cultural order (Hennig 1933: 3; Arntz 1936: 28). The 'primitive' and martial elements of classical culture, including the ideal body of the classical statue, were also celebrated.

Although the use of the term Nordic derived initially from an identification of the Aryan homeland with northwestern Europe, subsequent debate did not necessarily restrict the original homeland of the Nordic race to this location. The problem of reconciling the present-day German *Volk* with this mythic-racial origin remained, since the creation of the German *Volk* was nonetheless the product of a migration and process of settlement, and therefore also of conquest of territory. Günther stressed the need to link the origins of the Nordic race to the origins of the Indo-European peoples, and this pointed to central and southern Europe (Günther 1934: 227ff.). Hans Weinert (1934) argued that the Nordic race had emerged with the freeing of 'Germany' from the last ice age and the transitional middle Stone Age or Mesolithic period. The racial history of the Germans could be fitted into a wider history of humankind, in that the branching off between humankind and the other primates, and the branching of the human races from a common human ancestor, precede the formation of different races in different climatic zones: 'This is the history of the development of humanity, clear and comprehensible in its broad outline; it offers us the only possibility of grasping the nature of our being [*Dasein*], and it loses nothing in dignity and significance, if it once began with the history of anthropoids [*Menschenaffen*]' (Weinert 1934: 31).

Nordic versus Aryan

We can contrast Nordicism with Aryanism in a number of ways. A shift from Aryanism to Nordicism involved a shift from linguistic to racial indices of identity, and in the location of the ancestral homeland from the east to Europe. The evidence for the existence of an original Aryan people was primarily linguistic. The starting point for the Nordic ideal was the proportions of the human body. Aryanism was grounded in relations between words as the key to history: it was in this sense 'logocentric'. An Aryan world-view could be inferred from study of the Aryan languages. Nordicism was concerned with the body as aesthetic sign (or 'icon'): the body was primary seen as an indicator of human identity. The Nordic ideal located the site of original perfection in northern Europe rather than in distant Asia. In this sense, it offered a more straightforward account of historical continuity than the convoluted debate about the origin and migrations of the Aryans. These had to take account of the link to India and other points in the east. The view that the Nordic race had been responsible for not only the great achievements of classical antiquity, and the civilization of ancient India, Persia, perhaps even China (Staemmler 1935: 16), was in effect a relic of biblical-linguistic Aryanism. This was also true of mystic Nordicism (Herrmann 1934).

Aryanism was in one sense more compatible than Nordicism with modern German nationalism, since the Aryans, like the Germans, were understood as a *Volk*. Nordic was a racial category; there was no contemporary Nordic racial community, but there was a German *Volk*. There was a Nordic racial element within the German people, but the nature, extent and role of that Nordic element was highly controversial. In this sense, the German *Volk* could have a historical mission and be capable of mobilization to seize its destiny; the Nordic race was embedded within many different *Völker*. In the contemporary context, it lacked a capacity for independent, concerted action. Individuals were frequently discussed in terms of their membership of a race, as well as of a *Volk*. Lenz argued however that it was impossible in a racially mixed population to determine to which race an individual belonged: people could not be categorized like plants (1934: 181).

Aryanism and Nordicism were not always clearly distinguished, and Nordic racial discourse fused various scholarly disciplines. Eugen Fischer (1923: 15) listed the following 'synonyms' for the Nordic race: 'Kymric, row-grave type, Germanic, Teutonic race, *Homo Europaeus*, *Nordicus*, etc.' ('Kymer, Reihengräbertypus, germanische, teutonische

Rasse, *Homo Europaeus, nordicus* usw.'). Nordic was (and is) also used as a linguistic category, and Aryan was used as a racial term. Scheidt (1930b: 501) argued that the shifts over time in usage from 'Aryan' to 'Germanic' to 'Nordic' represented a gain in precision, though Scheidt himself was critical of what he saw as a substantially oversimplified presentation of the purity of the Nordic regional type (1930a: 140ff.). Neither Aryan nor Nordic was consistently distinguished from 'Germanic' (*germanisch*), itself a linguistic term with racial associations. The categories could be reconciled by postulating an original congruity. For Reche, the original Aryans, i.e. the Indogermanic peoples, were of Nordic race (1936b: 312). Similarly, Lenz argued that the Nordic racial element was common to all the Germanic peoples (1934: 189). In theory, 'Germanic' was distinct from 'German': 'Germanic and Germanicness are to German and Germanness what (classical) Roman and Romanness are to Italian and Italianness' (Mees 2004: 257), but there were clear ideological pressures in favour of the compression of these distinctions. Terms like *Germanentum* could gain rhetorical precision by being set up against 'Jewishness'.

There was also considerable overlap in ideology between these strands. Both Aryanism and Nordicism were oriented towards a lost perfection and implied an ill-defined hope of the restoration of that unity within modernity. These were nostalgic formations, looking back to lost essences, and lamenting the fall of superior peoples or races into racial hybridity. Under the impact of racial anthropology, the notion of a superior Nordic race became in part a substitute for the historically over-complex and confused notion of Aryan.

The Aryan hypothesis was originally associated with an eastern origin, but the further the authentic or symbolic origin was from Germany, the greater the narrative tension. While there was a gain in mystery and historic grandeur, the chain of connectivity from that mystic origin to the present was potentially highly complex, and subject to vicissitudes in intellectual fashion in a wide range of disciplines (comparative linguistics, archaeology, prehistory, etc.). An understanding of the Aryan conquest of India, or the archaeology of prehistorical Europe, was at the same time a potential theory of the nature of the German *Volk*. The prehistorian Gustaf Kossinna (1858–1931) quoted the nineteenth-century German historian Heinrich von Sybel: 'A nation which fails to maintain a living connection with its origins is close to withering away, in just the same way as a tree which has been separated from its root. We are still today that which we were yesterday' (1936: 1). But there was no clear agreement as to how to define the identity of that former self.

A transitional figure between Aryanism and Nordicism was Karl Penka (1847–1912), who argued for the origin of the Aryans in north-west Europe, so that the Aryan race was in effect a Nordic race. Penka also argued that the Nordic race did not survive well in warmer climes, leading to the 'de-Aryanization' (*Entarisierung*) of many peoples speaking Aryan or Germanic languages, unless there was continual renewal from the Nordic heartland (Riedel 1937; Penka 1883, 1886; Schmitz-Berning 1998: 430).

Northern Europe offered an ideologically propitious site of origin for a number of interrelated reasons. There was an association of racial and moral purity with cold climates, in contrast to the sensual excess of the tropical zone (Stepan 2001). The great ice age which was held to have preceded the emergence of the Nordic type could be understood as a particularly severe process of natural selection, out of which emerged a purified and homogenous human type. There was a powerful set of metaphorical associations, with snow and ice, white skin and blondness representing purity. The mountainous terrain of northern Europe, in the Romantic imaginings, could be seen as a pure realm, an abode of the Gods.

Darré accepted the proven northwestern European origin as demonstrating the natural-scientific correctness of the term 'Nordic' (Darré 1930: 188; Schmitz-Berning 1998: 431). This locus of identity had clear advantages in grounding the category Nordic in a simpler form of historical continuity, but the notion that the Nordic element was diluted, and threatened by migration and by its entry into the lives of nations, evoked a peculiar vulnerability. However, there was still a narrative tension with this model, since the superior racial element was understood to have come to Germany from outside. Günther conjectured that all peoples were composed of two popula-tion strata: an indigenous inferior race ruled over by a superior immi-grant race. Once this superior, creative racial element dies out, the *Volk* will decline (Günther [1922] 1934: 200–1).

The Nordic and the Jew

In racial theorizing, there was both a fundamental contrast and a strong parallel drawn between the Nordic race and the Jews. On the one hand, the Jews were frequently understood as racially a 'desert people'; the Nordic race had been formed out of the last ice age. However, both were understood as international, influential, racially defined sub-groups. Just as there was a Nordic element in all the

European peoples, so there was a Jewish one. But, crucially, the Jews were not a single race but a *Volk*. Thus, in contrast to the Nordic race, they were able to operate directly upon history as a collectivity. The Nordic race had fallen into racial hybridity by combining with other European races in the European peoples. The strict academic position was that it was not possible to find an individual who was 100 per cent Nordic; however, one could find individuals who were 100 per cent Jewish. Far from being intrinsically inferior, Jews were superior in their ability to adapt to the conditions of modernity and the city, viewed as toxic to the Nordic race (Fischer 1910: 22; Fischer and Günther 1927: 6).

The concept of the Nordic race as a transnational elite, playing a vital role in the development of high culture wherever it was present, suggested a powerful racial force which operated within, but independently of, modern nation states. It was the racial dynamo which had driven the otherwise ordinary racial mix of the German *Volk* to its historical achievements, and which exercised a decisive influence out of proportion to its numbers. Not only that; in order to operate historically, the Nordic race had left its own homeland in northern Europe; its historical achievements were at the cost of sacrificing that original relationship to homeland and to language.

Viewed from this angle, there was a suppressed parallel with the Jewish people. Egon Freiherr von Eickstedt (1934a: 359) even spoke of an enormous 'Nordic diaspora'. The Jewish people had also left its homeland and entered into history. It operated as a racial force within different nations; its influence and impact was out of proportion to its numbers. A small number of Jews had such power and influence that they could threaten to dominate the life of the *Volk*. Here the contrast with the Nordic race is instructive. The Jewish people had abandoned its original homeland, unlike the Nordic race which still had a dominant presence in its heartland. The Jewish people could thus operate entirely as a deracinated people, and unlike the Nordic race, which was threatened by the modern urbanized culture into which it was being dragged to its destruction, the Jewish people was able to thrive. The Jews were the ultimate case of acclimatization, of universal adaptability, though Eugen Fischer found this quality both in the Jews and the Chinese (1927b: 32). The Nordic race, or, more generally, the Europeans, seemed by contrast the least adaptable of all races. Fischer argued that the northern European was maladapted to the tropics (1927b: 32). Lenz reported that the whites were being outbred by the Negroes in South Africa (1927a: 266). The Nordic race was vulnerable to degeneration outside its traditional homeland and its original rural life-style. Its entry into history was a perpetual sacrifice. Lenz at least saw no similar problem with Nordic settlement in the Slavic east, where the population was a strongly Mongol mixture, and wide territories were open to colonization (1927a: 268). In modernity, the Nordic was however the weaker 'twin' of the Jew.

From the point of view of racial anthropology, the Jews, like the Germans, were a *Volk* not a race. There was no 'Semitic race', but this did not mean that there were no significant racial differences between Jews and Europeans (Fischer 1923: 174). Günther stressed that the linguistic expression of the Oriental race soul should be sought where Ernest Renan had looked for it, i.e. in the Semitic languages (1933: 55). The Jews were therefore a racial mixture, the main elements being the Near Eastern race (which according to Günther shared a common ancestor with the Dinaric race (1933: 51) and the Oriental race (1933: 56). In the opposition between Jews and Germans, Günther discerned an underlying struggle between the Nordic race and the Near Eastern race for mastery of the entire earth (1925: 124–5, 1926: 114).

As a *Rasse* not a *Volk*, the Nordic race was not a functioning collectivity; it was not an organic community, but a latent or potential community. In this sense, it needed the German *Volk* in order to act as a historical agent. We can compare this with the anti-Semitic construct of the Jews as international elite. Seen as dynamic and resourceful, Jews were capable of hollowing out from within the culture of different nations. The Jewish people was a *Volk*, not a *Rasse*, that is it was *not* a virtual community. It could interact and join with other *Völker* without losing its own collective identity. It had this key advantage over the Nordic race, which likewise sought to determine the fundamental nature of the German *Volk*, but which could not act independently of it.

This particular anti-Semitic model was not premised on the racial inferiority of the Jew. This is to misread entirely the racial pessimism that gripped a substantial portion of the German intelligentsia in the run up to the Nazi seizure of power. The familiar repertoire of anti-Semitic rhetoric was remodelled and recycled by *völkisch* ideologues, and this had an impact on racial anthropologists' description of the 'racial character' of the Jews. But there was no suggestion among racial anthropologists that Jews were inferior, as this notion was understood in the racism that was directed at Africans or other 'backward' or 'primitive' groups. The Jews were radically different or 'other', in a very specific sense. They were not racially bound to territory; they were not racially vulnerable to the effects of urbanization; they could adopt national forms (language, dress, culture), simultaneously operating at a transnational level. In the strict

Darwinian sense of 'the fittest' (i.e. fitness relative to environment), Jews were the biologically best adapted to modernity.

One solution for the Nordicist was likewise to seek to colonize the German *Volk* from within. If this were successful, the German *Volk* would become increasingly Nordic, rather than 'Jewish'. This could be done by measures designed to promote the Nordic component, on the assumption that the socially elite or superior elements were also the Nordic. But in this struggle for control of the German soul, the Nordic race needed first to be awakened to awareness of its own collective existence, whereas the Jew, as it were, never slept. Günther characterizes the Nordic person as having no special inclination to penetrate the 'inner life' of foreign races (1933: 60). This ability was, however, the special province of the Jew, though this Jewish-German identity was often understood as a kind of inauthentic mimicry.

The promotion of the Nordic race raised the question of whether, say, the Dinaric or Mediterranean racial elements in the German *Volk* could be seen as racially inferior. This had implications for any understanding of the regional make-up of the German *Volk*, and was highly sensitive in relation to the strong regional, cultural and confessional divisions in German society. Further, the eugenic concern with inherited pathologies, such as alcoholism, criminality, mental and physical disease, implied that the *Volk* contained many sub-standard elements which could not be categorized as 'racially foreign', but also recognized variations in leadership qualities, character, intelligence, bodily fitness. This might be expressed in a class analysis of the genetic quality of the German people. If the Nordic race was identified with the superior racial element, then should not the racially inferior elements be eradicated from the *Volk* in the same way as other foreign racial elements?

Conclusion

As noted above, the transition from Aryan race to Nordic race was effected by the location of the original homeland in northern Europe, which offered one solution to the problematic vagueness and dislocated historical trajectory of the Aryans. One fundamental problem with the diversity of theorizing about origins and homelands was that it was endlessly decentring. If the Aryans had erupted into history from a high Asian homeland, then where was the historical centre of the identities that linked themselves to those Aryans racially and symbolically? If all the world's major cultures showed racial or cultural vestiges of a past Aryan or Nordic glory, was not the whole world a chain of ruins, and were not the physical and spiritual descendants of those great forebears in diaspora, just like the Jews?

The Jews had a spiritual homeland which had been given to them by God. Even though the Temple was in ruins, there was a clear historical narrative recorded textually with the authority of scripture, and a clear teleology to Jewish history linked to that homeland, a teleology taken over in secular form by Zionism. The Jewish homeland could further be understood as a textual homeland, one that could not be conquered, in the sense that the texts and rituals that sustained or embodied Judaism were independent of physical territory and could be memorized, studied and carried from place to place. Jewish history thus had a well-defined teleological structure, looking both backwards, to a place (Jerusalem), and forward, to the coming of the Messiah and a return to Jerusalem. Jewish culture was logocentric ('The people of the Book'); it existed in texts and as law (a so-called 'nomocracy', Chamberlain [1899] 1932: 386) realized as a history of readings and commentaries. Racial anthropology stood in tension with logocentricism, since it was based on images of the human body. It was grounded in an anti-logocentric aesthetic of purity and racial beauty, but needed textual and mathematical interpretation or 'readings' to operate within the conventions of modern universities and the politics of science in modern societies.

There was no authoritative original document for the Aryan-Nordic-Germanic Germans. Even if the Vedic scriptures could be read as confirming an Aryan invasion and conquest, this did not supply a clear original point, and even if it could be understood that way or one could be found, it failed to supply teleology through return to a lost origin. If some Orientalist-Aryanist interpretations of British colonialism in India understood it as a home coming or reunion of long-separated branches of the Aryan family, no such clear narrative was available for the German *Volk*, for which the most pressing political problems lay in the political geography of Europe. While a mystic origin in the high plateaus of Central Asia was appealing to the plethora of secret Germanic and Aryan (Ariosophical) cults, its value as a concept for political mobilization was limited. It also raised a serious question about the relationship to territory of the present-day Germans, as to whether they were the descendants of conquerors or the conquered. If they were the descendants of both, this raised complex questions for an understanding of the racial composition of the German *Volk*. Was Germany, like India, a mixture of Aryan remnants lost among the 'Dravidian' masses?

8

The Nordic Race and the German *Volk*

Introduction

In the first decades of the twentieth century there was intense debate within racial anthropology concerning the idealization of the Nordic race. The implication, not always clearly spelled out, was that the German *Volk* represented the product of the racial fall of the Nordic race. Modern Germany had in effect replicated the Aryan fall in ancient India, albeit with a less dramatic racial contrast between the superior and inferior racial elements. Günther argued that a comparison between Norway, Sweden and Germany would confirm the leading role of the Nordic race, or of racially predominantly Nordic individuals, in Germany. While the overall percentage of Nordic types was higher in Norway and Sweden, in statistical terms Germany had many more, and this was the decisive factor. The Nordic race had a particular mission in relation to the German people (Günther 1925: 36). The countervailing view was that the Nordic race, although it had many fine qualities, had only achieved its greatest heights when it left Scandinavia and mixed with the other European races. Thus, the intellectual, cultural and political achievements of the German *Volk* were far superior to those of the racially purer Scandinavians. The question of racial hybridity was fundamental to debates about the nature of the German *Volk*.

Nordicism was suffused with nostalgia and racial pessimism, though there remained the hope that the Nordic race and the German *Volk* might yet be saved. By contrast, eugenic science, in its pure form, was technocratic and 'progressive', in that it argued for the engineering of a future bio-utopia. Some eugenicists identified the best genetic elements of the German *Volk* with the Nordic race, but in principle eugenic principles applied independently of racial classification, so that in any population or racial group there would be fitter and less fit members. Thus, Bernhard Bavink (1879–1947) supposed that any thoughtful person, even though they belonged to a race seen as inferior by the Europeans, would be concerned with the genetic health of their population (1934: 9).

Questions were continually raised about the relationship between eugenic policies and the concept of a Nordic race. Ploetz's notion of 'biological collective' or *Vitalrasse* stood in uncertain relation to the categories of racial anthropology and to the concept of the Germans as a *Volk*. This had been recognized by the eugenicist Wilhelm Schallmayer (1857–1919) in his questioning of the favouring of the Nordic element above other racial elements of the German people. Schallmayer argued that, leaving aside the fact that there were no pure human races, even within the Nordic component there would be fitter and weaker individuals (Schallmayer 1918: 385; Essner 2002: 43).

At one extreme was fundamentalist Nordicism, which argued for the absolute supremacy of the Nordic race. At the other, was the view that the German *Volk* had benefited from its hybrid quality, as each race had had a specific contribution to make to the success of the whole. Albrecht Wirth argued that the excessive emphasis on race put in danger the 'hard-won unity' of the German *Volk*: Racial anthropology should be confined to historical investigations and kept out of politics (Wirth 1914: 115, 128, 134).

Nordicism and nationalism

One position was that only the Nordic race was an 'original' race. Otto Hauser (1876–1944) saw the contemporary world as one without pure collective races, 'even among Negroes and Eskimos' (1930: 6). Each *Volk* might however display a number of more or less racially pure individuals, who tended to be geographically concentrated. Racial purity was thus the property of the individual, and if that individual mated with another racially pure individual, their children would most probably be of a pure racial type. The Nordic race was an originally pure formation; the Alpine and Mediterranean races, which were relatively recent, were mixed forms which had stabilized. The Alpine race was a product of a mixing of the Nordic with the Polar (yellow) race; the Mediterranean race arose from a mixing of the Nordic with the Negro race. The Nordic race was thus a pure product, unchanged since its origins, whereas other races were hybrids, albeit ones that had stabilized into a fixed set of features. The language of this original pure type was Indogermanic, and 'all the peoples who originally spoke this language were blond' (Hauser 1924: 52; Römer 1989: 69). But this model implied that the Nordic race was subject to a truly dramatic fall by its involvement in the German *Volk*.

A model slightly more congenial for German nationalism was that of Max Gerstenhauer (1873–1940), but tensions between Nordicism and nationalism are evident. Gerstenhauer rejected both Schall-mayer's concept of *Volk* as a reproductive community, as this deprived nationalism of its basis in science, and the notion that *Volk* was purely a linguistic and historical construct (1913: 21). Contrary to Ludwig Wilser's contention, the *Volk did* exhibit 'a commonality of type'. Gerstenhauer defined a *Volk* as 'the community of people sharing a common descent and a common national cultural identity'. A key factor in defining the unity of the *Volk* was a common lan-guage (1913: 9).

One could distinguish a white or European race, a black and a yellow race, but also other 'original races' (*Urrassen*). Within Europe, Gerstenhauer identified three original races: the long-skulled Nordic or Aryan as the actual white or lightest race (*homo europaeus*); a long-skulled but darker southern race (*homo mediterraneus*); and the further darker, short-headed, wide-faced Mongoloid race found in central and eastern Europe, a so-called Alpine race (*homo alpinus* or *homo centralis*) (1913: 18–19). There was a consensus that the German people consisted of two-thirds Germanics (*Germanen*), members of the long-skulled blond Aryan race whose original home-land was Scandinavia, and one-third non-Germanics, representatives of the Alpine race, who preceded the Germanic peoples in central Europe. On the threshold of their entry into world history, the Ger-manics had been, as Tacitus had testified, still 'racially pure, unmixed Aryans of the noble type, which had arisen through the harsh selec-tion process of the ice age' (1913: 19).

This model conceded the mixed nature of the German people, and implicitly that the admixture of non-Aryans involved a loss of purity, and therefore of racial quality. The Alpine component derived from the intermarriage of the Germanics with their indigenous slaves. This had happened in slightly different fashion in different parts of the area of settlement. In the conquest of west and south Germany (Flan-ders to Tyrol), a few of the previous inhabitants survived from the pre-Roman and Roman eras; in the east the enslaved population were Slavs, who though originally Aryan had mixed with racially darker elements; in the west and south, the originally Aryan Celts had been absorbed by the non-Aryan indigenous population, and the Romans who settled there were also no longer purely Aryan. These foreign elements were short-headed (Gerstenhauer 1913: 20).

While almost every German was of mixed race (*Mischling*), Gerstenhauer argued that each people (*Volkheit*) was a collectivity with its own individual and independent character. This collectivity was made up of new physiological building-blocks, which were the consequence of centuries of cross-breeding and propagation. Weismann's neo-Darwinism and Mendel's genetics taught that inherited characteristics were not destroyed, but that in the mixing of two racial groups the individual characteristics of each group remain latent in the total germ plasm (*Keimplasma*). Racial features were not erased and could recur. Someone with blond hair was not therefore necessarily predominantly Germanic, any more than someone with a short head was predominantly non-Germanic. The non-Germanic-looking individual could have latent Germanic features, and can even be Aryan in terms of dispositions and abilities. In this sense, a *Volk* could form a vital racial unity, a *Vitalrasse* (Gerstenhauer 1913: 23).

The German people, from its original formation around 500 BC, and with some exceptions had formed a relatively compact transmission group, so that the overwhelming majority of Germans had common ancestors. Expressions such as 'the folk body' (*Volkskörper*) and 'folk personality' (*Volkspersönlichkeit*) were scientifically justified; a *Volk* shared a common genetic inheritance (*Erbmasse*) (Gerstenhauer 1913: 24). Although the Germans were not racially pure Germanics, their nature was determined by the Germanic race ('germanisch rassenhaft bestimmt', a formulation attributed to Adolf Bartels). There were many intermediate individual variations along a continuum between the two pure racial types, both in bodily type and in individual psychology, but there was also an intermediate average type, a standard or average German (1913: 26). This evolved genetic collectivity had to be protected against further mixing and degradation (1913: 27).

In urging the Germans to protect their racial identity, it was relatively straightforward to ask them to resist intermarriage with foreign racial elements, as in the colonial context in Africa (1913: 40). But Gerstenhauer also considered whether racial selection might be possible within the German people, so that, applying Mendel's laws of heredity, one might recreate a purely 'Germanic' German people by promoting the breeding of those who show predominantly Germanic features. This, he stressed, was a matter primarily of psychological or mental attributes. It would be advisable for Germans to be more aware of this issue, so that they could select a spouse with the best characteristics. The decline in physical beauty illustrated the negative effect of mixing two physically incompatible racial types, such as the Aryan and the Alpine, so that the original, divine beauty of the Germanic people has been lost; but the effects on the psychological and mental constitution were more serious still. Lacking purity and harmony of type, persons of mixed race usually inherited the worst characteristics of the two races (1913: 41–2).

Gerstenhauer noted that some had welcomed racial fusion as progressive, a position which he rejected, but others had raised doubts about a purely mechanical approach to human heredity, as if the only important question was that of selective breeding. Scholars were far from agreed as to whether the production of long-skulled individuals actually would breed Germanic qualities (1913: 42). But these uncertainties should not prevent the Germans from acting; Otto Hauser had proposed that the purest Germanic types, Goths from Sweden, should be brought to Germany and given financial encouragement to start families (1913: 43). Gerstenhauer put more immediate faith in political measures to preserve the German peasantry and to create socio-cultural conditions in which the Germanic element of the population would flourish (1913: 43).

Eugen Fischer's view was a further stage removed from the pure Nordicist position, since he suggested that the German *Volk* had to a degree benefited from racial mixing between the European races (1923). Fischer nonetheless accepted the exceptional qualities of the Nordic race; with Günther he was a judge in a competition to find the best photographic representation of the Nordic racial ideal (Fischer 1927a). Biologically, each *Volk* was an 'enormously varied mixture' (1923: 68). Racial differences between *Völker* were only relative, in that the relative proportions of the races differed among neighbouring peoples; but even boundaries between these collectivities or physical types did not correspond exactly to language boundaries (Fischer 1923: 69).

Fischer also offered an intellectually more sophisticated model of the possible forms of interaction between conquerors and conquered. Conquerors from outside might be unsuited to the climate or other environmental factors, and undergo a process of decline. If the leading stratum of society underwent this gradual process of 'deselection', then the original conquered people might re-emerge as a type (though perhaps with a few genetic markers from the now lost conquering people), and with a different language and culture. The model for this particular interaction was ancient India (1923: 128–30). Another possible outcome was where a biologically well-adapted conqueror expelled the conquered group, but adapted some of the cultural forms of the defeated people (1923: 131). The fate of a people could be influenced by a host of environmental or other factors. Most crucial of all however was the quality of its racial composition, given the great differences in quality between the races, in particular in their mental gifts (1923: 131–2). Where the conquering stratum was in some way compatible with the conquered and able to take on a leadership role, the new *Volk* might experience a sudden rise in economic, political or creative energy. Whether such a particular combination would work or not was only discernible in retrospect.

While the analogy between the life of an individual and the life of a *Volk* was misleading, nonetheless it was possible for a *Volk* to fall into decline and degeneration (*Entartung*) (Fischer 1923: 1). Peoples might rise and fall, but what determined this above all else was the quality of their racial composition. A *Volk* might undergo an ageing process, but each race was unchanging and fixed in its nature – like a species of plants and animals – unless it was destroyed, that is 'dies an unnatural death' (1923: 132). In order to ensure the survival of the German *Volk*, it was essential to understand the nature of its racial composition and the rules which govern the interaction between racial difference, the individual and the *Volk* (1923: 2).

According to Fischer, the population of Europe consisted of four basic races: the Nordic, the Mediterranean, the Alpine and the Dinaric (1923: 134–40). The Nordic race was the carrier of the Indo-European languages, and its original homeland was in northern Europe, from which it spread out in waves of migration, and in some cases mixed with other racial groups. The Slavic type was in fact a mixture of the Nordic with the Mongoloid, and it was the historic mission of the Slavic peoples to form a buffer between the Mongol hoards and the Germanic tribes (1923: 142). The further this wave of Nordic settlement progressed from its homeland, the more likely it was to go under. These processes of dynamic change were present in the European peoples today, as changes in racial composition lead to changes in mentality (1923: 144).

This model then was based on the superiority of the Nordic race, and the dependence of the Nordic race on proximity to its homeland. Implicit in this model was a continuum within the German people, between the Nordic and the non-Nordic. The racial composition of the German people was fundamental to its survival, and that survival depended crucially on the defence of the Nordic element. Added to this was a powerful pessimism about the current racial drift of the German people, indeed of all the 'civilized peoples' (*Kulturvölker*), and a fear that the superior elements of the *Volk* were being gradually swamped by a rising tide of genetic mediocrity (1923: 326–9).

Fischer was anxious that southern Germany not be seen as a racially inferior zone, populated by the offspring of conquering Nordics and round-skulled slaves. Throughout his career, Fischer was preoccupied with the problem of the dominance of round-skulled types within the southern German population, so-called 'southern German brachycephaly'. In his early writings, Fischer had observed that skull type seemed to be inherited according to Mendel's laws, though the details were not all understood (1914: 14–15). However, Fischer increasingly attributed a significant role to environmental factors; in his view more so than other racial anthropologists (1933: 297). He regretted the misleading picture presented in racial maps of Germany which focused on the cranial index. Contemporary writings gave the quite erroneous impression that the Nordic race had largely disappeared in the south. This impression was due in great measure to the geographical representation of the cephalic index in the population. This was regarded in many circles as scientifically authoritative but 'there was no other hereditary feature about which we know so little as the proportion of hereditary and environmental factors in the shape of the skull'.

If the maps showed distribution of forms of the nose or the face or light colouring, then we would have a much better view of the presence of northern racial elements in the German population (Fischer 1936b: 298). The skull was not a mathematical precise entity with a few simple dimensions but an 'anatomical construct' (1940: 10). There was a general drift towards the round-skull shape, particularly in southern Germany, but also across much of Europe. This was not due to a change in racial composition but to 'peristatic circumstances', i.e. environmental factors (1940: 12). In similar vein, Hesch (1934: 68) attributed the predominance of round-skull forms to an increase in the width of the skull rather than a loss of length. Fischer's views on southern German brachycephaly illustrate the complexity of interactions between descriptive racial anthropology, Mendelian anthropology, Nordicism and political nationalism.

Critics of Nordicism

Nordicism was the target of a wide range of criticisms, both from within racial anthropology and in the general intellectual and political culture of the 1920s and early 1930s. The critiques discussed below came from within racial anthropology, and often shared key assumptions with the Nordicist wing. Wilhelm Schmidt (1868–1954), a Catholic priest of the Verbite order, offered a critique of Nordicism which was in part grounded in the terminology and conceptual scheme of the biblical paradigm. Schmidt attributed to the Nordic race a mixed origin, including Hamitic elements; the Germanic peoples or the Nordic race were not an original and mystically superior people. Their rise reflected the superior role which was taken up by all pastoral peoples, and the totality of cultural conditions rather than the specific characteristics of a particular race. The Indogermanic or Germanic peoples came third in a line of pastoral peoples, the oldest of which was the Ural-Altaic people (*Ural-Altaier*), followed by the Hamito-Semites (*Hamitosemiten*). Schmidt argued that it was this mixture that gave the Nordic race its special advantage, giving it both its conquering attributes, and, to a lesser degree, the artistic gifts of totemistic town-dwellers, as well as in a great measure the thoroughness, seriousness and conscientiousness of the matriarchal agricultural people (*Ackerbauer*) (1927: 41–2).

Rejecting what he saw as the partisan rhetoric of the Nordic enthusiasts, Schmidt's conclusion was that the Nordic race was a young race, one which had undergone many stages of composition, the final ones being in Europe. This gave it no more claim to be a European race than the Mediterranean race. The oldest links of the Nordic race stretched deep into Africa and Asia. Whether or not it had received the repeated influx of the blood from 'master peoples', it was no less true that it had been shaped by matriarchal, agricultural peoples. In this lay its chief distinctive character, distinguishing the Nordic race in particular from the Celtic. Schmidt denied that all superior achievements of the Indogermanic peoples were to be explained by the presence of Nordic blood, calling these ideas 'grotesque' or rather 'childish', especially given the often initially destructive impact of the Indogermanic peoples on other races and cultures, but also given the late arrival in history of the racially and culturally composite Nordic race. The white races of Europe could not claim to be distinct and separate from other races, nor could they claim a high degree of superiority. The internal racial differences were as great in many cases as those that separated the Europeans from a number of Asiatic and Asian races. There was however a strong cultural divide. On these grounds, Schmidt warned against the further rapid mixing of European with African and Asian peoples. He noted however that this has been done for reasons of pragmatic necessity. While it was regrettable that England and France had stationed foreign troops in

Europe, did anyone doubt that Germany would not have done the same if they had had colonial troops?

As far as the racial profile of Germany itself went, Schmidt – applying the principle that the Germanic peoples reached their highest level of achievement at the end of their migrations in areas of racial mixing – argued that this had occurred along the Rhine and the Danube, not in Scandinavia or on the North and Baltic Seas. This cultural formation, characterized by the second Germanic sound shift (e.g. $p > pf$), was so successful that High German culture has become dominant over Low German culture, language and literature. The Nordic movement was in effect a reaction against this southern dominance, and Schmidt rejected the idea that the cultural achievements of the south were only to be attributed to the influx of Nordic elements. If this were so, then the highest achievements would be found where the Nordic elements were at their purest. Schmidt argued for the complementary nature of the Nordic and pre-Nordic elements in southern Germany.

Both the Low German and High German cultures were in need of official protection and support, not merely the Low German (Schmidt 1927: 60). To protect the racial balance of Germany, measures needed to be taken to harmonize the relationship of town and country. The Nordic racial element would benefit most from these efforts, since it was concentrated to a larger extent than other races in the urban centres of northern Germany, and suffered the adverse effects of the overcrowding there. The Nordic element would then balance its efforts between the city and the country, and in achieving a balance between the town and the country both parts of the German people would be able to regain some leadership over their own affairs, and the excessive influence of urban culture as intellectual, business and administrative centres would be curbed. In particular, Schmidt expressed concern about the power of the large industrial concerns. The need was for a truly organic cultural leadership (1927: 61). Schmidt argued for the importance of large-scale agriculture remaining in the hands of the long-standing pastoral aristocracy, rather than being bought out by racially foreign international capital, or falling under the control of the urban proletariat, as had happened in the Soviet Union.

Schmidt's diagnosis of Nordicism as a reaction to a traditional conception of south Germany as the racially and culturally purer region reveals how debates within racial anthropology must be read against the deep cultural-historical (and class) divisions in German society. This north–south divide was the theme of Robert Gradmann's (1865–1950) discussion of the cultural and racial make-up of southern Germany. Gradmann noted Bismarck's view that the northern Germans had greater mixed blood than the southerners (1926: 135). This was due to absorption by or mixing with the Slav population, particularly east of the Elbe. However, Gradmann did not associate purity of blood automatically with loyalty to the *Volk*. Racially mixed populations of ethnic Germans outside the political boundaries of Germany often showed extremely high national consciousness. Southern Germany was not the original heartland of Germany, but it had become so by conquest, after migrations due to the loss of territories in the northeast. In the south, the original inhabitants had been systematically exterminated or expelled; this had led to the south becoming the stronghold of German culture and language.

Gradmann recognized that Rudolf Virchow's (1821–1902) anthropological survey of the population of Germany had shown that the greatest concentration of the blond-haired was in the north, including east of the Elbe. Virchow had concluded that the return migration of Germans east of the Elbe had driven out the darker-haired Slavic population, and that southern Germany was a zone of mixing between German elements, Celts and Slavs. The traditional understanding had been turned on its head by racial anthropology. The data could not be challenged, but the conclusions drawn were questionable, especially the equation of blondness with German origin. Not all blonds were members of the Nordic race, not all members of the Nordic race were Germanic, and Germanic and German were not equivalent (Gradmann 1926: 138).

For Gradmann, the blond-haired population of northern Europe was essentially a mixture of two different races, the Nordic race and the East Baltic (*ostbaltisch*) race, newly identified by Günther. The original Germanic peoples of the Roman era were purely Nordic; the East Baltic race did not have this original Germanic link at all. The Nordic race, defined by the long skull, was also in part Slavicized, as grave-finds had shown. In this way, Gradmann sought to reconcile the traditional view of the north as being heavily Slavicized with recent anthropological findings. His interpretation of racial history involved a denial that southern Germany was historically a mixed Celtic-Germanic zone. Rather it had an original and strong Nordic inheritance, so that southern Germany was nine-tenths Nordic at the onset of the Middle Ages (1926: 139). The apparent hybridity of the present-day south was due to factors of selection within the original Nordic population, and was not due to migration from outside and the mixing with Jews and Gypsies, which had been too small to be significant. The factors that had led to the decline of the Nordic were explained by the relationship of racial variation to geography, so that there were

climatic-racial zones, arising after the last ice age, which were organized from north to south (1926: 141–2). The racial make-up of the
south was due to inner selection within the Nordic element, a process
which could be explained by Mendelian genetics (1926: 144). The
northern zone was the optimal homeland of the Nordic race; the
processes of inner selection in the south had been accelerating with
urbanization and the ills of modernity. The southern Germans were
the descendants of a fundamentally Nordic base; in addition, some
specifically 'German' characteristics, such as musicality and a fanati-
cal love of order, were perhaps due to racial mixing (1926: 146).

Gradmann was caught between a desire to defend the racial
quality of the German people and respect for the Nordic ideology.
He evoked the Nordic race as a tragically doomed sacrificial race,
leaving its homeland to build civilizations and high culture, and then
falling victim to hostile climate and environment. Was southern
Germany due to fall victim to this process? Gradmann was not totally
pessimistic, as the proportion of blonds was still relatively high in the
south, and at least three-quarters of the southern population had one
or more racial characteristic of the Nordic race. Furthermore, while
a very high proportion of high achievers had Nordic racial characteristics, so did some criminals and feeble-minded individuals whose
basic intelligence was less than a quick-witted Negro (1926: 148).
There was no need for the south Germans and Swiss to feel inferior
to the Nordic, since one could assume that the psychological or
mental characteristics of that race had been inherited to a greater
degree than the physical characteristics (1926: 148). While the optimal
zone for the Nordic race was in the north, which was the homeland
of the Indo-Europeans, there was a greater need than ever for unity
and exchange between the different parts of Germany, particularly
as the northeastern territories were now once again threatened with
assimilation (1926: 148).

One model which more directly rejected the Nordicist emphasis
on racial purity was that of Max von Gruber (1853–1927), the president of the Bavarian Academy of Sciences in Munich. Von Gruber
saw the German *Volk* as beset by inner divisions, and was a strong
critic of Günther and popular Nordicism. Although the German
people was made up of at least three anthropological races, which differed quite considerably in their external appearance (Nordic, Alpine
and Dinaric), its current weakness was not attributable to racial
mixture or hybrid character. Both the English and the French had
strong national feelings but were no more racially pure. Even more
striking was the example of the Jewish people, which was made up of
several very different races and two anthropologically distinct groups,

the Ashkenazim and the Sephardim, but they nonetheless showed the longest-standing national ties (*Volksverband*) ever seen. A common language, tradition literature, etc., made a stronger union than a common origin: the racially heterogeneous Jewish people was bound together by the idea of the chosen people (von Gruber 1927: 244).

Marriages between different races often went wrong due to different traditions and culture, not race; this was also true of cross-confessional marriages. Children of such marriages often suffered a lack of integration into the national community (*Volksgemeinschaft*), so marriage with a 'racially other' (*volksfremd*) partner should be avoided. The most important thing was the creation of a unified national feeling or consciousness and the rejection of the divisive elements. Von Gruber hoped that the shared suffering that the German *Volk* had been through would achieve this. He denied that the unequal nature of racial elements was a barrier to national unity, arguing that when one looked at the vastly different types from different parts of Germany, their 'Germanness' (*Deutschheit*) was unmistakable. Did not all Germans feel for the unhappy situation of Germans in South Tirol as well as in the lost lands in the north? (1927: 244). But the German people had an excessive number of inferior (*minderwertig*) individuals; there was a need for a proper process of selection (*Auslese*) among those capable of reproducing (von Gruber 1927: 245)

The large-scale racial blocks that made up the human species certainly had different characteristics, but did it follow from this that the three 'German' races had psychological make-ups that were different in value ('höchst ungleichwerte Psychen'), so that one could make an inference from an individual's appearance or somatic type ('äusserliche Merkmale') about his psychological make-up (von Gruber 1927: 245)? Even if it were possible, it was not a good idea, as inheritance was too complex and multifactorial. We can see a clear physical difference between a 'Hottentot' and a blond blue-eyed Nordic from Niedersachsen (1927: 246); things would be simple if there were clearly different psychical characteristics, if there were racially specific thought-associations and racially inherited world views, as was often maintained, but these did not exist (1927: 245–6).

There were racial differences in intellectual make-up and in the direction of drives (*Triebrichtungen*) but no inborn concepts (*Vorstellungen*) or ideas. There was a continuum in ability between the races; there was no intellectual quality to be found in the most intelligent races that was completely absent in the least intelligent. There were no totally amoral races (von Gruber 1927: 246). In terms of ability, the extremes within one and the same race were much further apart than the average representatives of the different races – even the so-called purest race was not uniform (*einheitlich*), but rather consisted of countless lines of inheritance (*Erblinien*) which in spite of all commonalities exhibited great differences in value or quality ('Abstufungen der Wertigkeit', 1927: 246). Von Gruber argued that there was generally a natural sexual repulsion between distant races, but that between close European races for example the 'foreign' was a special attraction. It had been shown scientifically that the result of a cross between a high-standing race and a low race, e.g. a white person with a female 'Hottentot', was not good for the higher race as the offspring would lie in the middle. However, planters and breeders did not recognize any rule that racial crosses were always inferior (1927: 247).

The Nordic race was the purest and had achieved great things but it was not solely responsible for west Asiatic and European culture. The cultures of India, Persia, Greece, Rome had all grown up *in situ*, were not created on the Baltic where the Nordic race was based. Not all great men in German history were Nordic; they were all of mixed race. None of the races in the German people was an ideal race which was to be pursued (von Gruber 1927: 247). Even if it were possible to breed out a pure Nordic element from the racial mixture, this would not be a worthwhile goal, since the Nordic race also had its severe faults. The salvation of humanity did not lie in the past but in the future; there was a need to promote all the ideal lines of inheritance (*Erblinien*). The best genetic quality had to be selected and bred, wherever it was present, whereas the lowest quality genetic lines had to be eliminated as painlessly but as thoroughly as possible. The aim of eugenics was the creation of people who – in addition to having great strength, talents, firm judgement, a will to work and a dutiful nature – were born with compassion and a willingness to sacrifice oneself. This would lead to the creation of a natural elite which could serve the whole (1927: 247). Whether these superior peoples contained brown-eyed or dark-haired individuals or whether the blonds and the blue-eyed were in the overwhelming majority seemed not to be of decisive importance in the future of the German people (1927: 247). It was not sufficient to judge by appearances; it was no good choosing a healthy-looking wife if her intellect or personality was not up to standard (1927: 248).

Von Gruber concluded that among the noblest people he had met recently, there were remarkably many who did not appear Nordic, but that there were also many brutal or selfish individuals who looked particularly Nordic. The notion of anthropological race (*Systemrasse*) was of great scientific interest; the application of this concept in civil life was problematic. A Negro or a Hottentot or a Bushman, an alcoholic, a habitual thief or con artist, a sexual criminal would have to accept a strong prejudice against his genetic inheritance, but was this prejudice justified against a brown-eyed German, even if he had a snub nose or a round head? The notion of anthropological race should not be allowed to create further trouble among the members of the *Volk* (1927: 248).

The paleoanthropologist Franz Weidenreich (1873–1948) did not deny the existence of racial types, nor of racial superiority and inferiority, but rejected what he saw as the dogmatism of much contemporary racial theorizing. Contrary to Günther and Fischer, Weidenreich contended that new, mixed races (*Mischrassen*) could be created (1932: 16). However, his critique of Nordicism shared an underlying framework with the more sophisticated defenders of Nordicism, namely that someone who was blond, blue-eyed and had a long skull was not necessarily 'more Nordic' than someone who had a round skull and brown hair. The most primitive races, such as the Australian aborigines, were extremely long-headed; there was no connection at all between long-skulled races and levels of intelligence and culture, and a look at leading intellectual and political figures showed no clear correlation between skull shape and genius. Though they may have had other Nordic features, Bismarck, Kant and Schopenhauer were extremely short-headed. A purely Nordic body might therefore contain an Alpine or Dinaric brain, with the attendant mentality and mindset. Lenz had argued that a dark-haired German could possess as many Nordic mental qualities as a blond-haired one.

Weidenreich noted that Ludwig Ferdinand Clauss had claimed that Beethoven was able to wring Nordic expression out of his Alpine body. But this kind of argumentation could lead to the same person being classified differently by different race scholars. In spite of his diminutive stature and round head, Günther had classified Napoleon as Nordic, whereas Ammon defined him as an eastern type, a Mongoloid. To further complicate the picture, Ernst Kretschmer had shown that different body types (*Konstitutionstypen*) reveal different temperaments even within the same race, and there were cases of psychological types housed in the wrong body type. Weidenreich argued that the individual should be evaluated on his own terms, since there was no way of determining the racial composition of a *Volk* at any particular historical juncture, and no way of determining or measuring racial psychology independent of all bodily and environmental factors. We have still not got past the beginning stage in our attempts to answer these questions about race (Weidenreich 1932: 23–7).

In the same series of lectures, Ernst Kretschmer (1888–1964) of Marburg University, whose theories on the relationship between body type (*Konstitution* or *Körperbau*) and character remain influential (Kretschmer 1931), complained that race psychologists were often simply venting their individual prejudices and political philosophies (1932: 59). Kretschmer argued that in Europe the greatest creativity and levels of achievement were to be found in transition zones of racial mixing. The impact of the Nordic-Alpine racial mix on modern European culture showed this, as did the achievements of ancient Greece and India (1932: 63). The racially purer areas such as Lower Saxony and East Friesland produced strong physical and mental types, but were poor in geniuses and in cultural productivity (1932: 64).

Kretschmer was particularly positive about the mixing of the Nordic with the Alpine races, which, although dissimilar, complemented each other very well. It was an error of the present idealization of the Nordic element to assume that the incoming Nordic race always 'brought the genius with it'. This could be seen if we looked at the Nordic race in its homeland settlements. Conquering or martial peoples were not necessarily superior or especially 'heroic', but came from geographically inferior zones in the far north or from deserts, as in the case with the Germanic tribes, the Mongols and conquering Indians or Arabs. We should not see the conquering peoples as the 'master race' (*Herrenrasse*) and the conquered as a 'slave race' (*Sklavenrasse*), unless we have strong historical evidence. What was decisive was the stage of cultural development of the peoples involved. If the indigenous culture was on the rise, then the incomers would be destroyed, whether they were Nordic or not. If the invaders met with a declining culture, then there would be conquest and racial mixing; and if the two tribes or races were racially compatible, then this might give rise to a new cycle of creativity. But this happened not in the native land, but in the territory of the conquered.

The historian Walter Goetz (1867–1958) of Leipzig University also gave a positive evaluation of racial mixing, and evoked a constant, dynamic change under the impact both of racial mixing and the environment. Goetz did not make a clear distinction between *Volk* and *Rasse*, preferring to use the term *Volk* (1932: 73), as he denied that races transcended historical change. Goetz argued that racial mixing was the prerequisite for the greatest human achievements, and – attacking directly the *völkisch* race theorists – he extended his praise to the case of the Jews, noting that Wilhelm Schmidt in Vienna, Fritz Kern (1884–1950) in Bonn and others had argued for the original unity of the Indogermanic and Semitic-Hamitic peoples (Kern 1927;

Goetz 1932: 77–8). Goetz did not reject the field of racial or physical anthropology as a whole; rather what he saw as its politicized use by *völkisch* thinkers (Goetz 1932: 78). Goetz, a leading member of the German Democratic Party, was forcibly retired from his university post in 1933 (Heiber 1991: 497; Haar 2000: 174–5).

Conclusion

Within Germany the Nordic bodily ideal fed a certain inferiority complex on the part of the 'average' German. Racial anthropology held up a mirror in which the Germans saw themselves not as a blond blue-haired ideal but as a miscegenated composite, though one perhaps with a Nordic soul to compensate for the misshapen body. The accusation was thus frequently made that the Nordic ideal was destructive of the unity of the German *Volk*. Ignaz Kaup (1870–1944) complained in effect of intra-German racism (Kaup 1925: 13–16; Günther 1925: 43). The idealization of a Nordic race, taken to its logical extreme, did indeed involve the promotion of a transnational racial elite, rather than a narrowly nationalist agenda. The claim of modern race theory to scientific status was grounded in a rejection of the pre-modern, popular and perceived nineteenth-century academic confusion of races with human groupings such as peoples, nations and linguistic communities (Scheidt 1930a: 5). According to Eugen Fischer, this distinction, as a distinction between a natural scientific concept and one from the humanities, was particularly emphasized in Germany (Fischer 1955: 274). The distinction between race as defined scientifically or biologically and *Volk* as defined culturally reflected a philosophical and methodological division between the sciences, on the one hand, and the humanities and social sciences, on the other.

One solution was to argue that it was inner qualities which made someone racially superior or 'Nordic'. But this seemed to reduce to meaninglessness the category 'Nordic' itself, since Nordicism drew its cultural impact and vitality from the aesthetics of bodily superiority. It also made nonsense of the claims of racial anthropology to offer a new, explanatory science of the human body. A second solution was to argue for the benefits of racial hybridity for the Nordic race. But this position was tantamount to advocacy of the benefits of racial hybridity in general. While in principle the distinction between *Rasse* and *Volk* was perfectly clear, the strongly holistic tendency of Nazi thought in the early years of the regime, and the political stress on both race and people or nationhood, created a considerable degree of doubt and confusion. This was particularly true in relation to the idealization of the Nordic race, since the relationship between this ideal race and the linguistic and cultural construct, the German *Volk*, was both politically salient and theoretically ill-defined.

In debates about the survival of the German *Volk*, the parallel in this model between modern Germany and ancient India was fundamental. In modern Germany, as in India, intermarriage had taken place between a superior population and a slave or subservient one. In the case of the ancient Aryans, the consequence was racial fall and disappearance. The obvious solution was to prevent further racial mixing and to undo as far as possible the mixing that had occurred. Modern science offered possibilities in this direction, which had been not available to the Aryans of old. But should this model be applied in all its rigour to present-day Germany? How could the inferior elements of the population be identified and what measure should be taken against them? From the radical Nordicist point of view, the German *Volk* was not threatened solely by the presence of racial inferiors (i.e. non-Nordic Europeans), but by the presence of the Jews, who were racially 'other' rather than conventionally inferior. Anxieties about hybridity and decline, entangled in the politically uncomfortable model of racial diversity, were projected onto a Jewish threat to the unity and survival of the *Volk*.

9

Germany as Nordic Colony? Confusion and Anxiety Post-1933

Introduction

The seizure of power by Adolf Hitler and the NSDAP in 1933 was presented as a victory for the German *Volk*. Many ideologues, philosophers and social theorists believed that their time had come, that their alienation from the state was over. They saw in Nazism a new, revolutionary organicism or holism, in which the family and the state, the private and the public, the individual and the collective could be brought into harmonious alignment. In the universities, advocates for Nazism rejected traditional academic boundaries such as those between science and humanities, or between 'life', politics and the university. An ill-defined concept of race was heralded as the new intellectual key, and a whole range of ideologues and theorists emerged to claim their role in the 'New Germany'. The coming of the Nazi regime led to an intensified interaction and competition between different methodological and political strands within the academic study of race, as positions which had been clearly defined in the 1920s and early 1930s faced a new political reality. Racial anthropologists, offering an explanatory model which aimed to transcend the divide between humanities and science, and between academic theory and social policy, looked to be in a highly advantageous position. Nordic ideologues were strongly represented in political and academic Nazism, and the early years of the Nazi regime saw attacks on those who were seen as insufficiently committed to the 'Nordic idea'. However, this strand of Nazism was politically and intellectually marginalized, falling, like the category 'Aryan' before it, to the problematics of *Rasse* and *Volk*.

There was great optimism among Nordic ideologues that the decline of the Nordic race could now be halted, since a regime had taken power which took that decline seriously and had the political will to act. But there was considerable disquiet in the population, occasioned by concern that measures would be taken to promote the blond-haired, blue-eyed and long-skulled Nordic elements of the German *Volk* against their squat, brown-haired, round-skulled fellow citizens. For if the Nordic race was 'the creator of German culture' (Paul 1936: 462) and if the Germanic forefathers were of the 'Nordic-Phalian' race who came from the north to conquer the present German territory, then Germany was to become in effect a Nordic colony. Internal colonialism would create a category of second-class Germans, who would be ruled over by a Nordic elite, as the dark-skinned Dravidians had been in ancient India. The psychologist Ernst Rittershaus diagnosed an 'inferiority complex' in circles where there was an ignorance of racial anthropology. This had led those who did not measure up in appearance to the Nordic ideal to oppose the promotion of an ideology based on race (Rittershaus 1936: 183).

The problem of hybridity

There was a degree of confusion about the definition of Nordicism. One ideological strand hostile to the Nordicism of Rosenberg and Günther was *völkisch* Protestantism, as exemplified by Helmuth Schreiner (1934) and Walter Künneth (1935). In his attack on Rosenberg and Günther, Schreiner made use of a range of arguments, including the need for the political unity of the German *Volk* and the recognition of the contributions of all Germans. He quoted Fritz Lenz (Lenz 1927b: 287; Schreiner 1934: 63) as objecting to 'the privileging of the Nordic race within the German people'. It was not appearance that counted, as 'even most of the dark, heavy-set, round-headed Germans are predominantly of Nordic race' and traits such as 'blondness, slim build and long-headedness make up only a quite minor part of the inherited characteristics of an individual'. Lenz had stressed that the Alpine and the Dinaric racial elements in Germany, i.e. the Mongoloid element, were a mixed formation on a Nordic foundation (Lenz 1927b, cited in Schreiner 1934: 64).

Schreiner's conclusion was that there was no future for a German *Volk* based on a policy of Nordification (1934: 69). His more substantive theological argument was that race could not be the measure of all values, since a 'religion of blood' left no room for religion. But this did not imply the rejection of a relationship between religiosity and blood or race. There was such a relation, analogous to that between body type (constitution) and character. Nor did it imply a rejection of eugenic attempts to improve the quality of the German *Volk*, in which the promotion of the Nordic race also had its place. But, in these matters, the scientific study of heredity was the sole authority. Schreiner's objection to Nordicism was that it had trespassed both on the territory of religion, by implying a direct relation between 'pure blood' and a 'pure heart', and on the domain of science (1934: 76).

The response of Nordic ideologues to anxiety about the promotion of the Nordic race was to emphasize the need for the leadership of the Nordic race in the interests of the *Volk* as a whole. While Germans were indeed largely *Mischlinge* with Dinaric and Alpine blood, the Nordic race was what united all Germans (von Hoff 1934: 145). In some accounts, this unifying factor was the 'Nordic-Phalian' race (Ruttke 1937b: 10), and the virtues of the Nordic-Phalian hybrid were argued in Rauschenberger (1938). The Nordic race was called to dominate and lead, the Phalian race was distinguished by its love of liberty. The combination of these two defined the Germanic type both physically and psychologically (1938: 275).

Martin Otto Johannes (1934) argued that the Nordic question had to be approached with tact and objectivity. The dissemination of ideas about race had sometimes been badly handled, giving rise to uninformed discussion of race in educational contexts, which the Party was now rightly seeking to bring under control. It had to be stressed that the Nordic component was the unifying bond between the racial elements of the German people, and that physical or bodily dispositions (*Anlagen*) could be separately inherited from mental or psychological ones, so that the phenotypical appearance of the individual was not the primary criterion for evaluating racial value. Johannes denied that he was merely promoting a politicized race nonsense to which the *Führer* had given his stamp of approval, or promoting some superficial kind of Nordification. Johannes himself was brown-haired, and his 'objective' approach to race had been criticized by some in the 'pro-blond' faction, but he knew very well that 'colour and bodily form' were not decisive. The most important factor was 'Nordic spirit, Nordic soul and Nordic mindset' (1934: 112).

Nordicists, while acknowledging the racially mixed nature of the *Volk* ('mixed with elements of other indigenous races'), stressed that the German people was in its essence 'of Nordic blood' and that it was permeated through and through with Nordic character and spirit. Given the central role played by the Nordic race in world and

German history, this race was in need of particular protection. The paradox that this revealed was that the Nordic race, in spite of its great achievements and qualities, was particularly vulnerable. The Nordic race was more prone to exhaustion than other racial elements, a fact which was linked to its superior gifts.

Increasingly, the rejection of racial mixing with Jews and 'racial others' was emphasized in order to deflect attention away from the sensitive question of the hybridity of the German *Volk*. In Otto Rabes's (b. 1873) concise introduction to genetics and eugenics (1934), the percentages of each racial group in the population were given in a table, with Nordic making up 50 per cent, Alpine 20 per cent, Dinaric 15 per cent, East Baltic 8 per cent, Phalian 5 per cent and Mediterranean 2 per cent (1934: 44). Rabes laid out the superiority of the Nordic race unambiguously: 'Without wishing to damage the sense of worth of each individual race, it must be said that the maintenance of the Nordic race is of fundamental importance for the continued survival of the essential characteristics of the German people' (1934: 43). Pupils were offered also a visual representation of what would happen to the 50 per cent component if for example its members married on average at age 33 and had three children, whereas the rest married at 25 and had four children. After 100 years the 50 per cent would fall to 17.5 per cent; after 300 it would be at 0.9 per cent. Thus Germany needed to work to keep its current racial mix, and for that reason it was necessary to oppose the further migration of eastern Jews (1934: 44).

Otto Reche (1879–1966) followed more or less the standard model popularized by Günther, but emphasized that the superior racial elements were also the indigenous ones (1933). The long-skulled were indigenous to Europe, and the round-skulled were originally from Asia. The six races thus broke down into the indigenous (Nordic, Phalian and Mediterranean) versus the incomers (East Baltic, Alpine, Dinaric) (1933: 10). The round-headed groups arrived at the end of the ice age, either through gradual migration or sudden conquest, and have long since been highly 'Europeanized'. They were thus now composite races (*Mischrassen*). The original homeland of the Nordic race was, as far as is known, northwestern Europe; that of the Phalian race the central west; of the Mediterranean, southwest and southern Europe (1933: 10–11). The two answers that scholars could give to the question of what united the German were: the Nordic race and German language and culture (Reche 1933: 5).

Race was not a matter of mere physical appearance, understood as a reflection of the environment and climate, but rather of inherited predispositions which had arisen in ancient prehistory. These were transmitted with great fidelity and according to unchanging natural laws. These genetic dispositions or qualities were physical (bodily), spiritual/mental and psychological characteristics ('körperliche, geistige und seelische Eigenschaften') (Reche 1933: 11). Although environment and climate were not factors in the creation of this racial diversity, different races were adapted to particular climates, so that the Nordic race was ill-suited to southern European and tropical conditions (1933: 10). It was necessary to distinguish clearly phenotype from genotype. An individual could have a Nordic appearance, but be of a quite different psychological make-up, and vice versa. Thus, many of the pioneers of the Nordic ideal were not particularly Nordic in appearance, but were nonetheless possessed of Nordic mentality and abilities. Investigation of an individual required expert analysis of as much of the extended family as possible, and in this way an expert – and only an expert – could evaluate the individual (1933: 30–1). In an individual in whom the phenotype and genotype were in harmony, we would see the totality of the racial ideal in its organic unity (1933: 32). This reflected the organicism or holism (*Ganzheitsbegriff*) of what Reche refers to as recent 'philosophy'. Reche's model shows a clear tension between the ideal of the organic unity of the racially pure individual, and the implications of Mendelian genetics, which undercut the necessity for such unity.

One way to express the key relationship between *Rasse* and *Volk* was through metaphor. Accepting the view that no advanced or civilized people was composed of a single race, Gustav Paul (1936: 21) used the metaphor of metal alloy. Some alloys were hard and durable, and others were soft and of low quality. Similarly, a change in the racial composition of a *Volk* would bring about changes in its character, and for the biological historian these could be the key to the explanation of specific events and processes, as the racial core of the *Volk* was decisive in determining victory or defeat. The moral of this for the German people was the centrality of the Nordic racial component, given its military, political and intellectual achievements (1936: 21).

For Jakob Graf, organicism operated in natural science by showing how the entire genetic inheritance (genotype) was present in each living cell (1935: 206). This organic conception of part–whole relations could now be extended to higher organisms, such as races and peoples, and this led to a conception of race as an organic totality, in which reproduction does not destroy or split the unity but realizes it. In this sense, a race was outside time and history. It was an original living formation ('ein lebendiges Urbild'), and even though its original internal harmony could be disturbed by racial mixing, its survival as a totality was never lost, as long as there were people who carried this race within them (1935: 208). A *Volk* was a living organism (*Lebenseinheit*) in which the dominant race determined the specific nature of the collectivity. It was not an aggregation of millions of individuals, but a living totality animated by the inner law of the pre-dominant race (1935: 210). Race, while it might become atomized in the individual person, always operated as a totality in the life of a people (1935: 210–11). In the case of the Germans, this racial unity was provided by the Nordic race, and this racial element created an overarching unity in thought, feeling and action (1935: 259).

Graf was an advocate of the Nordification of the German people (1935: 262). He discussed the objection that this had opened up a rift in the German people, with those who were Alpine in appearance feeling denigrated, and others of Nordic appearance taking on supe-rior airs. Graf however stressed that any criterion by which we judge was relative to the racial group that was making the judgement, and thus comparison between races could be made only with reference to particular points, such as resistance to particular diseases, adapt-ability to different climates and suitability for a particular culture or form of moral civilization (*Gesittung*). In the case of the German people, since it was determined by its Nordic racial base, it was only possible for it to apply the standards of that race, with the proviso that the emphasis was not only on physical characteristics, but on the mental, psychological and spiritual disposition (1935: 262). What mattered was the inner nature of the individual seen against his or her ancestors and relatives (1935: 262).

The Nordic race was the leading or dominant race (*Führerrasse*) and united the German people. The state needed to create conditions that were ideal for the flourishing of this race. To those who felt slighted in their racial type, it should be pointed out that almost no one was a pure Nordic type, but that Nordic blood flowed in the veins of every German. Everything that had been written about the divi-sions between the Nordic and the Alpine races could only be hurtful to someone who was still caught in a self-centred, egotistical mode of thought, rather than partaking in the organic unity of individual and *Volk*. The question to be asked of each person was how compatible their achievements and inner outlook were with the Nordic-German way of being (1935: 263).

This racial relativism was also found in Philalethes Kuhn (1870–1937) and Heinrich Wilhelm Kranz's (1897–1945) popularizing presentation of the problematics of *Volk* (1936). There was no universal framework within which to judge the worth of a particular race, and each *Volk* would see foreign (*artfremd*) racial elements as less valuable than its own compatible (*arteigen*) ones. A racial element that was beneficial to one people will be destructive and harmful to another. Just as the nationalistic-Zionist Jew wished to drive out the foreign mindset from the Jewish people, so the German people had not only the right but the duty to root out mercilessly all foreign elements from the German people, and to promote the dynamic and creative Nordic element.

While recognizing the superiority and excellence of the Nordic race, they also paid tribute to the beneficial effects of the other racial elements of the German people in combination with the Nordic, for example the contribution of the Dinaric element to the production of musical geniuses. The Nordic race however determined the core of each German's being. There was no intention to eradicate the Alpine, Dinaric and Mediterranean racial elements from the German people, as they were part of the German way of being. But the inferior and the pathological in each racial element of the German people had to be prevented from reproducing, so that the Nordic component was not reduced further and remained the determining force. What had to be destroyed was foreign (*artfremd*), i.e. non-European, blood and influence. Marxists and pacifists argued that racial mixing was beneficial, and pointed out that the German people was racially hybrid. But the key was the *kind* of mixing: there were beneficial and harmful forms of racial mixing (1936: 57–60).

The German geneticist and dermatologist Hermann Siemens (1891–1969), a professor at the University of Leiden, conceded that 'each race has its own eugenic values' (1937: 135), but of course the eugenic health of one's own race was of most concern. He defined 'our race' as the 'central European racial mix' ('mitteleuropäisches Rassengemisch'); most of the key creative and scientific contributions to humanity had come from these races. The United States had had the courage to recognize the importance of a cultural evaluation of the races, and the greatest danger in Europe was the decline in the proportion of the Nordic race. Given the superiority of the predominantly Nordic type (which Siemens admitted had occasionally been somewhat overblown), its future must be protected. This was not to drive a wedge between the blond- and brown-haired population; nor should we favour a particular type over another in a mixed population. The determining factor was not the shape of the skull but the achievement and performance of the individual (1937: 137–9). What was needed was a sense of racial pride. The original Hawaiians had been swamped by outsiders, and this was now happening in France, where the weakness of the government could lead to civil equality for Negroes and other racially foreign peoples: France had betrayed the white races (1937: 140–2).

The view from psychology: Gerhard Pfahler

The psychologist Gerhard Pfahler (1897–1976) was concerned about the dangers of inner alienation, given the racial diversity of the German *Volk* (1938: 152). It would be a mistake to represent the German people as being of a single racial style. While it might be possible to have a Nordic psychology in an Alpine body, if all the members of the *Volk* were to claim that they were Nordic, then the whole discussion would have become a farce (1938: 127). Either there was a fundamentally valid principle of the connection between body and psychology, and this connection determined ineluctably the racial fate of each person; or the German *Volk* was, in spite of all the bodily variation, made up of individuals who were all more or less Nordic. But if this was the case, why should we take race so seriously? The second position made nonsense of racial anthropology (1938: 151). Pfahler argued that it was a mistake to ascribe a Nordic soul to people of other races; this would be the end of racial anthropology (1938: 150). We should not try to pretend that all Germans were Nordic (1938: 125); nor should we allow the misconception that children could be made more Nordic by the will of their parents (1938: 126).

If the Nordic race was the ultimate source of all racial virtues such as discipline, self-composure and loyalty, then every member of the *Volk* would have to count as Nordic. But this would be to undermine the fundamental tenets of racial anthropology, and the link between body and psychology or soul. If it were accepted that there were different races in the German *Volk*, then one single race could not have a monopoly on these virtues. Each core racial element (*Rassekern*) in the German *Volk* would then play its own special role in laying the foundations of the new *Reich* (1938: 127). There were real correlations between race and hereditary personality (1938: 131), and these forms of hereditary endowment could not be wished away. Each core race had its own mission within the *Volk*.

Pfahler's basic answer to this problem was that it was the task of education to unite the *Volk*, to shape and protect its unity (1938: vii). Where there was a danger of inner division, the shared history and a common moral system would create a strong bond. It was the task of education to create these bonds, and this was why education maintained a central role in the life of the *Volk*, within the mission laid down by National Socialism. Each race had its own possibilities and could attain its fulfilment in the service of the *Volk* – there thus remained a zone of freedom of action and potential within the unchangeable framework established by hereditary nature. Outside the *Volk*, there was no possibility for the individual to exist (1938: 162–3). It was the task of hereditary psychology (*Erbcharakterologie*) to give an account of the boundary between hereditary characteristics and environmental influences (1938: 24). However, this did not entail recognizing the equality and equal worth of all members of the *Volk*; education could not overcome these fundamental differences.

The key question remained: what was the correct understanding of the relationship between bodily type and racial psychology? In the third edition of a work stressing the importance of education in spite of the fundamental role of heredity (*Warum Erziehung trotz Vererbung?*) Pfahler argued that the measure of an individual's worth within the *Volk* was their contribution and achievements (*Leistung*) in its service. Racial anthropology (*Rassenkunde*) and hereditary psychology (*Erbcharakterkunde*) were now reconciled, as were racial anthropology and the study of human constitutional types (*Konstitutionslehre*), as it had been shown that each race showed the same basic variation in constitutional types, i.e. that these were separate dimensions of body–mind relations to those given by race (1938: 127–8). However, in his *System der Typenlehre*, Pfahler, while he named 'race' (*Rasse*) and 'heredity' (*Erbe*) as the twin pillars of the new social order founded on the *Volk* (*Volksordnung*), had nothing to say about the categories of racial anthropology (1943: xiii).

Conclusion

The dilemma of Nazism was that it emphasized the fundamental importance of a scientific concept of race and a biological concept of heredity, yet the organizing concept of political Nazism, the *Volk*, was not defined in either of these terms. It was neither *Systemrasse* nor *Vitalrasse* (Ruttke 1937b). Both these theoretical options were seen as potentially including Jews and other racial outsiders in the *Volk*, in that they gave a scientific or biological basis to a cultural category which had sometimes been understood as including Jews. A malign focus on the Jews masked deep confusion, as it became increasingly clear that racial anthropology did not have the intellectual tools to disambiguate the nature of the German *Volk*.

The fact that the German *Volk* was not constituted out of a German race (*Rasse*) was clearly problematic both intellectually and politically. While Günther had supplied the various races that made up the German people types with their own psychological and cultural characteristics, the situation was unsatisfactory, in particular if race theory was to be politically mobilized. While German culture recognized regional types, in part based on physical characteristics, these regional types were also linguistic, cultural and confessional. While Günther's categories might pass for scientific in some eyes, the Nordic race aside, they had no direct reflex in popular culture or the popular imagination. What were these races? What was their history? What would be their future interaction? Whereas the German *Volk* could be presented as a historical force with a historical mission, nothing similar could be claimed of the Dinaric race. What great battles had it fought?

Ultimately, as Walter Gross, the senior Party official with responsibility for race, made repeatedly clear, there was never any question of the Party and state authorities yielding their final authority in such matters to purely scholarly criteria. In any case, the scholars themselves, for all their bluster, did not have coherent or convincing answers to offer. The regime increasingly sought to keep academic and scholarly discussion of race separate from race propaganda in the public sphere. This was to maintain control over the ideological messages being communicated to the general public, and to prevent racial anthropologists from setting themselves up as ideological authorities.

For political or propagandistic purposes, the concept of *Volk*, unlike that of *Rasse*, was relatively unproblematic. Academic debate about the composition of the *Volk* was not suppressed, but there was no political benefit to be gained from introducing definitional confusions into the public sphere in an attempt to influence established popular usage (Sieg 2001: 263). While Nordicist racial anthropologists sought to exclude hybridity, the agreed 'facts' of German racial history forced them to come to terms with racial mixing. Even the Nordic race was frequently understood as related to, or hybridized with, the Phalian race. However, the Phalian race had no political or historical resonance, and the popular image of the blond, blue-eyed Nordic race had become a potential political liability.

10

The Neutralization of Intellectual Diversity

Introduction

After the Nazi seizure of power, many academics and ideologues who already had long-standing involvement with the NSDAP, often in alliance with pro-Nazi students, sought to move closer to the centre of power and to marginalize those they regarded as insufficiently committed politically. The opportunity that Nazism represented was the chance to gain institutional influence and prestige while guiding political decisions.

In racial anthropology and genetics, the 'Berlin group' associated with the Kaiser-Wilhelm-Institut (Fischer, Muckermann, Verschuer) initially lost ground to the more politically radical Munich eugenicists, led by Ernst Rüdin. Figures such as Fischer were often seen as insufficiently committed politically, or as having contacts with undesirable elements. In Fischer's case, this was a reference to his colleague at the Kaiser-Wilhelm-Institut, the Catholic eugenicist Hermann Muckermann. Fischer, however, consented to Muckermann's dismissal (Lösch 1997: 243). A series of intellectual controversies from the early years of the regime are sketched briefly below. The intention is to illustrate the process of political coordination (*Gleichschaltung*) as it affected intellectual debate and controversy, and the process whereby contentious policy issues debated by scholars were gradually removed from the public domain.

Georg Schmidt-Rohr and the worship of mother tongue

One opponent of Nordicism and 'race-mysticism' who encountered political problems in the early days of Nazi rule was Georg Schmidt-

Rohr (1890–1945). Schmidt-Rohr, a conservative nationalist, stressed the fundamental role of language in the formation of *Volk*, arguing that language outweighed racial factors in the process of identity formation (Schmidt[-Rohr] 1917:22). Schmidt-Rohr's *Die Sprache als Bildnerin der Völker* (1932) must be understood with reference to the perceived threat from theories emanating from racial anthropology, in particular Nordicism, to the unity of the *Volk*. Schmidt-Rohr represented the pre-racial concept of *Volk*, one grounded in the writings of Fichte. In this tradition, there was no absolute racial barrier to assimilation, as the concepts of racial anthropology had not been fully absorbed into what was nonetheless a xenophobic model (Bartels 1920: 231).

Schmidt-Rohr's work was also welcomed as a strike against racial dogma, seen as threatening the *völkisch* position (Thierfelder 1932: 257). Schmidt-Rohr recognized and accepted the distinction between *Rasse* and *Volk*, but disputed the priority given to race over language by racial theorists (1932: 289). The idealization of the Nordic race emphasized the divisions within the *Volk*, and encouraged arrogance towards a large portion of the German people (1932: 289, 291). Schmidt-Rohr, while noting that Jews were over-represented in the divisive elements of the *Volk*, also attacked the racial anti-Semitism which claimed to distinguish those who could be assimilated into the *Volk* from those who could not. There was no relationship between language and race, in the sense that a particular race had a primordial relationship to a particular language. Jews were a sub-group (*Untergruppe*) of the German people (1932: 301–2).

Hitler came to power as the second edition of this work was being set in type, now entitled *Muttersprache* ('mother tongue'). In an inserted discussion (written subsequent to the passing of the 1933 Law for the Restoration of the Civil Service), Schmidt-Rohr spoke of the pressure to remove or alter his section on the Jews, but he had decided to retain it. This was not because he was a great lover of justice or friend of the Jews, but as a matter of theoretical principle. The real crisis of the *Volk* stemmed from the losses of territory and vitality, rising assimilation into other nations and the lack of internal unity. These problems could not be solved by persecuting Jews as an outlet for the embittered discontent of the masses: cheap anti-Semitism was no solution (1933: 309).

Schmidt-Rohr argued that so-called 'Aryan peoples' had a great deal of non-European blood; on average, more than the Jews themselves, who now belonged linguistically to the Aryans (1933: 311). In a further page of explanation inserted into each edition, Schmidt-Rohr stressed that he was arguing for the protection of Germans outside the Reich (*Auslandsdeutschtum*), and he wished to stress that the German language was the key to their continued membership of the German *Volk*. The German language played a 'maternal, holy function' in the creation and self-determination of the *Volk*, in the self-consciousness that was necessary for survival in the face of the threat of assimilation. Schmidt-Rohr acknowledged that his statements had led him to be misunderstood as a liberal defender of the Jews, but he had been writing out of consideration for overall political aims, i.e. the defence of the *Volk*. He now recognized that his attacks on the exaggerations of race theory and the mistakes of anti-Semitism had been overtaken by events. The text of this explanation also appeared in the journal of the German Academy (Schmidt-Rohr 1934). Schmidt-Rohr, who had joined the NSDAP at the end of April or early May 1933, was threatened with expulsion from the Party, but he was eventually rehabilitated by the Race Policy Office in 1939 (see extensive discussion in Simon 1979, 1985a, 1985b, 1986a).

What was required from Schmidt-Rohr was that he recognize that Jews were not part of the German *Volk*, and that he cease his attacks on the Nordic ideology and racial anthropology. This episode illustrates how the linguistic category of *Volk* – like that of 'Aryan' – was disambiguated in the early period of Nazi rule. Schmidt-Rohr represented the Herder–Fichte tradition, which stressed above all the inner unity and solidarity of the *Volk*. Linguists tended to distrust what they saw as the materialism of racial anthropology (as opposed to vitalism of linguistics), and its neglect of the fundamental role of language in identity formation (Debrunner 1932: 307; Römer 1989: 143). In this 'linguistic' tradition, cultural, psychological and descent or blood ties were not fully disambiguated. The language community was a total community of the like-minded, sharing a common 'world-view' and a common set of ethical and philosophical concepts that distinguished them from neighbouring peoples. This model of the *Volk* was in one sense more 'totalitarian' than that offered by racial anthropologists, who were required by their own disciplinary training to recognize the existence of a fundamental hybridity.

The effect of this controversy was not to marginalize *völkisch* linguistics in the Third Reich, but rather to emphasize the methodological separation between the study of race and the study of language. Language remained fundamental, since it was the outer sign of the unity of the *Volk*. The 'mother tongue' of each *Volk* was a precious possession which should be protected from all forms of violence; mother tongue was 'its inner eye, its forms of thought with all its possibilities of constructing the world. It is the voice of the childhood of the people, and of its future, its memories and its longings' (Vossler

1936: 362). Language – mother tongue – could unite across divisions of both space and time (Schmidt-Rohr 1934: 203). Schmidt-Rohr later published a summation of his theory in the journal *Rasse*, one of the major Nordicist publications. The piece ended with a plea for the recognition of mother-tongue ideology (*Sprachgedanke*) as compatible with racial ideology (*Rassegedanke*) (Schmidt-Rohr 1939b).

The controversy clarified for linguists and others that the word *Volk*, as used in academic and popular discourse, must be understood as excluding the Jews. The linguistics of *Volk* and 'mother tongue' as pursued by linguists such as J. Leo Weisgerber, Georg Schmidt-Rohr and others needs to be read in this light. Weisgerber stressed that the study of race belonged to the natural sciences, whereas language was a 'cultural phenomenon' (1933/4: 171 (issue 16)). Edgar Glässer, like Weisgerber a neo-Humboldtian, attacked what he saw as confusions in Schmidt-Rohr and Weisgerber's understanding of the relationship of *Rasse* to *Volk*, and stressed that race was fundamental for the study of language (Glässer 1939: 56). Glässer argued that his intellectual opponents saw languages as creating peoples rather than the reverse (1939: 57). However, Glässer failed to give any explanatory substance to his claim that languages were racially determined, and his attempt to merge race and language lost ground to Weisgerber's school. Weisgerber's neo-Humboldtian linguistics assumed the ascendancy in the Third Reich, and remained dominant in the Federal Republic until the 1970s.

Eugen Fischer and the Nordic race

Having delivered a talk in Berlin on 1 February 1933 entitled 'Race crossing and intellectual performance', (Fischer 1936a), Fischer came under attack for his views on race mixing. Fischer had argued that many of the great Germans had come from racially mixed areas of Germany, that the Nordic race in its pure state had not achieved as much as in a mixed state. There were examples of gifted *Mischlinge*, such as Pushkin and Booker T. Washington. The German *Volk* was fortunate in having benefited from not only the highly gifted Nordic race, but also from the other racial elements of the German people. The talk was reported in the press, and triggered an attack by Lothar Gottlieb Tirala (1886–1974) in the journal *Volk und Rasse* (1934a). Fischer also came under attack from the pro-Nazi Munich Society for Eugenics, being sharply criticized by Karl Astel and Bruno K. Schultz.

His name was removed from the masthead of the *Archiv für Rassen- und Gesellschaftsbiologie* (Weindling 1985: 316).

Similar views on racial mixing had been expressed by Hermann Muckermann. Muckermann argued that the contribution of the Nordic race was at its greatest where it had mixed in a harmonious way with other compatible racial groups. The mixing of the Nordic race with the Phalian, Dinaric and Alpine races was without doubt 'harmonious', and it made no sense to argue about which line of inheritance (*Erblinie*) was the most important. This form of mixing was distinct from that with 'racially foreign' (*fremdrassig*) elements (Muckermann 1933: 20–1).

Tirala argued as follows: At the turn of the century, racial anthropologists (*Rassenkundler*) rather than biologists were involved in measuring the body, skull, face, colour of hair, skin, eyes. They were concerned with the question of the mixing of races, particular the effect of racial mixing on skull shape. Opponents of racial anthropology had an easy target, as they could point out that long-skulled Sicilians became medium-long-skulled without racial mixing but as a result of environmental factors; and that short-skulled Jews of Near Eastern race in North America became more long-skulled. The racial anthropologists had no answer to this. It was with the help of modern genetics that the idea of skull shape as genetically determined could be defended. Each measurable attribute was the expression of a 'reaction norm' (*Reaktionsnorm*), which was fixed genotypically. Thus, it was not a particular skull shape that was inherited, but a 'reaction norm', which allowed for variation according to particular conditions.

The example Tirala gave was of the plant *primula Sinensis* which bloomed a different colour when subjected to high temperatures. We would not say that the heat has created a new inherited feature. For Tirala, the stubbornly materialistic approach of many anthropologists had to be overcome in order to get a living notion of race and 'reaction norm'. This involved understanding that the organism does respond to the environment, without the environment having the power to create new inherited characteristics (1934a: 185). The environment did not have a creative input (*erzeugend*) but only a determinative (*bestimmend*) one (1934a: 186).

Fischer was further accused of suggesting that racial mixing was unproblematic, and that from an anthropological point of view there was no problem, so long as both parents were of equal racial value (*gleichwertig*). It was a matter of pure chance whether someone was blue- or brown-eyed, blond or dark-haired; this was little more than a question of aesthetics. This implied that the 'random mixing' of the main German races was not only unproblematic but actually desirable (1934a: 186). Tirala focused in particular on Fischer's use of the concept of 'hybrid vigour' (*Luxurieren der Bastarde*). Tirala argued that Fischer had exaggerated its importance, since it was not a general phenomenon, and often the second and third generation lacked vitality (1934a: 186). There was psychological vulnerability in the case of Lapp-Germanic and Jewish-Germanic racial crossing, particularly an 'inner conflict'; the offspring were less fit than their parents, and no great scholar or artist had been produced by such a union. What kind of 'hybrid vigour' could he show in relation to the Rehobother? Now that finally, after an era marked by promiscuous miscegenation, we were entering a period of racial consciousness, it was irresponsible for Fischer to claim that racial mixing was a positive phenomenon. There was a need for a careful process of selection, i.e. to do the opposite of what Fischer recommended, and revive the will of the Germanic forebears for the cultivation of the German stock ('deutsche Zucht', 1934a: 187).

The editorial board offered Fischer the chance to reply (Fischer 1934). Fischer had little difficulty in dealing with the first part of Tirala's attack, as he could show that he himself had been credited with the rejection of the old descriptive anthropology. It was Fischer who had argued for the importance of modern biology of heredity (*Vererbungsbiologie*) to racial anthropology, eugenics and population politics (*Bevölkerungspolitik*), and he had been the earliest (1913) and strongest advocate of the importance of 'anthropobiology' for eugenics. Fischer argued that he had shown that in some cases one could observe vigour, in others hybrid pauperization. He had stressed that the Rehobother were inferior to whites, and that they should never be allowed to intermix with 'our race'. Tirala was citing newspaper reports and other unreliable sources, which were reports from Jewish reporters (1934: 247). Fischer pointed to his long-standing warnings against the introduction of foreign 'genetic lines' into the German people, regardless of their eugenic quality, so as to preserve the unique racial character.

Fischer diagnosed the cause of the attacks in his warnings against the exaggerated idealization of the importance of the Nordic race. The culture of the German people could not be carried by the Nordic race alone; the great men of German history – Luther, Bismarck, Frederick the Great, etc. – were not purely Nordic in appearance. But Fischer emphasized that the achievements of the German people and of these great individuals would not have been possible without the intellectual character, sensibility, will, heroism of the Nordic race. The Nordic race was the most important element of the *Volk*. Hitler had called it the 'core' (*Kern*), but these achievements were those of the

German *Volk* as a whole. We should not see Germans with brown hair as inferior; there were peoples with a greater Nordic component who had fewer achievements on the world stage than the Germans. They also had high racial value, but why should this view of the achievements of our people be attacked? Could one say that the Scandinavians have given more to the common European culture than the Germans? The other 'German races' were not of inferior quality.

Fischer argued that he had been a pioneer in the recognition of the special value of the Nordic race, even before the celebrated Nordic ideologue, Günther (in Fischer 1923: 167), and at risk to his career. He had stressed that the common foundation of Indogermanic culture had been laid in its Nordic homeland. What upset many was the idea that racial crossing with closely related and equal races could produce particularly gifted individuals (1934: 249). This was shown by Greek high culture, one of the greatest products of the Indogermanic spirit. Did anyone want to say that the Greeks, for example Pericles, were racially pure Nordics? (1934: 249). There were other Mediterranean racial elements. Similarly, the Italian Renaissance had not been created by pure Nordics. Fischer was against any mixing with foreign races, including the Jews. Wherever the Nordic race was eliminated, the culture declined; but it was a serious mistake to argue that the entire culture of the Near East and Egypt and so on had been created by Indogermanic groups (1934: 250).

The *Volk* was a community (*Gemeinschaft*) and even if someone was born small of stature and dark-haired, that individual had the right to be associated with the Nordic spirit of the ancestors, and should have no feelings of inferiority in relation to his blood, as these bloodlines could be traced back to the original source of the entire German *Volk*. The new land policy of Hitler and Darré would promote those who made their living on the land, as the only true source of renewal and regeneration in the *Volk*. The community of the *Volk* was one to which each racial element could contribute for the enrichment of the collective national existence (1934: 251).

Tirala in reply (1934b) claimed he had relied on reports from experts; it was Fischer's fault if he had been misunderstood. These experts had all had the impression that he was warning against 'racial purity' (*Reinrassigkeit*). He should have made his views clearer before the coming to power of the National Socialists. Predictably, Tirala disputed Fischer's various claims to pioneer status, claiming priority for himself in advocating eugenics in 1905. Fischer had argued that there was a relationship between the rise of a collectivity and the racial mixing of the upper stratum with other social groups, and that such mixing was the cause of cultural development.

Tirala argued that he had been at the forefront of the struggle for the regeneration of the German people, and had attacked Spengler's mystical notion of racial decline in 1920, several years before Fritz Lenz. He had shown that the fall of peoples was caused by racial mixing, which led to changes in world-view (1934b: 356). Fischer had defended the Jesuit Muckermann, and had not wished to accept his resignation. Along with his Catholic friends, Fischer had preferred the term *Eugenik* to *Rassenhygiene*. But eugenics on its own ignored the specific racial quality of a *Volk*, and offered only general rules for all peoples.

Tirala remained sceptical as to whether Fischer supported Nordification or not. Where was his evidence of the exaggerated praise of the Nordic element? Tirala argued that the best elements of the German *Volk* needed to be promoted, and that this should be done on the basis of experimental genetics, so that the will to reclaim a particular type could be translated into the actual realization of that type, even if it had been severely diminished by racial mixing. The great men of the *Volk* had been of the 'Germanic race' (*germanische Rasse*), made up of the Nordic and the Phalian race (1934b: 356).

Tirala conceded that in the case of many great German figures, their phenotypical appearance included characteristics of the Dinaric and the Alpine races; but the question was whether these figures became great on account of this mixing, or in spite of it. The Dinaric and Alpine elements, Tirala argued, generally failed to bring any significant contribution to the make-up of genius, and more often than not they appeared as disruptive to the overall racial harmony of the individual (1934b: 357).

Tirala concluded by accusing Fischer of arrogance. There had been no need for our forefathers to wait for Fischer's insights in order to understand what 'eugenics' was all about; they carried it out unconsciously through the cultivation of the stock (*Rassezucht*). Fischer had boasted of his achievements in 1913, but in the USA they had known about this long before and had tried to stop black–white mixing. His dispute with Fischer represented a struggle between two distinct understandings of the world ('Kampf zweier Weltauffassungen', 1934b: 357). Tirala continued his attack on Fischer in his book *Rasse, Geist und Seele* (1935: 49, 52–3).

Fischer further clarified his view of the question of racial mixing in an interview with Charlotte Köhn-Behrens (Köhn-Behrens 1934). There, Fischer stressed the centrality of the woman in practical eugenics, in the avoidance of 'damage to our blood', in particular in relation to her following her healthy instincts in the choice of a husband. It was particularly important in the case of the woman, since her children would 'stay in the Fatherland'. This was not to say that the man was not to be condemned 'if he causes one of those unfortunate creatures to be born, which is what these Bastards are, because two blood natures (*Blutarten*) are at war within them'. Given that it was exceptionally rare for new racial characteristics to appear, if it were possible to eradicate all the negative lines of inheritance (*Erblinien*) in the *Volk*, then 'we would arrive at a total restoration of our health' ('eine vollkommene Gesundung'). Given that inherited characteristics persisted down the generations, each man and woman must respect the demand for racial purity (1934: 51–2). German culture, which had arisen over thousands of years, could only be sustained by the racial combination of the Nordic as the leading race (*Führerin*) and the Alpine and Dinaric races, which were to a degree its equals in value. Any admixture of foreign (*artfremd*) racial elements, for example of the Near Eastern-Oriental race (that is the Jews) was to be spurned (1934: 52).

Fischer argued for a legal duty for all lineages with hereditary illness to register, now that the Law on Sterilization had been passed. This would allow the processes of selection and weeding-out to take effect, 'which are found in exemplary fashion in nature'. The strong anti-Jewish policies would prevent this form of racial crossing from reoccurring (1934: 54). Fischer ended the interview with a panegyric in praise of higher birth-rates, to ensure that exceptional individuals were born (usually not the first-born), and to promote the vitality of the *Volk* in its competition with its neighbours. This was all summed up by a quotation from Friedrich Nietzsche: 'Give me the man who is fit for war, and the woman who is fit for childbirth!' ('Kriegstüchtig wünsche Ich mir den Mann, gebärtüchtig das Weib!', 1934: 54).

Fischer was the ultimate winner in the academic politics of the Third Reich, and Tirala, who clearly believed he represented true Nazi ideology in this exchange, was side-lined (Heiber 1991: 445–60; Weingart et al. 1992: 541). As part of his complex 'two-track' commentary on racial mixing, Fischer later attributed ugliness to disharmonious racial crossing. This ugliness was particularly prevalent in large cities and industrial regions, as opposed to the racially pure, more inbred rural populations. The race Günther referred to as the 'Alpine' race was frequently presented as the ugliest; but these were in Fischer's view mixed types of East Baltic, Alpine and often truly 'Eastern', i.e. Mongoloid. It was not generally possible to offer an accurate racial diagnosis of the face among products of such an array of different racial features. It was wrong to present such faces as representing racial elements of the German *Volk*: they were more properly seen as deterrent examples of uncontrolled racial mixing (Fischer 1936b: 192–3).

A German race?

Günther, following Fischer, had stressed that there was no possibility of the future creation of a 'German race' (Günther [1922] 1934: 255). However, this idea, representing as it did the future reconciliation of the categories of *Volk* and *Rasse*, had obvious intellectual and ideological, not to mention political, attractions. One logical conclusion of a positive evaluation of the hybrid nature of the German *Volk* was that as a collective it was, or could become, a race. One potential problem with this forward-looking or dynamic view of the biological status of *Volk* was that it did not sufficiently clearly exclude Jews and other racially foreign elements. It was redolent of the geographical concept of race (associated now with Lamarck), which implied that distinct racial lines could coalesce into new racial unities. It carried the potential implication that foreign elements would be included in the future German race by virtue of their absorption linguistically and culturally into the *Volk*. It also suggested that races could not only be created, but also die out as part of a strictly biological process. Fischer's adaptation of Mendel had offered reassurance that only external factors such as war and conquest could lead to the destruction of a race.

Egon von Eickstedt affirmed that Germany itself was defined primarily by its status as a political union – albeit incomplete – of speakers of the German language. Physical anthropology did not recognize a German race, or even a Germanic race. While he agreed that the German *Volk* was made up of a number of different races identified by Günther, this was not the end of the story (Eickstedt 1934b). The force that bound these disparate races into a single unity, the *Volk*, was culture – in particular language. While there was no equivalence between *Rasse* and *Volk*, there was however a relationship, since race was a physical collectivity based on blood relationships, whereas *Volk* was the cultural collectivity based on blood relationships (1934b: 11). Eickstedt argued that each *Volk* had a predominant race, and that in the German people the Nordic race was the dominant trait and harmonizing force (1934b: 11). Out of the ancient races and their sub-types (*Rassen* and *Unterrassen*) emerged new racial types, with their own sub-types (the terms are *Volkstypus* and *Gautypus*). It was the *Volk* not the *Rasse* which was the dynamic historical force (1934b: 12). Race was an end point, *Volk* a point of departure. In this sense, *Völker* were races in the making, and the biological carriers of the future of humanity.

On this model, the German *Volk* was the German race in inchoate form; a formation which was fundamentally formed out of the Nordic race, and in dialectic with the other races, was forging the racial future. But this raised a further problem. There were two foreign peoples in Germany, the Jews and the Gypsies (Eickstedt 1934b: 28–31). In addition, Catholics in the south of Germany, part of a population which was heavily Dinaric rather than Nordic, had a higher birth-rate than Protestants in the north. The German birth-rate was lower than other nations in Europe, and within Germany the birth-rate among the intellectual, skilled classes and independent farmers was much lower than among the unskilled and the criminal (1934b: 59–61). Eickstedt's dynamic model retained the xenophobic features of Günther's racial anthropology, but attributed the fundamental historical role to *Volk* rather than *Rasse*. His position however was not anti-Nordicist: it was not a matter of indifference whether the Nordic element increased or decreased, or whether there were stronger influences from east or west (Eickstedt 1934b: 56). Eickstedt did not go so far as to claim that there really was an existing German race.

A more radical view of this question was taken by Karl Saller (1902–1969), who argued that the German race had already come into existence. Saller, a student of Rudolf Martin, was something of a maverick. Saller was ambivalent about Darwinism, and his teleological language, and eclecticism with regard to biological theories, put him at odds with a developing academic orthodoxy grounded in neo-Darwinism. But he was also a *völkisch* thinker, who wished to put his theories at the service of the German people and the Nazi state. For Saller, the development of new races (*Rassenentstehung*) was in principle the same as that of new species (*Artwerdung*), since the development of a new race could be understood as a step towards the development of a new species. Saller rejected the conventional view of the present-day racial configuration of Europe, which held that the original races were found in a relatively pure form in a few areas, while other areas represented transitional zones of mixing. Rather, these so-called pure zones were the result of the isolation of a particular set of variants, which on account of their extreme development appear particularly striking. Even in prehistorical times there were continua between races and a transgressive variability of most characteristics, i.e. where there are offspring produced with phenotypes that exceed the parental extremes (1930: 214). In the case of recent forms, there existed clear continua in variation (1930: 215). The geography of human physical variation in Europe (as measured by eye colour, height, skull shape, etc.) showed fluid boundaries and irregularities, and it was therefore senseless to impose rigid boundaries on these phenomena on the basis of isolated extreme types corresponding to different peoples or *Völker*.

Saller made use of Kurt Gerlach's (1889–1976) studies of the distribution of different abilities and talents in the various regional branches or 'tribes' (*Stämme*) of the German people (Gerlach 1929) to conclude that though each individual branch might have its own characteristics, there was no evidence for designating one of the races in the German *Volk* as producing more creative, scientific, political or military talent. German culture was a creation of the interplay of regional identities. It did not arise in the heartlands of the so-called 'pure' races, but rather arose in the transitional and mixed zones, where several races overlapped. A sound *Volk* had to possess numerous possibilities of combination, the genetic material of which must be transmitted through different racial forms, and these forms must be able to interact in an appropriate way. Only a harmonious mixture of races (*Bastardgemisch*) was a sufficient buffer against vicissitudes, and gave sufficient breadth to its quality as a people (*Volkheit*). The specialized breeding towards particular types would always end in fiasco if they went beyond the area for which they have been specialized – this was true in the case of people, as well as in the animal and plant worlds. This was the lesson of the botanical researches of Friedrich Merkenschlager (1933, 1934).

Saller's conclusion was that it was not particular *races* that should be promoted – since there was such variation in any particular race that both good and bad qualities would occur – but rather proven individuals and proven lines of inheritance (*Erblinien*), the identities of which can be ascertained through the creation of appropriate environmental conditions (1930: 219). Saller insisted that races should not be seen as fixed and that the boundaries between them were fluid. Processes of mutation (a process about which nothing definite was known), as well as racial mixing within a particular community, could give rise to new races. The objects of research should not be forced into an abstract schema (1930: 220).

Both Merkenschlager and Saller had made themselves personally unpopular with various influential personages before the Nazi's rise to power. In an attack on Günther, Friedrich Merkenschlager (1927) had claimed that, with the Alpine and Dinaric component, southern Germany had up to 80 per cent 'yellow blood' from the Mongol race. Saller rejected what he saw as Günther's unfounded 'construct' (*Konstruktion*) of the Nordic race (Lüddecke 1995: 59ff.; Weingart et al. 1992: 318). What was important historically was the propitious mixing of racial elements: 'almost all the creators of modern European culture are bastards from the point of view of genetics'. It was impossible for a single pure race to have played the significant role that was ascribed to it (Saller 1932: 241).

Saller's model of human racial history paid little heed to anxieties about hybridity between east and west. Germany itself was understood as a racial crossroads between Romance influence in the west and Slavic in the east. It was these mixtures that gave the southern German *Volk* its dynamic character, in contrast to the relatively slow developments in the north (1932: 239). Further, there was no necessary correlation between the achievements of a people or race and its potential (1932: 239). In addition to his geographical use of the term, Saller also used 'race' in a 'vertical sense', i.e. to refer to the development of caste and class distinctions, and noted the rise of a high-achieving class of black Americans (1932: 241–2). (This use of the term 'race' was later held against Saller as the distortion of a concept which was foundational for the new order (Lüddecke 1995: 89).) The Jews were formed by a different racial composition to their European 'host peoples' (*Wirtsvölker*), by their separateness as a reproductive community:

> The importance of the Jews for the development of western culture is a matter of controversy. There is no question but that the Jew is essentially different in type from the western peoples. To this one should add that the frequent occurrences of hostility nowadays between the Jews and their guest peoples must be attributed at least as much to the similarity in their aptitudes as to differences in type, as this leads to an intensely competitive relationship. The Jewish spirit [*Geist*] is, next to the autochthonous culture, the main driving force in western culture (Lenz) and to this culture Jews have contributed with many brilliant gifts. Anti-semitism is therefore unjustified, in so far as it is directed against Jews as a matter of principle. It is only justified when it involves a rejection of far-reaching particularist demands and those activities which seek to undermine or fragment the state, activities which are associated with substantial *parts* of the Jewish people (Hennig). (Saller 1932: 253)

Richard Hennig (1874–1951) was a noted authority in geopolitics (Hennig 1931). On the evidence of this quotation at least, Saller was not a racial anti-Semite, but politically a *völkisch* one (see also Saller 1934: 56; Lüddecke 1995: 71).

Saller and Merkenschlager emphasized the dynamics of racial contact and interaction between races and landscape, and rejected the static taxonomy of Günther and the fixed racial characteristics described by Eugen Fischer (Saller 1963: 37). Race was understood as the dynamic interaction of environment and inheritance (Merkenschlager 1933: 27), rather than as a fixed inventory of racial features. Ideally, race was a state of equilibrium, one in which a race was grounded in the environment and nourished by it in an alliance of soil, plant and man (1933: 31). There were no pure races, and Germany's strength lay in its position at the crossroads of the Germanic, the Celtic and the Slavic worlds (1933: 47). *Volk* rather than race was the highest expression or principle of humanity; eugenics, and the artificial favouring of one race, were expressions of racial materialism (1933: 59–60).

Volk was the living organic community, united by and interacting through a common language, though not reducible to a linguistic community. The *Volk* was not defined by its links to an original biological community, but was itself an actual living community (Merkenschlager 1934: 43). The concepts of *Volk* and *Rasse* should be fused (Merkenschlager and Saller 1934; Lüddecke 1995: 80). In a work named after the fabled lost Germanic city *Vineta*, which developed Moeller van den Bruck's idea of the Prussian people as a synthesis of Germanic and the Slavic (*wendisch*) (Breuer 2001: 74; Lutzhöft 1971: 155–7), Saller and Merkenschlager evoked an ideal meeting place of east and west, and looked forward to a new age of exchange and interaction between different racial currents and temperaments symbolized by the Prussian people.

For Saller, Günther's model had wrongly portrayed the Alpine and the East Baltic races as inferior. In fact, this mongrel mixture or 'Bastardgemenge' was a stage on the way to a new, higher German race (Saller 1934: 17; Breuer 2001: 74–6). Germany's future strength was one in which all racial currents had a great role to play, i.e. those from the north, the south, the east and the west (Merkenschlager and Saller 1935: 139). This was an implied criticism of conventional paranoid fears of the Asiatic hordes to the east (Merkenschlager 1933: 59) and of the idealization of the Nordic race. It involved an unequivocal embrace of the vitality of a *Volk* as created by diverse and contrasting racial currents in their interactions with diverse landscapes. The idea of the German *Volk* as a meeting point of Germanic, Celtic and Slavic (*Wendisch*) was also in crass contradiction to the Nazi policy towards the Sorbs (known as *Wenden*), where the problem was understood in terms of a segregation into pure elements rather than synthesis (see below). This ideology of balance between east and west was however implicitly expansionist, since the German *Volk*, in order to rise again after the trauma of defeat and destruction, needed 'as much east as it has west' ('Deutschland braucht so viel Osten wie es Western hat', Merkenschlager and Saller 1935: 137).

Although Saller and Merkenschlager used the categories of traditional racial anthropology, these were seen as undergoing constant change and interaction. These categories were less significant in themselves than the interactions of race within *Volk*. Rather than the static, materialist category of anthropological race or *Systemrasse*, they gave priority to the concept of *Vitalrasse* (1935: 86–7). The evocation of direct interaction between 'soil, plant and man' involved a rejection of orthodox neo-Darwinism and Mendelian racial anthropology, as well as an attack on Günther's racial taxonomy. It was heresy to suggest that the environment and landscape could *directly* act upon the racial characteristics of a people (Rittershaus 1936: 181). This involved a rejection of Darwin's theory as the overarching explanation for evolution and change (Saller 1949: 26–8). In his post-war account of the relationship between race theory and Nazism, Saller identified the work of Darwin, Haeckel and Mendel as crucial in the shift from religious to biological, race-based anti-Semitism (1961: 23). For Saller, Nazi race theory (and therefore Nazism itself) was a product of scientific materialism.

Walter Gross and the idea of a German race

Like Fischer, Saller came under attack for favouring racial mixing. While Fischer needed only to shift his rhetorical ground slightly to avoid political trouble, Saller, by advocating the existence of a German race within a neo-Lamarckian framework, was on a collision course with the academic and political establishment. Saller saw in this idealization of the Nordic race a latent hostility to German nationalism, dubbing it the 'Nordic International' promoted by foreigners such as Gobineau, Vacher de Lapouge and Chamberlain (1934: 44). In the Nordicist journal *Rasse* Kurt Holler (1935a) poured scorn on their promotion of the idea of a 'German race'. This theory had been promoted by political undesirables such as Willy Hellpach, and by Jews like Hertz, Friedenthal and Weidenreich. The idea that any infusion of Slavic blood into the German *Volk* was invigorating had to be rejected. Holler called for the Race Policy Office to intervene.

Ludwig Leonhardt, an advocate of Nordification, attacked Saller for his acceptance of the ideas of the 'Jewish researcher' Franz Boas regarding the plasticity of races, for promoting the idea of racial mixing, and for his rejection of the priority of the Nordic race (1934). While the German *Volk* was a racial composite, that diverse racial composite would never have achieved its many-sidedness without the leadership of the Nordic race. Saller had argued that the German race was a product of the towns and cities, but this was where the Jewish influence had taken hold. Saller's work seemed to accord recognition to this Jewish component as part of the German *Volk*. It was wrong to equate the Nordic race simplistically with certain physical characteristics: Nordic qualities were as much psychological as physical (1934: 189). Without the Nordic ideal, our conception of the German *Volk* would be that it was 'colourless, uncombative, equalizing' (Leonhardt 1934: 190).

The idea of a single German race was clearly identified with opposition to the promotion of the Nordic race as the leading race (*Führerrasse*) within the German *Volk*. This was one area in which Walter Gross did indeed feel it necessary to intervene directly in academic debate. In a confidential circular issued from the Race Policy Office in Berlin dated 2 October 1934 (reprinted in Poliakov and Wolf 1983: 411–13; Saller 1963: 83ff.), Gross made it clear that any talk of the existence of a German race was both 'factually and politically erroneous and damaging'. The background to this contention was a desire to mitigate what Gross recognized was the exaggerated and one-sided rhetoric of the 'movement for the Nordic race' (*nordische Rassenbewegung*). While National Socialist ideology did not stand in need of academic proof, it was necessary that science played a role in the intellectual struggle with the enemies of National Socialism. In this it would be a disaster if the scientific findings on which its racial theories were based could be set aside for the sake of political convenience, thus allowing the enemies of National Socialism to deny or ignore the reality of the laws of inheritance. There was a German language, a German people, but racially Germany was a racial mix, and any racial description of the Germans must take account of this. The concept of 'race' was thus defined by natural science, and should be strictly distinguished from the sense in which we might speak of a German person or the German people.

Gross seemed to recognize that one possible motive for proposing the existence of a German race was that of demonstrating the unity of the German people. However, he argued that this use of the term race was characteristic of the enemies of National Socialism, in particular of 'Jewish-liberal and ultramontane' (Catholic) thought in which external factors, such as a common history, language or citizenship over blood lineage, were given precedence. This allowed Jews and Gypsies to be included in an Austrian or German race. Gross associated this viewpoint with the *Berliner Tageblatt*, and with the Austrian Chancellor Dr Engelbert Dollfuss, but he noted that comments from National Socialists such as Adolf Bartels and Achim

Gercke had been picked up and interpreted by enemies of National Socialism as indicating a weakening of the ideology.

The next point of Gross's circular returned to the question of the Nordic ideal and its potentially divisive impact, noting that he had a year previously expressed his opposition to the erroneous and one-sided promotion of the external characteristics of the Nordic race as an ideal. This could give rise to feelings of racial inferiority and damage the unity of the national community (*Volksgemeinschaft*). Gross did not however reject the Nordic ideal, but he suggested not discussing the German racial mix or at least underplaying it to avoid these unfortunate consequences. Talk of a German race should be quietly corrected in schools and other institutions, without making a public issue out of the question. If any public pronouncements were to be made, they were to come from Gross himself.

For Gross there were at least two levels to discourse about race. There was the full complexity of racial theory, with its attendant scientific debates and controversies, within which Günther's model of the racial composition of the *Volk* achieved semi-canonical status. Then there was public or popular discourse about race, in which the *Volk* was presented both as a moral and biological community. The problem for Gross was not so much that of reconciling these two levels of racial doctrine, but of keeping them from interacting in the public domain and causing confusion in the minds of the German public, thereby giving succour to the enemies of National Socialism. The consequence of this was that race theory as academic or intellectual discourse was much more politically sensitive than most other areas of academic inquiry, even where that discourse was being produced by approved ideologues or committed National Socialists.

Race theorists were subject to much greater political control than other academics and intellectuals. The question of the racial definition of the German *Volk* was particularly sensitive in relation to the eastern border between the German *Volk* and its racial others. In his final handout as a university teacher (17 January 1935), Saller made the following statement:

> Races are not fixed in nature, unchanging over many eons. Like all living things, they flow in a continual stream of change, in a tension between differentiation and levelling. Races are not merely of the body, they are of the mind and spirit. Thus history has led us from earlier races to our present German race and we have grown up to take our place in the community of peoples, a community in which we have always wished to assert our place though our own achievements in the great days of our history – this in the spirit of our dead brothers of the world war. (Saller 1935)

This Saller understood to be in keeping with the political leaders of the day, with Moeller van den Bruck, and with what Hitler had said after the Nazis had taken power. Saller's last words to his students were: 'But it does move! Long live the German race in motion!'. ('Und sie bewegt sich doch! Es lebe die deutsche Rasse in der Bewegung!') In addition to the allusion to Galileo, the word *Bewegung* also contained a dig at the Nazi 'movement', known as *die Bewegung* (Weingart et al. 1992: 540). *Vineta* was banned (as 'nationalist-bolshevik', Saller 1961: 61), as was Friedrich Merkenschlager's *Rassensonderung, Rassenmischung, Rassenwandlung* (1933). Merkenschlager was also imprisoned for a period (Lüddecke 1995: 87). The downfall of Saller and Merkenschlager was greeted with jubilation by the Nordicists (Holler 1935b). Michael Hesch (1935) noted that *Vineta* had been seen in Poland as justifying German expansionist claims in the east and was being used in anti-German propaganda. This alone justified banning the work.

Saller was unfortunate in being in key respects ahead of his time, in particular in rejecting the static model of racial anthropology and promoting a dynamic understanding of *Volk*. Similarly, his rejection (1934: 32–4) of the idea of a simple association of the Nordic race with the long-skull feature and his discussion of skull-rounding (attributed to 'self-domestication'), while it may have contributed in context to his profile as a anthropological dissident (Lüddecke 1995: 75), was not in principle at all out of step with the evolving mainstream position. Saller's support for closer links between eugenics and medicine was also prescient (Saller 1933; Weingart et al. 1992: 318–19; Lüddecke 1995: 72). However, Saller's model was suspect on grounds of environmentalism and neo-Lamarckianism. Saller's biological eclecticism, and an eastern-oriented model of the hybrid German *Volk*, were also political liabilities. There were also fundamental problems with the phrase 'German race'. The concept of a 'German race' was after all intellectually analogous to that of an 'Aryan race'. The diffusion of this concept would have created disarray in the public sphere and its established discursive order. In that order, the bridge between the academic and the popular was achieved by the concept *Volk*.

Hybridity and racial policy

On one level, nationality policy, i.e. racial and ethnic policy on assimilation or reassimilation (*Umvolkung*), was guided by a clear set of principles. In a memorandum produced by the Race Policy Office in 1939 ([Report 3] 1939), foreign elements were divided into two groups, regional minorities (*Minderheiten*) who belonged to a different, neighbouring *Volk* and 'parasites' (*Parasiten*), such as Jews and Gypsies. The Gypsies were defined as racially degenerate elements (*Entartungsteile*) of an original nomadic people. Four policy options in relation to foreign elements within the *Volk* were discussed (1939: 2–4): separation or isolation with degrees of autonomy (*Absonderung*); absorption or assimilation (*Aufsaugung*); sterilization (*Unfruchtbarmachen*); and elimination from the Reich by deportation (*Aussiedlung*) or annihilation (*Vernichtung*). Authentic assimilation took place between racially closely related peoples, as had happened with Huguenots in Germany and Germans in the United States of America and South Africa.

Examples of inauthentic assimilation were Negroes in the United States, Jews in all peoples, and the population of Polish origin in the Ruhr, which in spite of linguistic assimilation had retained its 'Slavic soul' and could never aspire to true German creativity. In these cases, there were merely pragmatic or material motives at work, and the assimilated elements could never grasp the true essence of the adopted *Volk*. The process of Germanization (*Eindeutschung*), which was in any case frequently re-Germanization (*Wiedereindeutschung*), had to be absolutely distinguished from these inauthentic forms of assimilation. In addition to the question of those ethnic Germans outside the political boundaries of Germany who were unambiguously part of the German *Volk*, the loss of elements of the *Volk* to other nations had created ruling elites of German or Nordic-Phalian (*nordrassig*) origin. This had energized otherwise uncreative and politically passive peoples (1939: 6). These racially valuable elements, if suitable, were to be drained from these foreign nations (*Auslaugung*) and Germanized, but should be settled in the interior of Germany rather than on the border (1939: 7, 19–29).

In addition to its hostility to Jews and Gypsies, the memorandum also exhibited virulent Slavophobia, in particular against Poles (1939: 8). The question of the eastern racial boundaries of the German *Volk* was much more contentious than that of the western. Estimates as to the extent of the Nordic-Germanic element in the eastern populations varied widely. One view was that the peoples to the east were fundamentally racially different, with only limited desirable elements, and that any assimilation had to be carried out with great caution. Many of the eastern populations (e.g. the Poles and Hungarians) were themselves highly mixed (1939: 21–6).

But when it came to the formulation of policy in specific contexts, the eventual result was theoretical confusion and the shutting down of public debate. Overall, National Socialist policy towards the Slavs did not follow a single, theoretical logic (Connelly 1999). This was the case in relation to the Sorbs. In contemporary terms, the Sorbs (*Sorben*) would be viewed as a Slavic-speaking ethnolinguistic minority living within the boundaries of the German state. For Nazi policy makers and racial anthropologists, the question was whether the Sorbs, known in German sources of the period as Wends (*Wenden*), were an original Slavic-speaking minority on German territory, or whether they were originally Germans who had become Slavicized (Burleigh 1988: 122). Otto Reche saw this as a chance to gain access to research funds and play a role as state ideologue (Geisenhainer 2002: 296–325). On the one hand, claims over territory required justification in terms of a relationship between *Volk* and geography. On these grounds, it was ideologically preferable to define the Sorbs as Slavicized Germans, who would in the natural course of events return to full membership of the German *Volk*. On the other, in the context of a general confrontation between *Germanentum* and *Slaventum*, there was general policy interest in emphasizing the differences between different Slavic peoples in a spirit of 'divide and rule'. This might suggest advantages in emphasizing the distinct status of groups such as the Sorbs.

Reche argued that the Sorbs were of 'Slavic race', whereas Hans Kleiner concluded that they fitted into the general profile of the German *Volk* in its regional variations (Geisenhainer 2002: 308–9). In 1937, there was an official attempt to create a united line among scholars on the Sorb question, and to prevent the development of nationalism among the 'Wends'. That line emphasized that the Sorbs were a Slavicized element of the German *Volk* (Burleigh 1988: 122; Schaller 2002: 146–8). The authorities sought to dampen down public discussion of the question, and a work by Reinhold Trautmann of Leipzig University on Sorbian–German place names was banned (Schaller 2002: 137–42). Questions of this kind ultimately fell within Himmler's expanding administrative empire as part of the general Germanization question in relation to the east. In the re-engineering of the east, those who failed to make the racial grade were to become part of a serf class (*Arbeitsvolk*) toiling for the benefits of the Germans (Burleigh 1988: 217–18; Geisenhainer 2002: 318–19).

A further controversy in relation to the contentious border between the German and the Slavic took place over the racial profile of the population of Silesia. In this case, there was a direct confrontation between German and Polish scholarly versions over the essential nature of the region and its population, including claims and counterclaims about the percentage of Nordic population in the German and Polish peoples. Eickstedt, who was at the University of Breslau, had completed a survey of Upper Silesia, but he was denied publication after the Ministry for the Interior had consulted Otto Reche. In a letter to Eickstedt (16 February 1937), Albert Brackmann noted that 'racial studies within frontier research are not particularly desirable at the moment' (Burleigh 1988: 97). In 1941, Reche attacked Fritz Arlt (the head of the Race Policy Office in Silesia) and Eickstedt for their research on Silesia. Reche objected to their claim to have discovered a Silesian racial type and to their model of racial hybridity in the population. Fritz Lenz was consulted and he argued that, according to the criteria applied, only one-third of the inhabitants were Nordic. This was politically undesirable from the point of view of pre-war Polish territorial claims (Burleigh 1988: 214; Eickstedt and Schwidetzky 1940). In addition to institutional and personal rivalry, there was a real theoretical difference between Reche and Eickstedt. Eickstedt's morphological method was an attempt to create an objective set of parameters for the assessment of the individual body in racial terms, but Reche objected that this failed to take into account the distinction between genotype and genotype (Geisenhainer 2002: 325–9).

The theoretical ambiguities of racial hybridity were deflected on a policy level by a focus on Jews and Gypsies. The racial anthropologist Robert Ritter classified the Gypsy population on a scale from 'pure Gypsy' to non-Gypsy, concluding that the vast majority were racially mixed, known as 'ZM' or *Zigeunermischling*. The association of this racial hybridity with a range of anti-social traits attributed to Gypsies gave anthropological justification for repression and murder (Finger 1937; Ritter 1939; Friedlander 1995: 246ff.). The attitude towards the small minority of 'racially pure' Gypsies (Verschuer 1941: 130) was however less clear-cut than that towards 'full Jews' (*Volljuden*). Those deemed socially well adjusted were frequently not deported and killed (Lewy 1999). Ruttke (1939: 20–1) quoted a decree issued by Himmler (8.12.1938), which required that full-blooded Gypsies be treated differently from *Mischlinge*, since most of the criminality associated with Gypsies was the responsibility of those of mixed race. The most pressing need was for a central registry and racial evaluation of all Gypsies and those adopting an itinerant life-style.

Ideological stalemate

The extreme range of potential categorizations of eastern populations, on a continuum from Nordic to Mongol or Asiatic, the vast expanse of space and the lack of clear geographical and racial boundaries made the east in particular a source of racial paranoia about the true boundaries of the *Volk*. On the basis of its geographical position, the German *Volk* was 'the most threatened of all the Germanic peoples by the penetration of the yellow race from the northeast and the Oriental race in its diverse mixed forms in the southeast' (Mollinson 1934: 48). If defensive measures were not taken, Germany would become like many peoples in the east: 'a partly mongolized, partly orientalized racial mix which would have to renounce for ever any claims for a leading role in the cultural development of Europe' (1934: 48).

The attempt to consolidate racially the German *Volk* and define an unambiguous boundary went together with a rejection of influence from the east. Opponents of the idea of an eastern or Asiatic origin of the Indo-Europeans, such as Otto Reche, were hostile to the whole tradition of *ex oriente lux* (Reche 1936a: 204, 18, 1936b: 313). The east, with its hostile climate and teeming masses of foreign races, had many times been the graveyard of the Nordic race (1936b: 316; Haase-Bessell 1939: 17). The urge to consolidate the eastern boundary of the *Volk* went together with the view that Germany, or northern Europe, was the traditional homeland and heartland of the Indo-Europeans (Kulz 1939). Hostility to the idea of *ex oriente lux* was directed at Christianity, with its roots in the Middle East, and at the Orientalist craze for exotic palaces and pyramids (Pastenaci 1935: 5–7). But racial anthropology could not provide a coherent or unanimous racial diagnostic of the true boundary with the east.

Direct attacks on Nordicism and Rosenberg were ill-advised, as he and his allies were willing to mobilize whatever power and influence they could muster to ban offending works or persecute ideological deviants. But in the wider scheme of things, Rosenberg was increasingly marginal. The conclusion of the early period of ideological foment was a kind of stalemate. Those like Fischer who used the language of racial mixing had received a warning that they should choose their language with care. Fischer responded by emphasizing that he was against any mixing with racially foreign elements, and by stressing his admiration for the Nordic race. Later in the Third Reich, Fischer co-authored an anti-Semitic volume with Gerhard Kittel (1943).

One consequence of the Nordic question was the strengthening of doubts as to whether external physical markers should be used in assigning individuals to superior or inferior groups. Professor Otto Aichel (1871–1935), the director of the Anthropological Institute at Kiel University, argued that race science and racial propaganda should be kept strictly separate (1933: 161), and that practical eugenic policies could not proceed on the assumption that, for example, 'blond, light-coloured eyes, long-skulled, tall' were qualities of high racial value, and 'brunette, brown-eyed, round-headed, short' were racially less valuable. Individuals could only be judged on the basis of the investigation of their family–kin group and their intellectual and psychological qualities (1933: 162).

Bruno Petermann (1898–1941) dismissed talk of static psychological characteristics (*Eigenschaften*) or features (*Merkmale*) in parallel with somatic racial characteristics. Psychology required the replacement of the popular concept of 'race' with a commitment to a truly scientific, 'genetic-functional' approach which involved understanding race character in the context of the processes of selection to which each race had been exposed. Popularizing and 'mythic-occult' presentations of race should give way to an understanding of race as a dynamic, biological interface between hereditary factors and environmental processes of selection (1935: 220, 222–3). Wilhelm Hartnacke's verdict was simply that the idea of anthropology carried out from a humanities perspective (*geisteswissenschaftliche Anthropologie*) was a contradiction in terms (1944: 226). In the applied domains of military and industrial psychology, race-typological systems were found to be dysfunctional: 'there were more supporters of typologies among academic psychologists than among military or industrial psychologists' (Geuter 1992: 122).

Nordic ideologues were clearly told to dampen down their 'exaggerated' rhetoric about the unique virtues of the Nordic race. Extreme Nordic chauvinism was discredited. The Nordic element was by consensus agreed to be the unifying bond of the German people. The corollary was that there was no clear relation between somatic type and intrinsic racial quality. This was the logical conclusion of Mendelian race anthropology, and allowed for an apparent reconciliation between the demands of unity of the *Volk* and the superiority of the Nordic race. One could have brown hair, a round skull, and still claim to be of Nordic character or mentality. A predominantly Alpine psychological make-up might be found in a predominantly Nordic body (Staemmler 1936: 119). This however reduced the Nordic ideal to at best an ideal set of character traits or at worst a mere slogan.

Theodor Viernstein (1878–1949), in an official handbook for doctors undertaking a racio-biological survey of the ancestral agricultural population (*Erbhofbauer*) of Bavaria, stressed that bodily racial type had no necessary relationship with mental or psychological type, so that 'a Nordic body did not necessarily imply a Nordic mentality'. By the same principle, 'an Alpine racial type can have the psychological qualities of the Nordic individual' (Viernstein 1935: 111). Walter Schultze stressed that there was no programme to 'breed' an ideal tall, narrow-faced, blue-eyed, blond type; no hereditarily healthy member of the German *Volk* should feel second-class or inferior on account of lacking these features. It was the psychology, the morality, the personality of the individual that counted, and the inheritance of external physical characteristics was a matter of secondary importance. The idea that racial policies took as their ideal a particular physical type was misinformation spread by the enemies of National Socialism (Schultze 1934: 16).

This principle also logically applied to Jews, in that one could not define a Jew as someone with a particular set of bodily features. The racially hybrid nature of the Jewish people meant that there was no single Jewish physical type (Thomalla n.d. [*c* 1935]: 125). Verschuer noted that someone physically of 'good Nordic type' might completely lack Nordic psychological qualities (1938a: 143). Further, someone with Nordic appearance might even be of Jewish character, and vice versa. This was recognized for example by Friedrich Keiter, who stressed the difficulty of identifying Jewish *Mischlinge* on grounds of bodily type alone (Keiter 1941: 179; Felbor 1995: 119).

The existence of a serious methodological problem was recognized, as was the lack of intellectual tools to deal with it. Theodor Mollinson for example stressed that it was the psychological and moral racial qualities which were fundamental to the future of the *Volk*, rather than the purely physical ones. But there was at present no precise statistical method which would underpin a science of race psychology. It was impossible at present to separate environmental or educational influences on the individual from those on the group. The only available methodology was to observe populations where one particular racial type was heavily dominant (1934: 35–7). It was self-evident that there was no tight connection between physical and psychological racial qualities. Most people were *Mischlinge*. However, it was unlikely that someone would inherit all the physical characteristics of one race and all the psychological traits of another (1934: 41).

The dilemmas of racial education can be clearly seen from the guidelines issued by the Ministry for Education in 1938 for biology teaching in schools, summarized by Kurt Holler in the journal *Rasse*. These required the teacher to stress that the phenotype was not necessarily a guide to race-psychological character, and that phenotype should be absolutely distinguished from genotype. A purely descriptive anthropology based solely on body measurements was not acceptable. However, the guidelines also stressed the unity of mind and body, so that children were encouraged to make links between physical and psychological or personality traits. In this way, the child would grasp race in terms of a 'living unity'. It should be made very clear that the Nordic race was the unifying factor of the German *Volk*. While the physical-chemical basis of life should be acknowledged, a purely mechanistic or mechanical presentation of biology was insufficient. Older children should be taught the limits of the scientific method, but also that the Nordic-Germanic drive to knowledge was constantly pushing back the frontiers of science, without getting lost in unreal conjectures. There was however no room for 'metabiological speculations' in the teaching of biology (Holler 1938: 469–70).

In 1939, Haase-Bessell dismissed the idea of a typology in which fixed physical and psychological characteristics were associated with individual races as 'superficial' (1939: 4). The major human races should be understood not in terms of purity or a fixed inventory of features, but as fields of variation in which genes showed particular statistical distributions. These variations arose through genetic mutation (1939: 4–5). The interaction of race with territory gave rise to peoples (*Völker*), and these peoples were the product of both horizontal (i.e. geographical) and vertical (i.e. social-hierarchical) processes of selection.

To a certain extent, Haase-Bessell's view of race paralleled that of Karl Saller and Merkenschlager, in that it rejected the idea of 'purity' and understood some forms of hybridity as positive. Within biology, the only concept that could express the idea of purity was absolute genetic identity. Given the diversity of conditions prevailing on the earth's surface, any race which was genetically absolutely fixed would inevitably fall victim to natural selection (1939: 4).

Haase-Bessell also seemed to blur the boundary between *Rasse* and *Volk*. Race was not defined as a set of shared features but as a higher-order unity (1939: 7). For example, the Nordic race was intrinsically variable. In addition to blue eyes, one of its features was brown eyes. This was common, particularly in northwestern Europe (1939: 7). *Rasse* and *Volk*, seen historically, were a single biological unit in that races interacted with territory (*Boden*) to give rise to peoples. Some peoples prospered and other declined, but there was no natural law dictating the life-cycle of a people.

The German people was only now finding its true biological unity ('seine volksbiologische Form', 1939: 16). In a clear reference to Nordification, Haase-Bessell rejected any idea of selective breeding with reference to a single scale of values. Aside from the dangers of subjectivity and of making judgements relative to a particular time and place, this kind of programme ignored what Haase-Bessell characterized as the 'three-dimensionality' of race. What defined a race was not purity but a harmonious equilibrium between diverse genetically transmitted traits. That diversity was itself functional for any major race which was spread over a large and variable territory (1939: 7).

However, there were important differences with Saller's position. The emphasis on mutation theory implied adherence to the neo-Darwinian theory of evolution, in which the environment did not act *directly* on the transmission of hereditary traits. Further, Haase-Bessell recognized the Nordic race as the driving force in the creation of the German people ('mother race' or *Mutterrasse*), as well as of the Swedish, Danish and English peoples. Each had acquired its own character as a result of dispersal and inner processes of selection. Haase-Bessell's discussion of hybridity made no mention of any other racial category, such as 'Dinaric' or 'Alpine'. Haase-Bessell used the term 'closely related' ('nahe verwandt') races, and thus avoided the question of the continuum between the German *Volk* and the non-Nordic peoples to the south and east. The evocation of the adaptive advantage of racial diversity was balanced by a strong statement rejecting the mixing of 'foreign blood': any admixture of foreign racial elements would destroy the harmony and balance of that inner diversity (1939: 7). The Jews were a parasitic people (1939: 17). In addition, pathological traits such as hereditary defects needed to be eliminated (1939: 7).

For Haase-Bessell, *Volk* emerged out of *Rasse*; it formed an organic unity derived from the interaction of race and territory. One analogy for *Volk* was with the concept of a non-unified energy field (*heterogenes Feldes*) in modern physics:

> Although a self-contained whole, the equilibrium of such a field is always unstable; it is not static, but rather subject to a particular dynamic. One can compare the energy lines (*Kraftlinien*) to the blood-lines (*Blutlinien*) of a people, which are characterized by different abilities (professions) and different levels of rootedness in the soil (*Bodenständigkeit*), but it is precisely in the totality that the special character of the people emerges. The image of an energy field brings out well the unity but also the elastic character of a people – provided it deserves to be called a people. (Haase-Bessell 1939: 8)

Another way of representing a *Volk* was through the statistical modelling of its genetic lines, so that the genetic profile of a *Volk* at a given point in time could be represented in three dimensions (1939: 8ff.).

Conclusion

This gap between academic discourse on race and popular racial stereotypes was functional, in the sense that it allowed for the autonomy of science in relation to vulgar Nazism. The separation of academic from popular racism prevented the complexities of academic debate from interfering with the political message. But there was also considerable confusion within Nazism over the relationship of body to mind, and of body and mind to race.

Racial anthropology had an important role in stressing that some elements were clearly harmful to, and to be excluded from, the *Volk*, and, through Mendelian racial anthropology, in affirming that the modern German *Volk* had not merged irretrievably with the foreign racial elements that had entered it. This also lay behind the rejection of the notion of a German race, since this seemed to embody the fundamental error of confusing racial with linguistic identity, and the 'unscientific' notion that racial mixing meant racial blending.

The whole topic of the racial composition of the German *Volk* had been shown to be at best a nuisance, and at worst a serious distraction from the main political messages of the regime. In addition to the Nordic question, there was the sensitive issue of the eastern boundary of the *Volk*. Could this be drawn clearly, i.e. could a racial line be shown between Germans and Slavs? If not, where was the 'true' border? One simple answer was that it was the linguistic border. But this was also unacceptable, given widespread assimilation. Mendelian genetics as applied to race suggested that the border was an abstraction rather than a line on the map. Racial anthropology could not draw a clear line around the *Volk* in relation to the geographical neighbours, and there was no clear single answer to the question of how these relationships were to be understood. Racial anthropology could however point out some elements within the *Volk* that were racially foreign and undesirable. The disciplines of *Volk* (linguistics, folklore, history, culture, human geography) might claim to offer criteria for a clear external boundary. But they were unable to point to the 'inner boundary', that between 'real Germans' and those assimilated Jews who were native speakers of German.

This, combined with the admission that the most important racial attributes were psychological, suggested very clearly that racial anthropology was neither scientifically coherent nor politically unproblematic. The notion of the German people having a collective 'Nordic soul' looked quaint, when set against the rising sophistication of evolutionary biology and human genetics. Racial anthropologists had shown their usefulness in making clear that Jews and other undesirable elements were not part of the *Volk*, and in clarifying that the *Volk* could not be defined purely in linguistic terms, but they had no coherent answer to offer in relation to the positive definition of the German *Volk*.

This is not to say that racial anthropology was banned or persecuted as a discipline. Racial anthropologists were key personnel in the state's profiling of its population, and in the preparation of racial evaluations of individuals and groups. The courts however did not always accept their opinions (Müller-Hill 1999). Walter Scheidt (1895–1976) was exceptional for refusing to undertake anthropological assessments on behalf of the authorities, though he was a scientific purist rather than an ideological opponent of the regime (Felbor 1995: 97–9; Massin 1999: 19, 41–2). Kaupen-Haas (1986: 120) dates the influence of racial anthropology within the Ministry of the Interior to the period from 1933 to 1939, and notes that this Ministry declared racial anthropology to be 'unscientific' in 1941 (1986: 118). Racial anthropologists were necessary for the state, frequently resenting the drudgery of racial evaluations which took them away from their academic careers. Given the acceptance of the distinction between genotype and phenotype, the emphasis in racial profiling was as much on the gathering of family medical history and genealogical information (*Sippenkunde*) as on the measurement of the individual human body. Church records and other family documents had a central role to play in this, as it was assumed that before 1800 there had been very few conversions from Judaism to Christianity (Schulle 2001).

Discussions about the Nordic race had thrown the whole question of the definition of *Volk* into relief. There was no political benefit to be obtained from seeing the *Volk* as a kind of imperfectly realized underlying race, as in effect the result of the fall of races from their original purity into hybridity. This presented a negative image of the *Volk*, suggesting it was somehow a second-class kind of grouping (Alnor 1935: 33). This was not to say that the purely linguistic or cultural definition of *Volk* was acceptable. The 'Schmidt-Rohr' affair demonstrated this quite unambiguously, since the notion that languages had the power to create and define peoples or *Völker* could be taken to imply that Jews were members of the *Volk*. Although an outspoken anti-Nordicist, Schmidt-Rohr survived his brushes with the authorities to promote a disambiguated ideology of the German mother tongue in the Third Reich (Simon 1985b, 1986a, 1986b; Hutton 1999). A 1939 article in the journal *Rasse* was prefaced with words of praise from Walter Gross, a clear sign of Schmidt-Rohr's rehabilitation. Gross saluted the appearance of the piece as a sign of developing intellectual consensus between different approaches, i.e. between racial anthropology and linguistics (Schmidt-Rohr 1939a: 81).

Nordicism survived as one available rhetorical answer to the problem of the unity of the German *Volk*, and to the meaning of 'racial elite' as applied to other European nations. But the radical agenda of Nordification (or re-Nordification) was politically dead. Gross had clearly signalled the requirement that racial anthropology adopt a lower public profile, and the official turn against Nordicism, which was the strongest ideological offshoot of racial anthropology, added further to its political marginalization. This political-intellectual stalemate left evolutionary biology and human genetics in an advantageous position compared with racial anthropology. The disciplines of *Volk*, notably linguistics, provided they respected the boundary between *Volk* and *Rasse*, also benefited from this stale-mate. The decline of racial anthropology left a space for an intermediary discipline between the humanities and the sciences. That discipline was psychology, which was better placed to mediate with the disciplines of *Volk*, since it was concerned with the interaction between the individual and culture. It also had an important role in the human sciences, since it was concerned with the boundary between what was inherited genetically and what was acquired socially and culturally. Advances in hereditary psychology offered the possibility of a new, scientific understanding of the relationship between body (understood as a set of inherited genetic qualities) and mind. There could be unity of mind and body at the deep level defined by hereditary psychology, rather than the superficial, quasi-popularist readings of the body offered by racial anthropology.

The fate of Nordic ideologies in Nazi Germany was a complex one, both ideologically and institutionally. Nordicism was effectively marginalized by 1936, and though the invasion and occupation of Denmark and Norway in 1940 raised the hopes of German Nordi-cists for a Nordic alliance, these were not realized (Simon n.d.: 1). Lutzhöft finishes his narrative of Nordicism in Germany in 1940, the point at which, he contends, Günther realized that his project had failed in the face of the modernity of Nazism (Lutzhöft 1971: 24). This move allows Lutzhöft in effect to separate Günther's career from Nazism. A more accurate way of understanding Günther's career and Nordicism in general was that it was ultimately a failed project *within* Nazism. It had however played a key role in the dialectic of *Volk*.

In the posthumously published contribution to the Baur-Fischer-Lenz textbook (Baur 1936), Erwin Baur discussed the scientific basis of selective breeding. Thus many lay people thought it would be possible to take the racial mixture of the modern European city and breed from it pure racial types. But this was to overlook one important fact. Racial characteristics were inherited according to Mendel's laws, i.e. independent of each other. If we selected for the most prominent characteristics of the Nordic or Mediterranean races, there was no way of ensuring that the psychological qualities of the Nordic – strength of character, firmness of will, intelligence – would be present. All that would be achieved is a degree of superficial Nordification of appearance (Baur 1936: 93–4). Junker and Hossfeld read this conclusion as a rejection of Nazi ideology (2002: 236; Junker 2004: 492), but on the contrary it is entirely in accord with the direction of racial thinking in the Third Reich.

11

Dynamics of Nazi Science

Introduction

In terms of intellectual culture, National Socialism was different in character from the Soviet totalitarian model of the 1930s. In the case of Nazism, persecution by a particular state agency or official could be neutralized by support from another power centre. Many academics and intellectuals who were broadly supportive of Nazism were later to claim falsely that they were persecuted by the NSDAP when they had in fact fallen foul of interpersonal or institutional rivalry. Except where an issue directly impacted on core state policy and ideology (e.g. Marxism, Judaism), there was room for debate and discussion. Frequently the result of too vigorous a public debate in areas of potential policy relevance was marginalization, and the topic would be removed from the public domain.

An example of one such controversy was the question of the eugenic status of illegitimacy. Under National Socialism, there was debate about the status of family values and illegitimate children. Gross and Lenz saw illegitimacy overall as an indicator of eugenic degeneration. Paul (1940: 159) saw the cases of high-quality illegitimate children as exceptions, and was concerned about the Romantic view of illegitimacy. Günther stressed the central importance of the institution of the family (1940). Heinrich Himmler however wished to see more offspring of high racial quality, regardless of civil status (Lenz 1937, 1940; Lilienthal 1985: 27; Pine 1997: 42–3; Grunberger 1971: 313–19). The publication of a book by Günther defending the eugenic status of the family and monogamy was eventually banned – apparently on the wishes of elements in the SS, and in spite of the support of Gross (Lutzhöft 1971: 390–402).

A further complication of Nazi intellectual life can be illustrated by a polemical exchange between the philosopher Kurt Hildebrandt (1881–1966) and the mathematician Pascual Jordan (1902–1980). This exchange has been represented as an internal ideological conflict within Nazism, between a '*völkisch*, traditional German and somewhat romantic-mystical' idea and a stress on 'modern, especially military technology' (Segal 2003: 376 fn., 377; Jordan 1935). Hildebrandt was a scholar of Goethe (Hildebrandt 1942). Jordan was however not a straightforward defender of scientific objectivity. He rejected the 'mechanist-materialist reduction of the physical world, its elimination of life as a special category for organisms' and its political individualism (Wise 1994: 225). Jordan saw in the ideology of scientific objectivity a moral cowardice which lent support to egalitarian notions. Nonetheless modern science, with its 'objective efficacy' (*objektive Wirksamkeit*) offered a kind of technological truth (Wise 1994: 226). The complicating factor here is that modern physics itself denied the existence of a straightforward kind of physical objectivity; for Jordan, the moral relativism of Nazism could be reconciled with modern theoretical physics. But this form of physics, in particular Einsteinian physics, had been seen by Aryan ideologues as 'Jewish'. Here we can see a clash between two stereotypes of Jewish thought. For Nazi ideologues in the tradition of Goethe, the Jews symbolized materialism and universalism antithetical to *völkisch* values; for scientists who rejected the new indeterminacy in the physical sciences, Jewish science meant subjectivism and relativism understood as a chaos of values. There were however moves to apply this notion of indeterminacy to the study of race and heredity (Haase-Bessell 1939; Verschuer 1944).

Science and ideology

The holism, organicism, bio-vitalism, anti-materialism and teleological nature of much scholarship in the early phases of the National Socialist period can be set within the context of the elitist revolt against modernity, in particular the evocation of a historical elite shaping the destiny of the *Volk*. The idealization of the Nordic race reflected this nostalgic elitism and ambivalence about new scientific understanding of human biology. These trends reflected a desire to break down the barrier between the humanities and the natural sciences and between scholarship and ideology. Nazi academic ideologues showed revolutionary distaste for the ivory-tower scholar, and for what they saw as the shallow materialism of modernity and the machine age. The philosopher Martin Heidegger (1889–1976) saw in Nazism the possibility of an end to the alienation of authentic 'being' within modernity. Ludwig Klages (1872–1956) lamented the destructive effect of regimenting mechanistic *Geist* on the freedom of rhythm and the 'pulse of life' (*Lebenspulsschlag*) (1934).

Holistic thinking (*Ganzheitsbetrachtung*) attempted to transcend the opposition between vitalistic and mechanistic views and mind–body dualism. It was a universal model, applicable not only to biology but to all living systems, including sociology and history (Meyer[-Abich] 1934: 8–9, 18). Ecological thinking, the idea of the living, harmonious equilibrium between organism and environment was seen as inseparable from teleological thinking (Friedrichs 1934). Holistic thinking was critical both of a positivistic approach based on precise but superficial measurement and of genetics, with its ontologically ill-defined notion of genotype (Keudel 1935). Some holistic thinkers sought to make a direct analogy between holistic biology and the National Socialist understanding of *Volk* as an organic unity. An individual was not an isolated element (*Element*) of an aggregation but a part (*Glied*) integrated into a whole. This was reminiscent of Hitler's statement: 'You are nothing, your people is everything' ('Du bist nichts, dein Volk ist alles', Keudel 1935: 402–3).

One key factor in the intellectual climate of the Third Reich was the accelerating mobilization and militarization of the state as the level of international conflict increased. A four-year plan was declared in 1936 for the rearmament of the state, with high-level state commitment to applied science and technology. This led to the increased dominance of a technocratic mindset (Sieg 2001: 258), and impatience with ideological posturing and academic debate in sensitive policy areas. In this sense, 1941 was very different from the *völkisch* spring of 1933–6. In 1937, the 'radical romantic' Johannes Stark (1874–1957) was replaced by 'the opportunist pragmatic Nazi' Rudolf Mentzel in a key position in the German Research Foundation, the Deutsche Forschungsgemeinschaft (DFG) (Segal 2003: 397). The journal *Deutsche Mathematik*, which promoted a *völkisch* approach to mathematics under the editorship of Ludwig Bierberach (1886–1982) had declined in '*völkisch* content and National Socialist rhetoric' by the late 1930s (Segal 2003: 410). The Nazi educational philosopher Ernst Krieck (1882–1947), who associated Darwinism with materialism, was highly critical of the increasingly technocratic spirit of the Nazi state and what he saw as its neglect of the humanities (Krieck 1936; Müller 1978: 131; Paletschek 2001: 50). At the end of the 1920s, the humanities received 30 per cent of funding from DFG; by 1943–4 this had fallen to 15 per cent (Sieg 2001: 264).

One marked feature of Nazi academic culture was a process of neutralization of the more extreme academic views and extreme forms of academic politicization. Views and ideologues that were at odds with scientific orthodoxy, as defined by scientific norms, tended to lose out in the long run. There was an underlying dynamic to intellectual developments in the Third Reich, which ultimately militated against theories that specifically set themselves against scientific orthodoxy. That orthodoxy was defined as a commitment to the phylogenetic and biological unity of humankind, to Darwin's theory of evolution – as it had been elaborated by August Weismann (1834–1914), drawing a clear distinction between the so-called 'germ line' (*Keimplasma*) and the 'somatic line' (*Soma*) – to Mendelian genetics, to population genetics: in other words to the so-called neo-Darwinian synthesis which established itself internationally in the 1940s. This involved the rejection of neo-Lamarckianism, in particular the notion of the inheritance of acquired characteristics, and the marginalization of approaches to science which drew too overtly on vitalism, relativism, Goethean science or any of the metaphor-rich theories of evolution which had run in parallel to neo-Darwinism.

One attempted characterization of Nazi ideology has been that of 'materialism' or 'race materialism'. But, as Harrington (1996) shows in her review of holism in German science, 'mechanistic' or 'materialistic' were the polemical epithets of choice for a wide range of vitalistic and holistic theories, including pro-Nazi ones. While the horror of mass civilization and its materialism provided much of the intellectual power behind the *völkisch* movement, eugenics, racial anthropology and Nazism itself could plausibly be presented as a product of this same mass culture of modernity. Alternatively, from the Nazi point of view, Soviet civilization could be presented as offering a soulless mechanized vision of life, in which the individual was crushed by a state system that was entirely alienated from the natural world, and in which the prevailing philosophical spirit was an imposed uniformity and 'mechanistic materialism' (Antonowytsch 1942: 54–5, 70, 95). The charge of 'materialism' was used by almost everyone against everyone else, and it thus has little to offer as a label for Nazi ideology.

Darwinism and the intellectual background to Nazism

One way to chart the question of science in Nazi Germany is in relation to Darwinism. Darwinism can be defined, following Walter Marle's 1936 medical dictionary, as: 'a doctrine that a struggle for survival takes place among organisms produced in excessive numbers (the so-called 'struggle for life'), which, by means of natural selection, has the consequence of the survival of the fittest, and finally, on grounds of inheritance and adaptation, gives rise to the emergence of new species' (1936: 226). 'Excessive numbers' points to the influence of the population theorist Thomas Malthus (1766–1834) on Darwin's work.

On the conventional reading of evolutionary theory, there is no goal or teleology to the processes of natural selection: 'evolution is a mindless, purposeless, algorithmic process' (Dennett 1996: 320). Superiority is always local; there is no global sense in which a complex organism is superior to a simpler one, and a variant which is selected is only superior under the particular prevailing conditions. This reading can be challenged by citing Darwin himself, who claimed that 'as natural selection works solely by and for the good of each being, all corporeal and mental endowments will tend to progress towards perfection' (Richards 1998: 592; Darwin 1859: 489). Richards argues that both Darwin and Herbert Spencer shared a view of progress in evolution. However, what the theory of natural selection denied was that there was an innate Lamarckian tendency in the organism towards perfection (1998: 599).

Both Darwin and Alfred Russell Wallace (1823–1913) saw racial struggle as giving rise to hierarchical racial difference (Stepan 1982: 56–8). However, natural selection operated without reference to any divine ordering of the universe. Nature was at best its own teleology. In Germany, Haeckel managed to construct a form of natural religion on the basis of this idea, but for many thinkers evolutionary theory drained meaning from the natural world. This was a more profound intellectual shock than the scientific assimilation of human beings to animals, one to which *völkisch* thinkers responded with their own meaning-creating teleologies. For socio-political theories, the problem was not so much the fitting of a set of metaphors of struggle and competition onto Darwin's theory, but the stark nature of pure neo-Darwinism. Disavowing any teleology (*Zielgerichtetheit*), neo-Darwinism was however not itself incompatible with teleological thinking.

The reception of Darwin was central to intellectual developments in the second half of the nineteenth century. Darwin's work was translated into German by Julius Victor Carus (1823–1903), and promoted by the scientist and social theorist Ernst Haeckel (1834–1919). Haeckel rejected both Christianity and Kantian idealism and humanism (*Anthropismus*) as falsely elevating humankind out of nature. Heavily influenced by Goethe, Haeckel tried to negotiate a position between a materialist view of matter and what he saw as the dualist mysticism of vitalism and neo-vitalism with its concept of 'life force' (*Lebenskraft*) and related teleological theories of nature ([1899] 1922: 55–6, 280). Haeckel's Monism asserted the fundamental unity of humanity with nature, and of organic and inorganic substance: so-called 'pan-psychism'. In practice, the Monism of Haeckel and his followers was not always distinct from pantheism and indeed from holistic vitalism, and it took on an increasingly *völkisch* form, over-lapping with various strands of pan-Germanism, paganism and occultism. However, Monists lacked a commonly agreed political agenda (Gasman 1971). Haeckel's most famous intellectual slogan of 'ontology recapitulates phylogeny' was highly influential within biology and on theories of the mind, including that of the racial typologist Carl Gustav Jung (Noll 1997: 104–6).

Following Haeckel's vision of an organic state, and the reformulation of Darwinism by August Weismann, neo-Darwinism became fundamental to the eugenics movement in Germany. Haeckel stressed that modern civilization led to the suspension of a process of natural selection. Modern medicine worked counter to natural selection; he contrasted this with the Spartan practice of exposing babies to the elements as a form of selection (Weingart et al. 1992: 76–7).

Late-nineteenth-century racial anthropology in Germany, under the leadership of Rudolf Virchow, was in general politically and racially liberal, monogenist and resistant to Darwinism, associating it with radical political materialism and socialism. Virchow however did not dispute Darwin's importance as a scientist. A rapid shift took place at the turn of the century, towards a synthesis of neo-Darwinism, racial anthropology and eugenics. On Virchow's death in 1902, the intellectual tide, which had been running against Virchow, turned, and Hermann Klaatsch and Gustav Schwalbe in particular began to promote Darwinism (Massin 1996: 114–15). Carl Stratz (1858–1924) (1904: 1–23) saw Haeckel as having harmed the reception of Darwinism in Germany by his lack of intellectual caution, and at the dawn of a new century welcomed the arrival of a transformed anthropology on the foundations of biological science, as exemplified in the comparative anatomical studies of Hermann Klaatsch (1863–1916). Klaatsch had thus 'sown the seeds, the fruits of which we hope to harvest in the twentieth century' (Stratz 1904: 23).

Ludwig Woltmann produced a merger of Darwinism and *völkisch* organicism, and argued that the leaders of the Italian Renaissance were descended from the Goths and Longobards (Mosse 1998: 102–3; Woltmann 1905). For Otto Ammon, Darwinism rather than economic theory provided insight into the fundamental nature of social processes, and revealed the intellectual poverty of social democracy (1893, 1900: 1–14). Ammon dismissed Lamarck's theory of the inheritance of acquired characteristics as irrelevant, but not contradictory, to his social theory. Since the theory was built on Darwin's theory of natural selection, Ammon argued that it could not stand or fall by whether there was an additional mechanism allowing the inheritance of acquired characteristics (1900: 8–9).

Although the eugenic pioneers in Germany, following their French models, assumed that social hierarchies represented, or should represent, a hierarchy of eugenic fitness, and took for granted the superiority of white Europeans over other races, they were little concerned with questions of racial classification, and were not uniformly anti-Semitic. Their pessimism was formed by a biological understanding of socio-political developments, and this directed attention to the theoretical and practical aspects of social engineering on eugenic lines. The aim might be to create a eugenic utopia, which would as far as possible resolve the conflict between Darwinism and humanitarian-socialist ideals (the view of Alfred Ploetz, Weiss 1990: 18), or to restore or protect the biological vitality of the nation by encouraging the best elements to reproduce at a higher rate (the view of Wilhelm Schallmayer, Weiss 1990: 20–1).

Friedrich Nietzsche saw Darwin's theory as manifesting 'scientific nihilism' (Call 1998: 11), and opposition to Darwinism had deep roots in German intellectual culture. In the Weimar intellectual culture, intellectuals in many fields rejected what they saw as a utilitarian, mechanistic and technological mindset: the cry was 'Back to Goethe'. In psychology, Kurt Goldstein (1878–1965) and Max Wertheimer (1880–1943) reconciled traditional empiricism dialectically with 'Gestalt seeing' or *Schauen* (Harrington 1996: 27, 29). Many intellectuals looked back to Goethe's morphology and other scientific writings for an alternative theory of biological change. Intellectual trends such as ecological biology, vitalism and neo-Lamarckianism interacted with this 'Goethean' science in complex ways. The key to these alternate intellectual trends was the assertion of some form of teleology in evolutionary change.

In his autobiography, Houston Stewart Chamberlain (1922: 82ff.) admitted to having been an admirer of Darwin in his youth, though even at that time he had felt a mistrust for the rigid abstraction of purely 'systematic' classification systems. An intuitive grasp of organic relationships had eventually led him away from Darwinism. An unpublished work by Chamberlain, *Die Lebenslehre*, was to offer a new understanding of the form of living beings and the relationships between organisms. It was written under the influence of

Goethe's scientific writings, and of Indian and Kantian philosophy, and in the hope 'of striking a death blow to the crudely empirical theory of evolution' (1922: 127). Chamberlain saw causal theories of evolution as gigantic intellectual structures built up on minimal observation (1922: 128).

The *völkisch* movement contained strong elements of hostility to Darwinism. For example, the anti-Semitic *völkisch* feminist Mathilde Ludendorff (1877–1966), together with her husband General Erich Ludendorff (1865–1937), attacked Darwin's theory for its purely materialist-mechanistic account of the origin of life (Strohm 1997: 37–8). The *völkisch* ideologue Julius Langbehn attacked the narrowness and materialism of modern science, preferring subjectivity and Goethe's 'total wrongness' to Darwin's partial truth (Stern 1974: 125). One of the most prominent representatives of this intellectual trend was Oswald Spengler (1880–1936), who compared his historical or morphological method to Goethe's organicist approach to the natural sciences. Goethe's call for the study of 'living nature' was echoed in Spengler's 'the world as history' ('die Welt als Geschichte'), in which a mechanistic, mathematical understanding of nature as causality was rejected in favour of 'the law of form' ('das Gesetz der Gestalt'), and the understanding of cultures as following life-cycles. This method involved 'empathizing, observing, comparing' (Spengler [1922] 1993: 35). In the 1920s, many ideologues had written off Darwin, but the theory continued to gain ground (see Seiler 1928: 405).

In a work published in the aftermath of the Nazi seizure of power, Spengler distinguished between a zoological sense in which someone might belong to a race, and race qualities that one possessed (1933: 161 fn). In this latter sense, he argued for a selection within the *Volk* of the elements with the highest racial quality, elements which should be chosen without regard to wealth or background (1933: 161). The Germanic race was 'the strongest willed race which has ever existed', but this was not race defined in the sense of anti-Semitism in Europe and the United States. This fashionable view of race was Darwinist and materialist. For Spengler, racial purity was a 'grotesque' expression, given that for thousands of years there had been racial mixing, i.e. outsiders of good racial quality being welcomed by healthy, martial groups, regardless of which 'race' they belonged to. Those who spoke too much about race showed that they lacked 'race': 'It is not a question of the purity of the race, but rather the strength of the race, that a people [*Volk*] has within it' (1933: 157). Facing the twin dangers of 'class war' (*Klassenkampf*) from below and 'race war' (*Rassenkampf*) from outside, Spengler feared an alliance of the European proletariat with the coloured races ('die Farbigen') which might end the white domination of the world. Looking to the future, he foresaw the unleashing of a transformative, martial 'Prussian' spirit which would ultimately transcend the boundaries of the nation state (Spengler 1933: 164).

The disdain for zoological race theory and materialism was shared by the political scientist Eric Voegelin. In addition to looking back to Goethe, Kant and Johann Friedrich Blumenbach, in particular Blumenbach's notion of 'formative drive' (*Bildungstrieb*), Voegelin saw in the racial anthropology of Carl Gustav Carus (1789–1869) the culmination of the Goethean tradition. Subsequent developments had represented a decline into a vulgar form of race materialism. Voegelin represented a philosophical organicism which he perceived as threatened by various forms of modern materialism, including liberalism, Marxism and racial anthropology (Voegelin [1933] 1998: 23–4). This elitist philosophical anthropology was ambivalent about contemporary racial anthropology and eugenics, seeing in them expressions of modern materialism and mass culture. The crudity of the understanding of natural form through measurement and classification, and the treatment of human beings as domestic animals, seemed a vulgarization and popularization of the idea of the 'well-born man'.

Other important representatives of this philosophical-organicist elitism and anti-logocentrism were the 'characterologist' and vitalist Ludwig Klages and the anthroposophist Rudolf Steiner (1861–1925). Klages blamed Darwin's 'English mentality' for narrowing the vision of the second half of the nineteenth century; Darwin's unconscious metaphysic followed the dominant paradigm since the Renaissance, namely rationalism, with its assumption of a utilitarian drive behind an objectified nature, and its assimilation of human expressivity to reflex mechanisms (Klages 1936: 208–15).

The advent of the Nazi regime led to the exile or dismissal of *Gestalt* biologists and psychologists who were politically or racially undesirable, or who rejected the *völkisch* interpretation of holism. The vitalist biologist Hans Driesch (1867–1941), an internationalist and pacifist, was dismissed from his post in Leipzig on political grounds, and was forbidden to hold public lectures in 1935, though his work was a fundamental influence on vitalist supporters of Nazism such as Adolf Meyer-Abich (1893–1971). The main proponent of a National Socialist form of holistic and vitalist biology was Ernst Lehmann (1880–1957), the editor of *Der Biologe*, and follower of the holistic theories of the *völkisch* biologist and ecologist Jakob von Uexküll (1864–1944). The Goethean concept of *Gestalt* was celebrated by Karl Lothar Wolf and Wilhelm Troll (1942), and metaphorical parallels between the inner form of an organism and the ideal inner harmony of a National Socialist *Volk* were drawn. The Jew, predictably, often stood for the mechanistic or the chaotic.

This organicist holism could also be turned against the 'mechanistic mentality of Mendelism' (Grabe 1938: 148). However, in 1936 the holistic trend associated with Karl Kötschau (1892–1984), Ernst Lehmann, Adolf Meyer-Abich, Wilhelm Troll (1897–1978) and others – which like its counterpart 'Aryan physics', was associated primarily with Alfred Rosenberg and his followers – began to come under attack from more technocratically oriented geneticists and racial anthropologists from Himmler's Ahnenerbe, in particular Karl Astel (1898–1945). The implausible accusation was made that this form of holism was a disguised form of Jesuitical doctrine. The Ahnenerbe took over control of *Der Biologe* in 1939, and announced a new emphasis on scientific facts. A number of factors were at play here, including a shift towards a more pragmatic science as power shifted within the state to the army and the SS. This was one symptom of Rosenberg's relative weakness in the face of his arch-rival Heinrich Himmler (see Harrington 1996: 175–206). Another was the closure of the Race Policy Office in 1942 (Benz et al. 1997: 658–9), as Himmler increasingly took charge of ethnic and racial policy, now focused on the occupied territories in the east.

Reflecting his ambivalent place in neo-Darwinist orthodoxy, Haeckel had both National Socialist admirers, such as Ernst Lehmann, and detractors, such as Günther Hecht (1902–1945) of the Race Policy Office (RPA) of the National Socialist Workers Party (Bäumer 1990: 217–19). Lehmann saw in Haeckel a forerunner of National Socialism's striving for a relationship to nature, stating: 'The deepest essence of the National Socialist world-view is the striving for a connection to nature. National Socialism is itself politically applied biology' (Lehmann 1934a: 132). In contrast to Marxism, the National Socialist world-view was built on race (Lehmann 1935: 378).

Hecht contrasted Haeckel's materialist Monism with the *völkisch*-biological world-view of National Socialism, and urged that Haeckel's intellectual legacy be confined to discussions with the scholarly sphere, without any attempt being made to apply it to matters falling within the responsibility of the Party and its organs (Hecht 1937: 284). However, this opinion should be understood in the context of Hecht's assertion that National Socialism could not be defined by reference to any thinker or scholar. Echoing the stance of his boss, Walter Gross, and their ultimate superior, Alfred Rosenberg, Hecht asserted that National Socialism was a political not a scientific or scholarly movement. Neither Lamarck, Darwin nor Haeckel, nor their successors and opponents, could provide the political tenets of

National Socialism. National Socialism was a political-ideological (*politisch-weltanschaulich*) movement for which Hitler and 'his political soldiers' alone were responsible. It was not the scholar but rather the leaders of the National Socialist movement who had the ultimate authority to determine what was harmful to the 'health of the people' (Hecht 1937: 290).

It should be stressed that not all neo-Lamarckians were hostile to Darwin. Those who worked broadly within the conventions of contemporary natural science accepted that Darwin was an important, groundbreaking thinker (Plate *c.*1909), but rejected the neo-Darwinian view that the inheritance of acquired characteristics played no role whatsoever in evolution. Darwin after all 'had recognized the interaction of selectional and Larmarckian factors' (Plate 1932: vii). Neo-Darwinism, however, was central to the claim that National Socialism was grounded in, and drew on, scientific truth. In this sense, Lamarckianism and vitalism were thus both scientifically and ideologically vulnerable. Ferdinand Rossner (1900–1987), the Austrian zoologist Konrad Lorenz (1903–1989) and Paul Brohmer (1885–1965) argued in their different ways for Darwin's importance in understanding the nature of human races and for National Socialism (Wegner 2002: 71–2). Konrad Lorenz in particular applied this notion of domestication (*Haustierwerdung*) as part of a 'process of reciprocal legitimation' between Nazism and his thinking (Kalikow 1980, cited in Deichmann 1996), reflecting both Darwin and Ernst Haeckel's Monism (i.e. his rejection of a firm distinction between humans and animals). Domestication was seen in the effects of civilization, in which certain hereditary traits come to the fore: 'overcivilized big-city man has a whole series of hereditary traits that would readily mark any other animal life-form, exhibiting them as a typical domesticated animal' (Lorenz 1940: 5; Deichmann 1996: 186). In the wild there was an equilibrium between mutation and selection; this was not the case in the domesticated state, which led inevitably to deterioration (Nachtsheim 1936; Paul and Falk 1999).

Thus, while there were anti-Darwinian figures within the *völkisch* movement who sought a role as Nazi ideologues, it is misleading to read these as representative for National Socialism as a whole. Otto Haas (1887–1976) of the American Natural History Museum saw the dismissal of the theory of evolution as symptomatic of National Socialist ideology (1941: 40–1): 'Evolution seems to be especially suspect because it appears to be contradictory to the invariability of species and races, required as dogma by the "Rassenlehre", and is in consequence, stigmatized by Otto Muck as "Theorie des universalen Art- und Rassenlosigkeit" [a universal theory denying of the distinct nature of species and race]'. Haas did note that the Nazi scholar Hans Weinert had described these objections to Darwinism as 'pseudo-scientific', but noted he also sought to support his scientific ideas 'politically' (1941: 41).

Walter Gross: balancing the claims of science and ideology

In two public lectures held at Berlin University on 26 November 1935 and 20 January 1936, Walter Gross addressed a specifically academic audience. Gross spoke in the spirit of Alfred Rosenberg in promoting the transcending of a false opposition between research (*Wissenschaft*) and life (*Leben*) (1936: 31), a message which contained both implied promise and threat to the university community. Gross attacked disciplinary isolation, apolitical distance from the concerns of everyday life and disdain for the destiny of the *Volk*, evoking a holistic vision of academic striving in which, now that the political and economic power had been brought under control, a new intellectual front would be opened up (1936: 9–11). This involved a rejection both of individualism and a universal humanity; the roots of all intellectual striving should be in the *Volk* as a true community. It is this *Volk* from which meaning is derived, and the intellectual task is that of contributing to the perfection (*Vollendung*) of its vision (*Weltbildes*) (1936: 13–14).

Gross did not argue simplistically that science was subordinate to ideology. He recognized the scientific domain as having its own rules and standards, and argued that National Socialist ideology could not exist in contradiction to established scientific fact. It could however draw attention to facts that had been overlooked, or interpret particular facts in a new light. The construction of National Socialist vision on the basis of these facts was fundamentally a product of lived experience and belief (1936: 20). Gross rejected the idea that National Socialist ideology was a product or offshoot of scientific research, specifically the natural sciences and biology, and that the race science (*Anthropologie*) and biology of the previous decades could claim to be the source of the new racial-folkish ideology (*rassisch-völkische Denkweise*). Natural science had much more claim on our attention than the humanities: 'the findings of natural science demand recognition' (1936: 22). Gross described the worlds of modern science and National Socialist ideology (*völkische Weltanschauung*) as independent if overlapping and mutually supportive domains, each with its own autonomy (1936: 22). In a similar vein, Gross asserted that the underlying laws of logic were the same for everyone, but that their value and application within a culture depended on the stage of evolution and was also racially determined (1936: 28).

Gross also defended Nazi thought from the charge of a deterministic materialism, in which the mental-psychological-spiritual (*geistig*) and the cultural were simply determined by race. He denied that the scientific view of race took this one-sided view, and argued, in the case of racial distinctions, that they embraced both the mental and the bodily-physical, without necessarily making any fixed statement about the relationship between these two aspects. Thus, the laws of inheritance applied both to the mental and the physical, but this did not imply there was a direct causal relationship between these domains (1936: 23). Again Gross stressed holistic unity and the totality of 'life', and rejected the artificial separation of mind and body, as well as the marginalization of the body in favour of the mental and spiritual, which had left an unhealthy attitude to physical needs and drives, leading to a belief in their sinfulness or their unnatural repression (1936: 24). This plea for a holistic and life-centred philosophy led Gross to plead for the alienation between the humanities and the natural sciences to be overcome 'in a new and fruitful synthesis', so that both in life and in intellectual matters the opposition between the mental and the physical could be overcome, leading to the total fulfilment of the human being.

Just as this brought together what had been previously wrongly separated, so Nazi ideology would separate where separation was the natural order of things, fighting against the internationalist tendency to blur national, cultural, linguistic and racial boundaries (1936: 25–7). A new awareness has arisen of the profound differences that exist among the races and the racially determined peoples of the world ('zwischen den Rassen und rassenbedingten Völkern', 1936: 27).

To his denial that Nazism was materialist, Gross added a denial that it was chauvinistic or imperialistic, noting that it recognized the subjectivity of values and rejected the false objectivity of the liberal world-view, which applied inappropriate standards to different cultures. Nor was it anti-religious, since it rejected superficial religious form and recognized that the profound inner experiences of a religious nature were also racially determined (1936: 29).

This model offered a means of reconciling science with the totalitarian demands of the state, and had the effect of separating ideology from science and preventing the kinds of confusion that had arisen in relation to racial mixing. This did not require the subordination of science to ideology; nor did ideology give the initiative away to science in the formulation of ideology and policy. This was also the position articulated by Heinrich Härtle, namely that science or scholarship (*Wissenschaft*) and ideology (world-view, *Weltanschauung*) should be kept separate (Härtle 1941; Geuter 1992: 170).

In an interview with Charlotte Köhn-Behrens, Gross described his role as neither research (the domain of the scientist) nor policy (the domain of the Ministry of the Interior), but rather the educating of the people. He was concerned with the unification of educational and informational efforts, so that in the public domain there should be complete unity on race matters, with only proven facts being propagated. Academic disputes and controversies should be carried on behind closed doors (Köhn-Behrens 1934: 74–5). Gross thus saw his task as central to the Nazi enterprise, since the German people could be saved only by a collective rejection of the false ideal of equality and by embracing wholeheartedly the propagation of the healthy elements of the *Volk*, and this was essentially a matter of public education and the dissemination of a political message (Gross 1935). Gross's commitment to holism and the breaking down of barriers between science and 'life' reflects his commitment to Alfred Rosenberg's vision of Nazi science. But Gross can also be seen as attempting to mediate between this rhetoric and the rising status and prestige of biological and genetic science, which did not require a direct synthesis between the humanities and the natural sciences.

Race theory on trial: the case of Ludwig Ferdinand Clauss

A chance to see Gross in action is afforded by his sustained attack on the race psychologist Ludwig Ferdinand Clauss, a former student of Edmund Husserl (1859–1938). What Gross objected to in particular was Clauss's apparent belief that he was an authority on race matters and could define the study of race in Nazi Germany. Clauss was particularly problematic for Gross, as he was a popular speaker and lecturer whose books sold well and were reprinted regularly.

In 1941, Clauss initiated proceedings in the Highest Court of the Nazi Party against Gross, charging Gross with obstructing his academic work and hindering the dissemination of his ideas. Although it was Clauss who had initiated the proceedings against his fellow-Party member Gross, it was Clauss, not Gross, who became the accused under the rules, since Gross was a Party veteran (*alter Kämpfer*).

Clauss, though in many ways an organic intellectual of race science, a popular author and a charismatic lecturer, was not securely positioned within the academic system. Clauss overestimated his ability to silence the upstart bureaucrat (Weingart 1995).

The trial had been triggered by letters sent by Clauss's wife to senior Party officials, including Hitler, denouncing Clauss for his close relationship to his Jewish research assistant, Margarete Landé. The gist of these letters was that German race theory in the person of Ludwig Clauss had fallen under Jewish control. Though the letters showed clear signs of mental instability, Gross sought to use this denunciation to bring Clauss to heel. In his initial deposition, Gross pointed to the lack of an empirical basis to Clauss's work, the paucity of the materials from which he made his generalizations. He objected that Clauss, by identifying race with style, had no way of distinguishing racial formation from environmental influence. His conclusions were not logically distinct from his premises

> It should be said that Clauss does believe that the 'mimetic method' of living with his subjects [*Mitleben*] makes it possible to distinguish between inherited race characteristics and those determined by the environment on the basis of psychological and physical architecture. ... Here the phenomenological method reaches the limits of its possibilities, and only in clear recognition of this can the scientific attitude of the investigator be shown. (Weingart 1995: 83)

The method was 'completely subjective'. Gross also poured scorn on Clauss's claims to have passed himself off as a Bedouin, noting that the Bedouin had had extensive contact with the British, the Turks and Germans, and were perfectly familiar with the modern world. Without dismissing Clauss's method in its entirety, Gross argued that it could only be validated by submitting itself to the methods of biological race theory, which Gross saw as transcending the mind-body dualism he attributed to Clauss.

Clauss, accused of living in close proximity with a Jewish woman, simultaneously found his authority as a race theorist and his research programme on trial. The case has great textual density, with Clauss seeking to justify his use of the research assistant by objectifying her as an object of study and arguing that his prominence as a race theorist put him above the normal restrictions of interracial contact. Landé, Clauss argued, was half-Jewish and thus had a valuable understanding of two racial psychologies; she was an indispensable tool (*Werkzeug*). In seeming contradiction to his own method, which argued that a researcher from one race can understand and even enter mimetically into the culture of another, Clauss reported that he had long tried to persuade Landé to use her special insight to live with and study Jews.

Clauss denied that he was insufficiently anti-Semitic, claiming that his work had made a fundamental contribution to the Nordic movement and to Nazism. He denied any sexual relationship with Landé, emphasizing her status as an object of study, a scientific specimen, but also someone with an intuitive racial intuition. In his efforts to save himself and Landé, Clauss made statements of the following kind:

> I am interested in Judaism in the way that a doctor is interested in disease. Against one germ I have put into action a counter-germ. Only someone who is part of that can really sense the Jew in the fullest way. I cannot live with Jews, no one can imply that of me. I can live as a Bedouin among Bedouin, but not as a Rabbi among Rabbis. I cannot share in the life of the ghetto. It is hard for Miss Landé, but she has this ability. I need someone of this kind, if you like in the way that the police need their informers. ([Report 1] 1941: 122)

Put another way, Clauss defined his task as drawing the boundary between Orient and Occident, part of his understanding that through the insights of his method 'we' can realize fully who 'we' are.

Gross's intellectual attack distinguished three kinds of race theory: materialistic or physicalist race theory; Clauss's mind-body dualism, with an emphasis on the mind or race psychology; and National Socialist race theory which was renewing scientific race theory, through the ancient Aryan idea of the unity of mind and body. Gross, while using the criterion of science to attack Clauss, nonetheless left final authority on race matters with a culturally privileged notion of mind-body unity. Clauss, noted Gross, had tried to present himself as the saviour of contemporary race theory through his critique of materialism and physicalism.

The criterion of science was also used against Clauss by an expert witness, the Tübingen Professor Wilhelm Gieseler (1900–1976). Gieseler argued that Clauss's method was not scientific in the sense that the methodology employed by Clauss was uniquely suited to him. It was not a methodology that could be taught and reproduced institutionally. While not unsympathetic to Clauss, and noting that he had always urged his students to read his work, Gieseler's evidence concluded: 'I cannot call this a scientific method' ([Report 1] 1941: 15; Weingart 1995: 111–21).

The Party verdict was indeed, as Clauss protested, the consequence of a trial of his race theory as a whole, rather than of his conduct in relation to Landé. In expelling Clauss from the Nazi Party, the court denied that Clauss's work had any significant role to play in National Socialist ideology, since his lecturing and other popularizing work had not been carried out under the Rosenberg Bureau. Were Clauss's work to disappear, it would leave no ideological gap. Clauss was an opportunist, and someone who looked to the Party for recognition, rather than seeking to serve the Party. Some of his ideas, when taken to their logical conclusion, were against National Socialist ideology, and the scientific status of his ideas was at least questionable.

In its judgement, the Party court emphasized that, the recognition of academic and scientific freedom notwithstanding, National Social-ism required discipline of its scholars, who should accept the priority of the Party to dictate matters of political importance. An example of this was Günther, who had responded to an instruction to moder-ate or suppress certain views with the required attitude, without claiming that this meant the end of academic freedom. No one who knew Clauss and his boundless overestimation of his own importance would expect the same of him ([Report 2]: 11).

The scientific gaze

Clauss's theory was grounded in an intuitive racial insight, and this stress on intuition was shared by a range of racial and biological the-orists. There was a strong association between *völkisch* ideology and the praise of the intuitive or 'natural' vision of the engaged observer. Modernity had led to the loss of the instinctual racial gaze of the ordinary people, and thereby blunted the racial instinct that had prevented interbreeding with distant races. Residues of this racial instinct could be found in folklore, e.g. in proverbs and popular sayings (Schwab 1937), in folk images, e.g. of the build and physiog-nomy of the devil (Kretschmer 1931: 1); and in a neglected history of eugenic thinking (Scheidt 1941).

Eugen Fischer offered ambivalent praise to Günther for combin-ing the scientist with the artist and poet. Acknowledging the criticism directed at Günther's work, Fischer stressed his role as an educator of the German people and his importance in preparing the way for National Socialism (1935: 220–1). Lutzhöft describes how the *völkisch* publisher J. F. Lehmann was deeply impressed by Günther's visual acuity in diagnosing the racial character of passers-by on an Alpine walking tour. He subsequently commissioned Günther to write his study of the racial profile of the German people, notwithstanding Günther's lack of formal qualifications in racial anthropology (Lutzhöft 1971: 30–1). Günther himself deplored the loss of a strong visual sense of race among the Europeans, in particular the Germans

(Günther 1924: 139). Even more than with Günther, vision and insight was the essence of Clauss's method. There was an intrinsic tension in Clauss's work between his work as a popularizer and his elitist insistence on intuition and insight. Clauss stressed the absolute priority that had to be given to the training of the gaze, to *Schauen* or *Hinschauen*; this – not abstract theory – was fundamental to the development of the racial sense or intuition that Hitler wished for the German people (Clauss and Hoffmann 1934: 3ff., 14ff., 40). In the same spirit, Hunke (1936: 91) talked of the scientist as 'researcher, visionary and artist'.

This intuitionist tendency in German science frequently – though not exclusively - drew inspiration from Goethe's 'remaining with the experience of the thing throughout the course of study', in which the emphasis was on the education of the vision of and kinship with the natural world (Seamon 1998: 9). It was essential to go 'with open eyes through the natural world'. The classification of the natural world into hierarchies of types was misleading, since some organisms were similar in one respect and different in another. The model of descent suggested by the genealogical tree was only part of the picture; Goethe's visionary insight into comparative morphology led to the recognition of a few basic forms (*Grundformen*) under the apparent chaos of the variety of natural organisms. The basic form was not an abstraction; it was not enough to strip away the differences between forms to reveal an underlying basic form. This form had to be *seen*, since it was always clearly visible (*anschaulich*) to the intuitive eye (Schaeppi 1940/41: 174–5, 184).

In mechanistic modernity, there was a visual deficit: the intuitive 'eye' was not valued. This was contrasted implicitly with the logocentric nature of formal education, in which the written word – both religious and secular – took pride of place. Praise for the eye, and for intuitive, searching 'pure' gaze can be found, for example, in Houston Stewart Chamberlain's intellectual autobiography, written as a letter to Baron Jakob von Uexküll. Uexküll's 'eye' is praised for its luminosity (1922: 66). This memoir is an account of Chamberlain's visual education, with nature as the tutor of his gaze (1922: 68, 69). The emotional impact of nature was greatest in his youth before he lost the 'innocence of the gaze' ('Unschuld des Anschauens', 1922: 77).

Although drawn to the study of botany, Chamberlain also realized that he was a visually intuitive observer rather than a systematizer, who had an intuitive sense of the 'inner connections' between organisms, a synthesizing gaze promoted by his short-sightedness. Shortsightedness was related to the imagination, as exemplified in the adventures of Don Quixote, during many of which he transformed reality (1922: 67). As a student, Chamberlain had brought together a collection of skulls with the intention of studying their form, but had given up, since he did not have the systematizer's eye, that is he could find no normal skull (*Normalschädel*) from which to measure the differences. The synthesizing gaze, once its attention was directed to the detail, found no natural stopping point in its perception of differences. By contrast, the systematizing gaze achieved its goal through a determination to be blind, to not see. The systematizer was akin to the philologist, in the admirable but violent rigour of the gaze, which achieved great successes, but which functioned in an anthropomorphic way, lacking the innocence of the pure observation of nature (1922: 83). From the eye of the landscape painter Hans Thoma (1839–1924) there shone a light of incredible power (1922: 69).

The pure eye was further contrasted to the blindness brought on by theory. Chamberlain praised the comparative anatomist Georges Cuvier (1769–1832), for whom, in contrast to Ernst Haeckel, 'the *eye* remains open and pure and is recognized as an irremovable, incorruptible law maker in the natural sciences'. Thinkers like Haeckel end up with objectively derived falsity (1922: 121). Hermann Fol's lectures in Geneva were 'an education in pure seeing' (1922: 94). Chamberlain insisted that mistakes in observation could lead indirectly to truths (1922: 96). Chamberlain pleaded for the liberation of visual perception from constraints: 'logic is not the goddess of truth, it is her maid; the eye is king, the ear is queen, the sense of touch is the wise counsellor' (1922: 128). The aim was not to offer an explanation, but to transform through perception realized as a conceptual schema (1922: 128).

The characterologist Ludwig Klages, while praising Charles Darwin's contribution to the study of expressivity in humankind ([1872] 1999) as a solid contribution, noted that he had no 'intuitive insightful vision' (*Hellblick*) which could take him beyond the confines of the scientific study of appearances (*Erscheinungswissenschaft*), and thus could not offer true insight or explanation (1936: 208–9). However, Wichler (1937/38: 368–9) defended Darwin against Alfred Wallace by praising Darwin's ability to observe 'in the full sense of the word'; Wallace was 'not a productive observer'.

These tensions were reflected in concerns about the nature of the observation (i.e. gaze) that racial anthropology involved. This philosophical issue took on political salience in the Third Reich, since the question arose as to whether the racially acute gaze of the anthropologist could be taught to the ordinary person or schoolchild, and if so, how. Many racial anthropologists, particularly those with a strong organicist or holistic approach, saw in racial anthropology possibilities of the training of the popular vision. Ernst Kretschmer, while he recognized the importance of exact measurement in the study of the human body, saw mathematical precision as insufficient: 'Above all however we must learn again to use our eyes, to see and to observe plainly and simply, without microscope and without laboratory' (1931: 2).

Ernst Dobers (1936), writing with regard to the teaching of biology, stressed the need to open the pupils' eyes to the world around them, to sharpen their vision and appreciation of detail (*Blickschärfung*), including the apparently irrelevant. This was important in awakening the 'feeling for life' which had been lost in the modern, urbanized world. This would contribute more to the future of the *Volk* than whole libraries full of specialized literature (1936: 383). This was particularly true with regard to race education (*rassenkundliche Schulung*), for which the teacher must develop a never-ending curiosity about processes and connections.

Dobers rejected the 'verbalism' of elementary education, and the over-reliance on textbooks. This could never achieve the desired effect of the 'biologizing' of the sensibility and mentality of the people (*Volksempfinden und -denken*). He favoured a dynamic model of pedagogy, in which the teacher, as a curious and engaged observer, would experience the continual movement of racial processes. These underlay and shaped the surface phenomena which we call 'world history'. The key was not intellectual 'book-learning' but an education of the senses (1936: 384). Examples of locales for this kind of observation were villages on the edge of a city, where the impact of urbanization could be seen; Gypsies living on the edge of a village; a station in Berlin where refugees were arriving from the Baltic – those arriving on long-distance trains could be contrasted with those on the commuter trains. Sport could be observed, as a good chance to see the Nordic type in action. One could observe soldiers marching by, or discover the contrast between town and country types.

Otto Reche argued that, in training the eye, high-quality illustrations, including photographs that could capture the racially important colouring, were necessary. Reche also argued that the photographs used in many textbooks were too confusing, given the inevitable variation that existed in the population; it was difficult for the beginner to identify the essential from the individual, and thereby to abstract the true 'racial type' (*Rasse-Typus*). The accompanying descriptions were not enough to compensate, and often the pictures themselves did not present the ideal features presented in the verbal description. To give life to these abstract racial ideals, Reche had ideal illustrations – combining all the ideal features of the racial type, both male and female, and eliminating this element of variation – realized as posters by an artist, Emil Fröhlich of Leipzig. Reche noted that it was necessary to have both male and female exemplars illustrated, as the racial characteristics were 'different in the case of woman from those of the man'. The portraits had been done from a frontal view and in profile, in the same way that anthropological photographs are produced, which was important for objective comparison, even though somewhat schematic from an artistic point of view. Reche recommended that the posters be hung in the classroom for at least a week, so that the pupils would become familiar with the significant characteristics. The black-and-white pictures in the books were more for orientation, as were the sketches of the primary skull types.

Reche stressed that these were racial types, and that these types rarely appeared in the pure realization of the German *Volk* (Reche 1933: 3–5). There is an educational paradox here. On the one hand, the intent was to sharpen the racial acuity of the *Volk* by awakening their visual sense. This was to be done by presenting ideal types, who represented the perfect realization of all the physical characteristics of particular races. But, outside these Platonic idealizations, appearance was in itself deceptive, since phenotype was not consistent with genotype. The consequence of this was that superficial judgements by lay persons based on individual appearance were to be avoided. Expert evaluation of an individual would be based primarily on an investigation of as much of the extended family as possible. Only the expert could reach a proper evaluation of the racial status of an individual (1933: 31). Reche insisted that racial evaluation was a matter for experts and experts alone.

This question also related to the tension between elitism and popularism in the Nazi treatment of race questions. Was every member of the *Volk* to become a race expert? Gross had clearly identified the political dangers of this popularization of theories of race. While the regime wished to raise consciousness about race, and impressed on Germans the importance of selecting a suitable marriage partner, it risked spreading confusion in the population if a serious attempt was made to spread the teachings of racial anthropology among the general population. It was surely evident that the subtleties of the phenotype/genotype distinction would get lost in the school classroom.

Neo-Lamarckianism and Nazism

The status of neo-Lamarckianism was complicated by its associations with Soviet ideology, on the one hand, and anti-Darwinian and teleological thinking in German biology, on the other. Neo-Lamarckianism, however, had deep roots in German scientific thought, with its explanations of evolutionary change as having an order or logic, as a process of striving for a goal (*Zielstrebigkeit*), and as following an inner necessity (*innere Notwendigkeit*) latent in the organism rather than being the result of random influences and mutations (Schneider 1934).

One important factor was the association of Neo-Lamarckianism with the plasticity of the human races. If, for example, environmental factors could impact directly on the germ plasma, then racial divisions were liable to be eroded among groups of different races living in the same environment. For this reason, Fritz Lenz associated Lamarckianism primarily with Jews, explaining that their preference for the theory derived not from any racial characteristic, but from a desire to see racial differences as contingent to and liable to be erased under the influence of the environment. If there was a possibility of acquired characteristics being inherited, then there was nothing standing in the way of the creation of a uniform human species ('eine Gleichartigkeit aller Menschen'). This, argued Lenz, was an attractive theory to a group who relied on their success as a minority among racially different peoples. In addition, there was great 'demagogic value' in any theory which presented the genetic differences between people as potentially erasable and therefore inessential (Lenz 1923a: 425). The idea that organisms could alter their hereditary nature by striving (*Streben*) for change (Fischel 1934: 514), even if it was not intended to apply directly to human races, also suggested the possibility of the willed assimilation of foreign races to the German *Volk*. From a neo-Lamarckian point of view, if modernity created increasingly uniform living conditions, i.e. a uniform environment, then all racial distinctions would gradually be erased, even without direct interbreeding.

The ideological climate in the early days of the regime was decidedly hostile to neo-Lamarckianism, but a debate did begin in the Nordicist journal *Rasse*. Kurt Holler (Leipzig) took the line that this view of human evolution suggested that Jews could become Germans by racial assimilation to the Germanic milieu (Holler 1934: 37–8). However, both the zoologist Ludwig Plate (1934) and Hans Böker (1934) argued that there were no grounds to reject Lamarckianism outright. Plate (Jena) rejected the notion that evolutionary change could be explained entirely by arbitrary mutation: there was no need for National Socialism to reject environmentalism (*Umweltlehre*) in its entirety. Plate, an outspoken anti-Semite, had belonged to a minority of professors who supported Günther's appointment in Jena

(Hossfeld 2003: 524). Böker (Jena) emphasized this distinction between Lamarckianism and environmentalism (1934:251).This view of evolutionary change was not to be identified with Marxism. For Böker, races were constant, but not species (1934: 254); his understanding of change was derived from the holistic Goethean strand of German biological thinking. This relied on the neo-Lamarckian concept of 'active, mnestic processes', i.e. changes which are triggered by repeated stimulation of the organism and leave behind an associative trace that can be transmitted to offspring (Böker 1937: 134). Rejecting the extreme mechanistic view which he saw as now discredited, Böker argued for a synthesis of dynamic and static thinking in biology (1937: 134).

One aspect of discussions of evolutionary theory under National Socialism can be illustrated by an article contributed by Jakob Hamacher to the popular science journal *Kosmos*. That the topic was politically sensitive was indicated by a note clarifying that the discussion was merely intended to describe the different views expressed on this topic. Hamacher was clearly a reluctant Darwinist, lamenting the lack of a clear teleology in the theory of evolution. While he recognized that the scientific evidence had come down on Darwin's side, including the neo-Darwinism of August Weismann, he could not accept the purely mechanistic view of change that Darwin's theory seem to promote, in particular the lack of an overall direction of change ('richtungslose Veränderlichkeit', Hamacher 1942: 14). From this point of view, Jean-Baptiste Lamarck's (1744–1829) vision of evolutionary progress as a striving upwards from simple organisms to more complex and perfect ones was more a congenial model, both socially and culturally (Hamacher 1942: 50).

How then could a reconciliation be effected between the mechanistic theory of Darwinism and the need for order and meaning? Hamacher's solution was a rejection of mechanism in favour of the notion of 'organism', whereby living organisms are understood to coexist within a holistic (*ganzheitlich*) system in which there is a relationship between units and processes. Hamacher denied that this was a mystical concept: 'Only with the methods of the exact natural sciences and with a strict separation of subject/object can we capture the fundamental phenomena [*Gegebenheiten*]'(1942: 150). This concept of holistic system involves a dynamic equilibrium, a system of self-regulation, as found in the thought of the Viennese biologist Ludwig von Bertalanffy (1901–1972) (1942: 50). This was captured by Bertalanffy's notion of 'organismic biology' (*organismische Biologie*), according to which impulses for change and transformation can come both from within and outside the organism (1942: 50–1). The final section of Hamacher's article was prefaced with a note from the editors, stating that the presentation of modern Lamarckian ideas was to serve the education of the educated layperson, but that these ideas have been misused in popular presentations (1942: 104). This indicates the political sensitivity of Lamarckian thinking, but also its relative marginality and insignificance in the evolving intellectual landscape of the Third Reich.

Conclusion: the problem of *telos*

In 1934, the zoologist Bernhard Rensch was strongly criticized for neo-Lamarckian sympathies (Rensch 1979: 77; Schmuhl 2003a: 26). Rensch had sought to make the case that Lamarckianism was not antithetical to National Socialism, but in the mid-1930s shifted his position. Rensch was a leading figure in the development of the neo-Darwinism synthesis in Nazi Germany. While neo-Lamarckianism was not totally taboo, it was politically suspect, and marginal to the scientific mainstream. However, the question of the purpose or direction of life (*telos*) remained. The key ideological problem in this was the ateleological character of neo-Darwinism. Many who sought to effect a fusion of science and Nazism looked to neo-Lamarckian, or to a range of holistic theories which denied the distinction between nature and *Geist*. This allowed for an underlying unity of purpose to the unfolding or evolution of an organism over time.

The National Socialist dilemma with regard to science can thus be framed as follows. Nazism was a political and ideological movement, intent on the mobilization of all sectors of the German *Volk*. This seemed to argue strongly for the fusion of science and ideology, such that the pursuit of learning and scholarship would be in step with the wider goals of the movement and the *Volk*. The destiny of the *Volk*, the nature of its world-view, needed to be expressed across the entire range of academic scholarship and science, from the study of literature to the most abstract mathematics. The criterion of race would be relevant across the entire spectrum of human endeavour, and the idea of a separation of the material from the spiritual, moral and intellectual would be rejected. This engaged form of science would be rich in metaphors of organic integration: will, duty, harmony, energy, mission, totality and struggle. It would break down the barriers between 'life' and scholarship, and between the humanities, the social sciences and the natural sciences.

But this proposed fusion of science with ideology had a number of drawbacks. It raised a question of authority, i.e. the question of who was to have the final say over what was politically correct and what was not. If the Party or the *Führer* determined what counted as good science, then in effect science was redundant. This model was also highly confrontational, as it involved a direct political attack on broad sections of the German professoriate. The status of that professoriate was understood in relation to the adherence to discipline-internal standards and norms of scholarship. This potential conflict was greatest in the natural, physical and mathematical sciences. Those disciplines which involved the study of *Volk* could accommodate themselves more readily to the teleological rhetoric of struggle, destiny and mission, or indeed were already cast in these terms. Yet it was not an option to exclude science and scholarship from political control.

Nazi ideology existed in tension between a merger of ideology and science and a strict separation. The dominant trend, it can be argued, was the second, and this had become clear by the late 1930s. The Party leadership of the regime was increasingly technocratic, working towards a modernized, corporate state, with a powerful military-industrial base. While there was no clear formulation or resolution of the problem in these terms, there was an underlying logic at work which made this direction functional within the Nazi state. The ideologically and scientifically most appealing solution to the problem of *telos* was the traditional distinction between natural science and other disciplines. This division of labour would give the disciplines of *Volk* the task of elaborating mission and teleology (under the tutelage of the NSDAP), and the natural sciences would pursue their research agenda without being required to talk in political metaphors. This is not to say that science would become apolitical. This did not preclude metaphorical echoes across disciplinary boundaries, but it did not require them. Applied science in particular would be highly politicized, but since National Socialism and modern science were not perceived to be in conflict, science could best serve National Socialism by being at the forefront of international science as judged by international norms. This model avoided a conflict between science and ideology, yet did not threaten the Party's ultimate dominance and control of both ideology and science. There was no room in this model for the interdisciplinary enterprise of racial anthropology to play a dominant role.

12

Nazism Beyond Race

Introduction

In 1933, the extreme Nordicist Herman Gauch (1899–1978) argued that the prime evolutionary gap was between the Nordic race and the rest of the animal kingdom, rather than between human beings and animals. Gauch thus distinguished between the Nordic race, on the one hand, and the Dinaric, Alpine, Negro, Mongol races, on the other. These were inferior *Untermenschen* akin to animals (Gauch 1933: 4, 79). Gauch's views on the nature of the racial composition of the German *Volk* were cited and mocked by the holistic biologist Ernst Lehmann (1934b: 63–4). In a moral sense, we can describe both Gauch and Lehmann as 'Nazi', but both became marginal within academic Nazism.

In 1937, Wilhelm Hartnacke (1878–1952) criticized Ernst Krieck's use of the term *Anthropologie* to describe his folkish-political ideology (Krieck 1936). Krieck juxtaposed his ideology with the 'rationalistic-humanistic' world-view, and set his holistic or organic (*ganzheitlich*) approach against materialist science. However, Hartnacke objected that to describe *völkisch* ideology as 'anthropology' was to confuse natural science with politics. While he had no objection to the promotion of *völkisch* values, the term 'anthropology' itself should be reserved for scientific approaches to the study of humanity. The *Volk* was not an organic whole in the same way that an individual organism such as a person was. To pretend differently was to be carried away by a simile. A *Volk* was not an anthropological racial unity, even if race played a role in its fate. To speak of a *Volk* as a 'holistic organism' ('ganzheitlicher Organismus') was to blur the boundaries between natural science and ideology. This confused the biological with the historical, linguistic and territorial ties that bound a *Volk*. The idea of an ideological anthropology was a contradiction in terms. Anthropology belonged to the realm of science and should be kept separate from the realm of politics. There could be no insight into the whole without the rigorous study of the parts. Science required precision, and Krieck's holism was intellectually muddled, and his model without any proper foundation. In the same vein, Haase-Bessell used the term 'totality' (*Totalität*) rather than *Ganzheit*, which she described as 'unfortunate' and 'frequently misused' (1939: 3, 13).

Two collections of papers indicate the intellectual direction of research into human heredity by the end of the 1930s. The first, on the foundations of human hereditary biology, *Die Grundlagen der Erbbiologie des Menschen* (1940), was edited by Günther Just. In his introduction, Just noted the recent rapid development of the study of human heredity, in particular experimental genetics. The collection included contributions by Gerhard Heberer (Jena), Kristine Bonnevie (Oslo), Nikolai Timoféeff-Ressovsky (Berlin), Paula Hertwig (Berlin), Ernst Harnhart (Zurich), Hans Nachtsheim (Berlin), Günther Just (Berlin), H. Zwicky (Zurich) and Ernst Rodenwaldt (Heidelberg). The intellectual agenda was the integration of the study of human heredity into the field of genetics. As Just observed, some of the contributors naturally made reference to 'race biological and eugenic questions' (1940a: v). However, the tone was one of scientific caution. Hertwig reported on experiments in mutation in mammals triggered by exposure to X-rays. Could the hereditary damage be compared to the effects of alcohol, smoking or nicotine? Although there was a possibility of damage to the germ cell (*Keimschädigung*), there was no evidence as yet, and it was the duty of the geneticist to exercise caution in making such judgements (Hertwig 1940: 284).

Just's concern was with the Mendelian genetic foundations of the human constitutional types as identified by Kretschmer, and while this did not imply a rejection of anthropological race (Just 1940b: 441), the racial taxonomy of Nordic, Dinaric, etc. was very much in the background. The concept of anthropological race, and that of the Nordic race, was at its most prominent in paleoanthropological and prehistorical discussion. Heberer's account of the racial history of the northern Europeans argued for continuity between the long-skulled prehistorical races of Europe (Chancelade, Cro-Magnon) and the present-day Nordic-Phalian race. There were two highpoints in the history of northern and central Europe: the development of distinctive Neolithic Indogermanic peoples, and the rise of the Germanic peoples. Given the racial characteristics of light hair and skin, there was no possibility of a migration from the east (Heberer 1940: 631–6; Grahmann 1936). Rodenwaldt, while not rejecting the importance of measuring the human body within physical and racial anthropology, noted that many measurements taken in the past by Rudolf Martin and others offered only a quasi-precision (*Scheinexaktheit*) and were no longer of practical relevance. Given advances that had led to the anthropobiological turn, attention was now focused on understanding the complex of hereditary and environmental factors that gave rise to the phenotype. All discussion of race biological variation was provisional until a better understanding of the ecology of races (*Ökologie der Rassen*) was obtained (Rodenwaldt 1940: 646).

In the autumn of 1942, Gerhard Heberer (1901–1973) completed editorial work on the second of these collections of papers, *Die Evolution der Organismen* (Heberer 1943). This work, produced under the patronage of the SS, represented the internationally ascendant scientific paradigm which had achieved the 'unification of biology' on the basis of neo-Darwinism, the so-called 'synthetic theory of evolution' (Junker and Hossfeld 2002: 223–4). One of the contributors was Nikolai W. Timoféeff-Ressovsky (1900–1981), the Soviet geneticist who had been working in Berlin since 1925 (Reindl 2001; Schmuhl 2003b: 340–2). In the introduction, Heberer stressed the fundamental role biology played in the world picture (*Weltbild*) or world-view (*Weltanschauung*) of the times. These terms were often used as a general description of National Socialist ideology. The previous era of debate and disagreement over the theory of evolution and its ideological role was now closed, and there could be no room for further discussion about its scientific status: 'The genetic understanding of life has now become a solid foundation stone of the natural scientific-biological world picture.'

For Heberer, those in the humanities (*Geisteswissenschaften*) who saw the theory of evolution as 'naive' and with an inappropriate sense of certainty merely showed how out of touch they were with the importance of the theory for an understanding of the world and the formulation of a clear understanding of reality. This was also true of a 'completely chaotic' literature which had been appearing until recently. This literature was produced mainly in Germany, and typically led to an unbridled mysticism. Ironically, Heberer quoted Goethe expressing despair at the Germans and their speculation, but also showing scorn for those who commented on a field of knowledge which they did not practise.

Heberer had in mind the 'pseudo-scientific literati', and diagnosed their rejection of evolutionary theory as a reaction to the rising recognition of the importance of biology as a foundational discipline. This was in particular true in relation to the integration of the human being as a totality into the natural scientific-biological concept of law-governedness. Things had come to the absurd point that some in the humanities had been arguing that modern biology had shown the theory of evolution to be erroneous. The work was intended to offer a comprehensive refutation of these sceptics, and to that end it brought together theoreticians and practical scientists, geophysicists, geologists, palaeontologists, zoologists, botanists, geneticists, anthropologists, psychologists and philosophers. The volume had been produced in the midst of the 'struggle for freedom' in Europe.

Noting that the volume was only superficially affected by the ideological context of Nazism, Junker and Hossfeld conclude that 'the widespread impression of a special relationship between scientific Darwinism and National Socialist ideology is not warranted by the historical facts' (2002: 243). But this comment begs the question of what that ideology was, and provides evidence for exactly the opposite conclusion. The fact that Nazi ideology made foundational use of Darwinism should not however be understood as implying any simplistic equation of the two.

Determinism and free will

The distinction between genotype and phenotype offered one framework for understanding the relationship between genetic determinism and free will. For, although the genotype laid down the 'deep structure' of biological inheritance, many factors combined to produce the 'surface structure' of the phenotype. What was inherited was a set of dispositions, which might or might not be realized (Rüsche 1937: 114–15). These dispositions laid down a variable range of reaction, a so-called 'reaction norm' (*Reaktionsnorm*), and the extent of their realization was dependent on environmental factors. In terms of psychology, the individual inherited dispositions and tendencies, which did not fully determine their realization; nor were the 'contents' (*Gehalte*) of psychological life determined (Rüsche 1937: 114ff.).

One model which showed the tensions between determinism and free will, directionless change and teleology, holism and compartmentalization, was articulated by Otmar Freiherr von Verschuer. Verschuer distinguished three levels of inherited characteristics, with different levels of predetermination (1944: 17–19). The first level

involved fully determined genetic inheritance (as in some genetic illnesses, racial characteristics); the second involved inherited characteristics which partake in a dynamic, open-ended system in which
other factors may determine how or whether these characteristics are
expressed, and if they are harmful in effect; the third concerned inherited talents and character, which were not dependent on the material
characteristics of genetic inheritance and of the environment, but
were dependent on education and upbringing, in particular self-
education (*Selbsterziehung*), though the ability in this respect was also
essentially genetically determined. In the case of the first level, there
was complete predetermination; in the second, there was no pre-
ordained outcome; in the case of the third, 'the battlefield lies open
before us, and it is largely dependent on the will of the individual
whether he remains on the field as a victor' (1944: 17). Even in the case
of absolute predetermination of inherited character, there was a role
for achievement and self-sacrifice. Verschuer gave the example of the
hereditary deaf-mute or blind, or even those with mental limitations,
who could contribute to society by their loyalty, love and sacrifice. In
addition, they would also have to make the sacrifice of not reproducing in order to safeguard the welfare of the *Volk* as a whole.

In the second case, there was a need for guidance in the individual's development, though again if there was a serious genetic ailment
then that individual should not have off-spring. In the third case, there
was a great range of developmental possibilities, together with freedom of the will (1944: 19). Verschuer (1944: 17 fn.) denied that there
was a contradiction between his genetic view of human destiny and
free will. Free will gave rise to responsibility. This model stressed not
only fate or destiny (*Schicksal*) but individual and collective duty, task
and mission (*Aufgabe*). Each individual had a responsibility to
protect his genetic inheritance in the interests of future generations.

Did this imply that the aim was a new racial elite, a new racial mer-
itocracy? If the future of the *Volk* depended on the gifted and the
fittest having sufficient children (Verschuer 1944: 21), did that not
imply that some people's children were more important than others?
Verschuer distinguished between the activities of the plant or animal
breeder, which were directed at the emphasis of particular features,
i.e. specialization, and the aim of eugenics (*Rassenhygiene*), which was
not the breeding of special types (*Spezialtypen*) but the promotion of
the genetic health and racial particularity of the *Volk* as a whole.
Although the idea of a 'superman' (*Übermensch*) had been seen as
the possible next stage of development, there was no way scientifically to predict humankind's future direction. Eugenics could not
take the development of a 'superman' as its goal (1944: 21–2).

Verschuer's approach focused on heredity within the *Volk*, seen in effect as a population rather than as a racially determined mix. The term *Rasse* was used primarily as *Vitalrasse*. While Verschuer recognized the category of 'race' as intermediate between humanity and the individual (1944: 20), the classical concept of anthropological race played a marginal role in the exposition, with no mention of its taxonomy of human racial types. Race in the anthropological sense was for Verschuer primarily a geographical category, as each race developed as a result of geographical isolation and through selection and mutation. As a result, each race was adapted to a particular environment, and its inherited make-up would also determine whether it could tolerate migration to a new environment. Migrations gave rise to racial mixing, but the factors involved in the formation of races (*Rassenbildung*) operated to restore harmony between humans and the environment. Verschuer stressed that human beings were not passive in relation to the environment, and were able to actively reorganize it. In this sense, the environment was determined by race (1944: 14–15).

Within each race there was a high degree of variability, and this was true as much for bodily characteristics as for ability, character and temperament. In addition, Verschuer was in no doubt that 'the culture and history of a people are dependent on race'. Although history was made by humankind, this was only on the basis of a racial prerequisite, such that great leaders (*Führerpersönlichkeiten*) arise, and peoples take on historical roles. Genetic make-up was a key to the rise and fall of peoples, but peoples could also be wiped out by violence or dramatic changes in the environment (1944: 15). Verschuer did not take a simply deterministic view of heredity and cultural achievement. He compared developments in eugenics to those in modern physics, which had shown that the classical laws of macrophysics did not apply in microphysics. In the study of inheritance and heredity, the same process had occurred. Classical 'race biology' (*Rassenbiologie*), of which Fischer was the pre-eminent exponent, had developed a set of key concepts based on Mendel, natural selection, phylogeny, physical anthropology. These concepts had found their practical application in the eugenic and racial policies of the day, and in rapid progress in genetic counselling and assessment. The range of applications of race biology were becoming greater and greater. However, its limitations had also become clear. Heredity and race had been too often seen from the point of view of a materialist determinism, as the only source for all aspects of human performance, in particular for culture and history. Modern genetics however had shown that there was diversity in the genetically determined nature of individual characteristics, particularly at the level of the psyche, in which heredity was often a prerequisite but only one of several conditions. Culture and history therefore could not be explained by race.

Though heredity was fundamental to *Volk* and the state, the determining role of *Geist* in culture and history should not be forgotten. Modern genetic research gave absolutely no support to materialism and determinism of any kind, and each individual had a responsibility to work at their own personal development in the service of the whole. Verschuer finished with a quotation from Goethe: 'Always strive towards the whole and if you yourself cannot become a whole then serve a whole as a part' (1944: 24–5). Recognizing but allowing the anthropomorphic and teleological metaphor (marked with inverted commas), Verschuer saw in natural forms a 'striving' towards health and harmony, a 'search' of the body for normality, the body being a self-regulating totality in which parts are subordinated to the whole (*Ganzheitsfunktion*) (1944: 10).

Biology and linguistics

The functional and ideological advantages of academic compartmentalization can be understood by looking at the relationship between evolutionary biology and genetics, on the one hand, and the central discipline of *Volk*, linguistics, on the other. For genetics, the *Volk* was a population made up of *Erblinien*, hereditary lines; there was no natural or genetic boundary to the *Volk*. The proviso within Nazi ideology was that the hereditary lines of racially foreign groups had been excluded. In the dialectic from the biblical to the genetic conception of *Volk*, racial anthropology in effect served as the antithesis, negating the so-called linguistic understanding of human identity, and identifying those elements which were to be excluded. In the synthesis, racial anthropology could be displaced by human genetics, which offered a superior form of science. Genetics was neutral as to the boundaries of the *Volk*, unlike racial anthropology, which directly undermined the status of the primary boundary drawn between one *Volk* and another, and imposed an independent racial grid on the European population. The idea of a language as an organic or holistic structure which expressed the world-view of its speakers explicitly defined a clear boundary between one language and the next. There was in this sense a complementarity to the relationship between genetics and the disciplines of *Volk*, and not a conflict. They were operating in parallel and autonomous domains.

A genetically oriented discipline of psychology offered the theoretical possibility of subsuming the undesirable racial traits identified by anthropologists under more general, non-racial traits associated with criminality, 'anti-social' mentality and indifference or hostility to community values and norms, in particular the welfare and unity of the *Volk*. These traits, as with physical handicap, could be traced as pathologies through the generations of particular families (*Sippen*). The switch in emphasis from the physical racial type to the psychological racial type was consistent with this possibility of transcending the intellectual opposition between *Rasse* and *Volk*, and between mind and body. Targeting genetically inherited criminal traits would be as effective as – or more effective than – targeting individuals on the basis of anthropological race. This required not a crude deterministic biology but a sophisticated and scientifically informed discussion of the interrelationships between heredity and environment.

Natural science, as defined by the neo-Darwinian synthesis, sought to understand the nature of genetic inheritance, emphasizing the fundamental but not absolute impact of heredity on human affairs. The humanities, in particular linguistics, were concerned with non-genetic or non-heredity forms of transmission, in particular language. Linguistic identity was not inherited, it was acquired. Language was the fundamental institution whereby inherited characteristics of the *Volk* were transmitted: its history, ways of thinking, its understanding of the world and the place of the *Volk* within it, its values and morality. This notion of the inheritance of acquired characteristics, which had no place in biology and genetics, was of course unobjectionable – indeed it was fundamental – in relation to human culture and language in particular. Similarly, a language had a direct and intimate relationship with landscape (Weisgerber 1933: 230), in contrast to the indirect relationship within the neo-Darwinist framework.

It was the German language, as understood in the theories of the key linguist in Nazi Germany, J. Leo Weisgerber, which embodied the acquired wisdom and world-view of the *Volk* in its struggles for mastery of the world and the maintenance of its particular world-view (Weisgerber 1939; Hutton 1999). There was no intellectual conflict between this view of the *Volk* and the biological and genetic understanding of human heredity. Weisgerber used a wide range of vitalist metaphors of energy, will and self-assertion, and strongly teleological language about the mission and historical trajectory of the *Volk*. Again, there was no conflict between this vitalistic metaphor-rich language and the anti-metaphorical stance of scientific genetics.

Weisgerber's rhetoric was suffused with organicism, with the idealization of the German language as a total (*ganzheitlich*) way of seeing, but this organicism was related primarily to the category of *Volk*, and only indirectly to race. A language was a particular mode of seeing, which was founded in the emotional bonds between mother's milk, landscape and *Volk*, but which also represented an ethical and cultural system and the acquired wisdom of generations of ancestors (Weisgerber 1933: 230). This mode of seeing was grounded in these intuitive bonds, yet, unlike the intuitive gaze, it had the precision that belongs to language, and was acquired by every member of the *Volk* who was born into an authentic German-speaking household. The acquisition of language was the acquisition of identity, a process which 'naturally' began at birth. The German language could speak for, indeed think for, the *Volk*. Race was mute. Weisgerber's understanding of languages as 'mother tongues' was no less a construct than Günther's concept of race. However, the logocentric construct of a language had much deeper intellectual roots than the aesthetic iconography of race, not least because of the cultural centrality of writing.

Like Günther's Nordicism, Weisgerber's linguistics had a clear anti-Semitic subtext, as loyalty to one's language was made a central moral quality of *Volk*. Within Nazi ideology, Jews notoriously lacked this natural loyalty to *Volk* and mother tongue, and to territory. Their concept of identity was based in a 'father language', Hebrew, and a set of texts. Here as elsewhere, Jewish adaptability was understood as an immutable characteristic (Gilman 1998: 80). This mutability was a sign that a deeper essence was untouched and unshaped by the mother tongue. Jews were 'eternally foreign' (Chamberlain [1899] 1932: 382). The Romance linguist Edgar Glässer, who rejected 'linguistic Lamarckianism' (1939: 8), sought to promote a 'racial linguistics' over Leo Weisgerber, but ultimately it was the fascist 'mother-tongue' linguistics of the former which emerged as the dominant intellectual and political force (Hutton 1999: 47–8).

In the division of labour, genetics would deal with those elements of individual and collective identity which were hereditary in nature. While there might be debate and doubt about the exact dividing line, there was no attempt to reduce the whole of human personality and culture to genetics. There was, for example, a complex and methodologically sophisticated debate about the relationship between heredity, environment and criminality. The simple deterministic model was not uncritically accepted, and 'there was a trend towards increasing conceptual and methodological refinement in criminological research during the Nazi era' (Wetzell 2000: 229). There was awareness that categories of crime were in part socially constructed, and that there was no simple deterministic relationship between heredity and criminal behaviour, or between race and criminality (Exner 1939: 47–71; Wetzell 2000: 179–231). These positions were intellectually much more sophisticated, but in essence no less racist, than vulgar Nazism within which Jews were a 'criminal counter-race' (*Gegenrasse*) (von Leers 1936; Wetzell 2000: 188). The specialist in hereditary psychology and twin research, Kurt Gottschaldt (1902–1991), recognized that intelligence 'was so complicated that even its hereditary aspect could not be carried by any single gene' (Gottschaldt 1942; Ash 1999: 289).

Mother-tongue linguistics offered a model of how the world-view of a community could be transmitted from generation to generation without compromising the scientific integrity and methodology of genetics. Linguistics offered an established discourse of difference, and it could show how the world-view of the *Volk* had been fashioned out of centuries of the operation of human will upon nature. A child born into a politically stable and homogenous speech-community would be inducted by the language into the *Volk*; it was not required that genetics explain every aspect of the world-view of the German people. An organicist or holistic (*ganzheitlich*) approach to linguistics meant seeing a language as a dynamic, meaning-creating unity; it did not require the demonstration of any direct relationship between race and language. This would have threatened the clear distinction drawn between *Rasse* and *Volk*. Once the *Volk* had been purged of foreign racial elements, then language could again become a true criterion of the boundary of the *Volk*. The hereditary quality of that *Volk* would then become the province of genetics.

This same pattern was seen, in a different form, in the rejection of the world-historical speculations (Gobineau, Spengler) that saw *Völker* as analogous to individual organisms. According to Leo Frobenius, culture was 'an organism independent of its bearers', and each was to be seen as 'a living creature which is born and passes through childhood, manhood and senility' (Frobenius 1921: 3–4, translated and cited in Heine-Geldern 1964: 415). This represented a confusion of modes of knowledge which were to be kept separate, and this confusion had led to ill-informed pessimism about the destiny of the German people. Biological metaphors were misleading when applied to historical epochs or nations (Verschuer 1934: 58). In his discussion of the role of the teacher as instructor in race (*Rassenkunde*), Josef Spelter stressed the importance of modern scientific knowledge, as defined by Mendel's laws, in refuting this widely held assumption. The eternal Reich of the Germans could thus be shown to rest not only on the vital and life-affirming will of the German people, but on the science of biology. Science and the *völkisch* world-view were close allies (Spelter 1937: 4). There was no conflict between *völkisch* world-view and science; indeed, science offered the *Volk* a chance at unbounded existence.

Racial anthropology and the role of psychology

This division of labour also simplified the relationship between the popular-political and the academic. Racial anthropology, in particular in its guise as Nordicist ideology, had sought to bridge this gap, since it both made a claim to reflect the findings of modern science and sought to mobilize political action. The resulting confusion led Walter Gross to insist on a strict separation of the two levels. Gross was concerned about the lack of a clear orthodoxy on race, and what he saw as a resulting 'free for all' in matters of race theory. By contrast, linguistics and other disciplines of *Volk* which participated in the traditional discourses of cultural nationalism and exceptionalism did not face any similar political problems.

The attempt by racial anthropology to create a synthesis of these domains had created confusion and political doubt, and had laid open National Socialist science to the charge of racial materialism, by way of a parallel with Soviet dialectical materialism. On this argument, race played a similar role within Nazi ideology to 'class' within Soviet Marxist-Leninism. Race in Nazism, in parallel to the economic base in Marxism, formed the individual in their basic identity and determined the socio-cultural and political superstructure of the collective. While these race-materialist tendencies were in evidence, there were strong intellectual and political arguments against allowing them to set the agenda.

The key discipline which emerged at the interface between the humanities and the biological and genetic sciences was not racial anthropology but psychology. This discipline was much better placed to operate in this way than any other, since it could pick up at the point where racial anthropology left off. For the outcome of the methodological debate over the status of racial anthropology had been to stress the importance of psychological and mental qualities. The shift embodied in the 'racial idea' against purely cultural explanations of human society and behaviour remained fundamental to Nazi thought. However, the debate increasingly shifted to genetics, and the question of 'nature versus nurture' fell to psychology. Psychology, at the intersection of the study of human heredity and the humanities, was much better suited to this intermediate role than racial anthropology, which had conceded that there was no direct relationship between inherited racial characteristics of the body and inherited aspects of the mind.

Dialectics of *Volk*

Racial anthropology, which for intellectual, political and strategic reasons, had needed to argue that racial types were permanent, could offer no dynamic, forward-looking vision of the German *Volk*. The notion that the Nordic component needed to be maintained and protected was apiece with the racial and eugenic pessimism to which Nazism sought a bio-political solution. It was a backward-looking, nostalgic, discourse which, while it was in tune with the reactionary cultural politics of a broad section of the intelligentsia, did not sit well with the radical and revolutionary eugenic and technocratic utopianism of the new genetics. The industrial-technocratic drive of the Nazi state and its militarization coincided with the increasingly radical policies of the leadership, culminating with the attack on the Soviet Union in 1941. The paradox of the expansion of the Nazi state was that inherent within European colonialism. The greater the area of territory annexed, the greater the hybridity of the population controlled by the state. The genocidal nature of that expansion, in particular in the east, reflected its radical settler-colonial agenda and the radical will to police the boundaries of the *Volk*.

The nostalgic pessimism of traditional racial anthropology and its intellectual cousin historical and comparative linguistics was grounded in what was an essentially biblical model of human evolution, in which history itself was constituted by an original racial-linguistic fall. The narrative of history enacted and re-enacted that fall from authentic racial being. The vision that this presented was of a contemporary landscape of ruins and relic forms. These were fragments of lost organic wholes which the race theorist or the linguist could discern amid the misshapen forms of modernity. By the exercise of scholarly alchemy, lost wholes could be restored, proto-languages reconstructed, an endless series of lost homelands proposed and debated, and pure racial types abstracted. But this was a paper exercise only, and no plausible political agenda could emerge from this. This had become clear in the early years of the regime when the Nordicist wing of Nazism had been effectively neutralized.

Racial anthropology thus operated dialectically within Nazi ideology, serving usefully to define the *Volk* negatively, yet ultimately marginalized in favour of two parallel, autonomous and complementary ideological formations, namely the humanistic disciplines of *Volk*, on the one hand, and genetic and biological science, on the other. The complex and ideologically contested area in between was the province of psychology, in particular hereditary psychology (*Erbpsychologie*). Theories that seemed to stress the dynamic relationship of environment to race, such as those of Saller and Merkenschlager, were silenced; those which offered a static but confused vision of the racial hybridity of the *Volk* were marginalized from the public sphere. There was a retreat from the simplistic holism of some pro-Nazi scientists in the early years of the regime, where every human phenomenon was related to the category of race, an approach which frequently went together with a vulgar ideologization of scientific discourse. That holism was frequently embodied in anti-Darwinist strands in German science.

Neo-Darwinism suggested that there should be a rigorous separation of the natural sciences and the sciences of culture. Neo-Lamarckianism, suspect because of its association with environmentalism and its status within Soviet ideology, did not merely shift the boundary between science and culture, but effectively merged the biological and the cultural. The notion that acquired characteristics could be directly inherited suggested that racial differences could be modified by social engineering. Neo-Lamarckianism suggested that races could merge under the influence of the environment, a form of hybridity that was anathema to the xenophobia of Nazism.

Yet Nazism needed to offer a definition of the boundaries of the *Volk* which allowed both for genetic inheritance and the inheritance of acquired characteristics. The option of deriving everything from biological race was problematic, in that, in addition to its methodological and philosophical failings, it offered no place for free will, culture and education. If the essential qualities of an individual or a collective were laid down by their genetic inheritance, then much social action, the striving for self-improvement might seem futile. This was politically problematic for an ideology which placed such emphasis on the individual and collective will, and which sought to mobilize the *Volk* politically. If the neo-Lamarckianism was ruled out on ideological grounds, the alternative was to adhere strictly to the logic of the neo-Darwinian synthesis. Racial materialism in its purest form offered no scope for the operation of the individual and collective will in influencing the destiny of the *Volk*, and no clear role for educational and cultural activism, since racial destiny was laid down in advance. This smacked of the pessimism of Gobineau and Spengler. This racial pessimism was the central intellectual target of Nazi science, and fuelled its embrace of neo-Darwinism.

Ultimately, there was a convergence of interest between political expediency and a re-affirmed distinction between the natural sciences and the humanities. The attempt by racial anthropologists to approach the definition of *Volk* holistically had ended in confusion. The concept *Volk* could best be defined by denying any direct causal link between the biological and the linguistic-cultural. This was not to say that there was no place for a holism, but that holism was not to operate globally between all areas of scholarly investigation. There was still room for political rhetoric about the need to forge a bridge between academic science and 'life', and for emphasizing the ultimate links between mind and body.

The underlying logic leads not to a popularized race theory but to a separation of racial anthropology from popular race propaganda. The aestheticizing racial anthropology of Günther fell precisely into this middle ground, in which the attempt to describe in 'objective' language breaks down and is drawn towards a comparative aesthetic of the racial body. While this aesthetic was fundamental to Nazi images at the level of propaganda, it was inadequate as a basis for a science of race. The picture (i.e. the photograph) and the accompanying text did not together amount to a definition that could be applied or operationalized.

If racial anthropology was the product of the subjectivity of the racial expert, if it was an aesthetic discipline, then the power to determine where the crucial distinctions lay was held by the anthropologist. This was not acceptable to the political authorities, who wanted a discipline that could serve the forensic needs of the state, yet which would not itself pronounce on the fundamentals of ideology. That role fitted much more closely the self-understanding of natural scientists, including racial anthropologists who saw themselves as being in alliance with genetics. The opposite of the intuitive aesthetics of Günther and Clauss in this sense was to be found in Reche's attempt to replace somatic anthropology with a racial diagnostic based on blood type (Geisenhainer 2002: 127ff., 169ff.). There were evident methodological reasons why it had to fail, in particular because the term 'race' is circularly defined within the theory (see Marks 1996). But had it succeeded, then the racial anthropologist would have evolved a technique which any laboratory technician could apply. It would be digital rather than analogue. Nazism ultimately needed a digital theory of human identity, and the disciplines that potentially offered that theory were human genetics, on the one hand, and the disciplines of *Volk*, on the other, with psychology operating at the interface in the central debate over the relation of mind to body, and genetic inheritance to environment.

Conclusion

The eugenic concept of *Vitalrasse* had lacked racial specificity, and seemed to imply that the mixing of distant lines of inheritance, provided they were genetically healthy, was beneficial. This was at odds with the strong political, ideological and intellectual currents that saw racial mixing as leading the German *Volk* to its doom. The taxonomic concept of *Systemrasse* or anthropological race expressed this concept of racial distance (see Duncker 1934) in unambiguous terms, even if it was in reality grounded in 'common-sense' perceptions of human racial diversity, and offered a scientific rebuttal of the arguments for the assimilation of the Jews in the German *Volk*. The Negro, the Gypsy and the Jew represented 'otherness', and a threat to the purity of the bloodlines of the German *Volk*. This otherness was also given aesthetic or visual form, and could be grasped in metaphors of contagion, corruption, degeneration, etc.

But racial anthropology could offer no such clarity with regard to the 'European races', and the racial composition of the German *Volk*. It was caught between two intellectual and ideological poles. The first involved the politically problematic racial elitism of the Nordic movement. The second accepted the equality or equal value of all the ('European') races that had contributed to the German *Volk*. This embrace of racial hybridity among the European races could be presented as a process of chaotic mixing and levelling to the lowest common racial denominator. Neither of these options offered a clear definition of the nature of the German *Volk*. The rejection of racial hybridity ultimately implied a rejection of racial anthropology.

The discipline that was best placed to define the uniqueness of the German *Volk* was linguistics. Linguistics could provide an account of the relationship between linguistic structures and world-view, between culture and landscape, and between the individual and the collective. Each language had its unique world-view, and the German language expressed the world-view of the German *Volk*. It could offer an account of how that world-view was transmitted from generation to generation, namely in language acquisition, in the induction of the child into the community of the 'mother tongue'. This was intellectually much more defensible than the aesthetic approach of racial anthropology, as it was grounded in the 'word' rather than the 'image'. But the linguistic definition of *Volk*, like the concept of *Vital-rasse*, did not automatically exclude the Jews from membership. That was the task of racial anthropology in the dialectics of *Volk*.

Once Jews had been excluded from the *Volk* (both at the intellectual-metaphorical level and in their progressive segregation within, and elimination from, German society), racial anthropology lacked a clear role in positively defining the nature of that *Volk*. The categories of racial anthropology were intellectually crude in comparison with the new genetics. Fischer's appropriation of Mendel had offered racial anthropology the possibility of a synthesis with genetics, but the idea of a race as an eternally unchanging set of characteristics did not sit well with the neo-Darwinian synthesis, a paradigm which was based on perpetual change. Genetics could offer a eugenic assessment of the *Volk*; linguistics provided an account of what made that *Volk* different from others.

Linguistics offered an unproblematic account of the inheritance of acquired characteristics, i.e. the transmission of culture and ethics; genetics within the neo-Darwinian synthesis denied that acquired characteristics were transmitted in heredity. The interface between these two was psychology, which had the task of distinguishing the culturally from the genetically transmitted characteristics. This model reconciled 'difference' (the uniqueness of the German *Volk* and its world mission) with an adherence to international standards in science and technology. It would also restore the 'authentic' relationship between being a native speaker of German and being a member of the German *Volk*. This *Volk* would also be protected by a powerful state with the will to police both its inner and outer boundaries. The insistence that there was no necessary link between bodily form and race-psychological character, combined with an insistence that there was a profound unity between the body and the mind ('die Leib-Seele-Einheit des Menschen', Meyer and Zimmermann 1942: 214), gave no serious role to racial anthropology.

The traditional distinction between natural science and the humanistic disciplines of *Volk* was ultimately more functional in relation to the needs of the state than attempts to merge the two into a common, holistic form of 'Nazi science'. This offered a means of reconciling 'directionless evolution' (Darwin) with vitalistic metaphors of dynamism, teleological metaphors of destiny and mission, and organic metaphors of holism and unity (the disciplines of *Volk* and political Nazism), without compromising the scientific integrity of the enterprise. The ambiguity of the term 'race' was functional in popular and political presentations of race ideology, and attempts to introduce scientifically precise meanings into the public domain had spread confusion and suspicion about the ultimate aims of Nazi population policy. However, any confusion of race with partly or wholly cultural constructs like nationality, peoplehood or language was systematically rejected.

Reactionary and pessimistic forms of 'Germanocentrism' and racial nostalgia could not offer a convincing account as to why the German *Volk* would not this time fall into degeneration and hybridity, as had happened to previous superior civilizations. Racial anthropology was hostile to the city, and nostalgic for an agricultural past based on a vision of an organic rural society. It viewed the city and modern mass society as the graveyard of the Nordic racial elite. Modern evolutionary science offered a framework within which such degeneration could be understood and avoided, and thus had a key role in the technocratic vision of a forward-looking Nazism based on a racially purified *Volk*. This model reconciled scientific universalism with *völkisch* particularism. It showed how the supremacy of nature and natural processes could exist in parallel with the demand that culture achieve mastery over nature. It defined a complementarity between determinism and voluntarism, and between science and ideology, and held out the promise of a vital and dynamic future for the German *Volk*.

National Socialism had no Jesus Christ or Karl Marx to provide it with teleological vision. Marxism offered the reassurance of historical science that the utopia of the future was latent in the murderous present. Nazism drew on biblical, and quasi-biblical or mystical, understandings of the *Volk* and its destiny. But reassurance that the *Volk* was not doomed like its Aryan predecessors could only be offered by modern evolutionary science, a science not available to the heroic but doomed forefathers. Courage, martial prowess, force of will and racial taboos were not enough, as the Aryan fall into miscegenation had clearly shown. The situation of the modern German was more desperate still than that of the ancient Aryans. The Aryans had faced an enemy who was racially inferior, though superior in numbers, but the modern Aryan, the German, was threatened not only by the faceless hordes of the east, the Slavs, but a more deadly opponent, the Jewish people. The Jews did not merely survive in modernity, they were comfortably at home there; Jews could take on the mask of national forms and languages, and were behind the universalizing ideologies of capitalism and communism. Crucially, unlike the Nordic race, the Jewish people had retained its racial instinct intact, whereas the hybridity of the *Volk* was a cracked mirror in which the German found racial self-hatred and paranoia.

All the key elements of this world-view had been constructed and repeatedly reaffirmed by linguists, racial anthropologists, evolutionary scientists and geneticists. Ludwig Plate observed that 'progress in evolution goes forward over millions of dead bodies' (Plate 1932: vii). For Nazism, survival in evolution required the genocide of the Jews.

APPENDIX I

Bibliographic Notes

The information below is intended to offer the reader a brief overview of further reading on subjects relevant to this book, in particular those concerning individuals, institutions and policies. The victims of Nazism, a diverse set of 'social outsiders' (Gellately and Stoltzfus 2001), fell into categories defined by political, intellectual, cultural or religious belief; racial or national identity; medical status; sexual orientation; perceived alienation from fundamental community norms. Crimes committed against these victims ranged from harassment, dismissal from employment, expropriation, loss of citizenship and other civil rights, social exclusion, sterilization, imprisonment, torture and abuse, deportation, forced labour and murder.

The search for the origins of Nazi ideology has proved an elusive one, with lines of continuity debated in relation to many thinkers and overlapping intellectual trends. One much discussed group are the Romantic theorists of *Volk*, Johann Herder (Dünninger 1938; Curran 2000), Johann Gottlieb Fichte (Kaufmann 1942) and Friedrich Hegel. The Gobineau circle around Richard Wagner, including the 'evangelist of race' Houston S. Chamberlain, is discussed in Field (1981). Nietzsche's views on race are surveyed in Schank (2000). Jones (2000) analyses Nietzsche's 'misappropriation' within Nazism. Ernst Haeckel was proposed as fundamental to Nazi ideology by Gasman (1971). Classic analyses of 'volkish thought', also in the context of Nazism, are those by Stern (1974) and Mosse (1998). Both Gasman and Mosse identify Nazism with a rejection of Darwinism. Aryan mysticism or 'Ariosophy' is discussed in Daim (1958) and Goodrick-Clarke (1992); the broader background to occultism in Germany can now be found in Treitel (2004). Steigmann-Gall rejects the view of

Nazism as fundamentally anti-Christian (2003). Georges Vacher de Lapouge is the subject of works by Hecht (1999, 2000, 2003) and Quinlan (1998). The history of German anti-Semitism is the subject of Rose (1990).

On Nazism and Enlightenment, see Max Horkheimer and Theodor Adorno's *Dialectic of Enlightenment* ([1947] 1973), where it was argued that 'Nazism was the final product of the Enlightenment' (Herman 1997: 305), and Bauman (1989). For discussion of the relationship between Nazism and modernity, see Levinas (1990), Beyerchen (1997) and Lindenfeld (1997). On the ambivalences of fascism and modernity in relation to images of the United States, see Gentile (1993). Bavaj (2003) gives a detailed overview of the literature, including discussion of Aly and Heim (1997).

In recent years, attention has shifted from the Romantic, *völkisch* and irrationalist origins of Nazi thought to the role of modern biological science. On the biopolitics of modern science, see Massin (1993) and Dickinson (2003). Darwinism and Social Darwinism are treated in Zmarzlik (1963) and Weikart (2004); on geopolitics and the theory of *Lebensraum* ('living space'), associated with Karl Haushofer, see Dijkink (1996), Graml (1993) and Murphy (1997); on irrationalism and the destruction of reason, Lukács ([1955] 1988); on German philosophical idealism, Brumlik (2002); on Enlightenment humanism, Lacoue-Labarthe (1987) and Rockmore (1995). Aly and Roth analyse the relationship between the registration and classification of the population, the dehumanization of the individual and extermination (2004). Anti-Semitism in the context of Nazi Germany is surveyed in Graml (1992). Brechten (1998) recounts the history of the so-called 'Madagascar solution' for the Jews, from 1885–1945. On sexuality and Nazism, see the essays in the *Journal of History of Sexuality* (volume 11, nos 1 & 2, 2002).

On the history of western race theorizing, see the contrasting studies by Hannaford (1996) and Malik (1996). Kiefer (1991) analyses the question of a 'Jewish race'. On race theory in the nineteenth century, see Stocking (1986, 1987, 1996). On the reception of race science, see Efron (1994) on Jewish doctors, and Dikötter (1992) on China. Gilman (1985) looks at ideas of bodily beauty and racial pathology in the western tradition. Colonialism, hybridity and race theory are approached from a post-colonial perspective in Young (1995). Aryanism and empire is the subject of a series of papers by Joan Leopold (1970, 1974, 1987), and is treated historically in Leach (1990), Maw (1990), Trautmann (1997) and Ballantyne (2002). The abuse of the human sciences is the theme of Gould (1981). The history of blood group genetics is treated in volume 18 of *History and*

Philosophy of the Life Sciences (1996). The genocide of the Hereros in Southwest Africa is treated most recently in Bridgman and Worley (2004). On German colonialism in Africa and racism directed at Africans and black Germans, see Grosse (2000), Eckart (1997), El-Tayeb (2001), Silvester and Gewald (2003) and Lusane (2003).

The best general introduction to the racial policies of the Nazi state is Burleigh and Wippermann's *The Racial State: Germany 1933–1945* (1991). Good general introductions to many issues of race policy and and eugenics are Proctor's *Racial Hygiene: Medicine under the Nazis* (1988) and Koonz's *The Nazi Conscience* (2003); see also, from a more specialized point of view, Kater (1989), Klee (1997b, 1999) and Weindling (1989). Müller-Hill (1988) has been highly influential. Eckart's (1997) historical study of German doctors and colonialism also looks at the Nazi period. Schmuhl (1992) and Burleigh (1994) deal with 'euthanasia' in Nazi Germany. On the institutional links between brain research and euthanasia, see Schmuhl (2002). A recent survey of the Nazi murder of disabled people is Gallagher (2004); an important study of sterilization policy in Nazi Germany is Bock (1986). The link between the euthanasia programme and the genocidal Final Solution is the subject of Friedlander (1995). On this integrated approach to Nazi racial policy, see Bock (1991). Meinel and Voswinckel (1994) offer a collection of papers on medicine, technology and science, including Lilienthal's study of Germanization (see also Lilienthal 1993). On the fate of the Gypsies in the Holocaust, see Oesterle (1998), Lewy (2000), Weiss-Wendt (2003) and Milton (2004). A survey of different elements of the Nazi elite is found in Hirschfeld and Jersak (2004). Kestling (1992, 1998) and Lusane (2003) look at the question of Germans of African descent; Bastian (2000) is a discussion of the fate of homosexuals in the Third Reich. Hale (2004) describes the SS expedition to Tibet in 1938. On the issue of polemics in relation to Nazi Germany, see remarks in Evans (2004).

A good introduction to the massive literature on the history of eugenics in the English-speaking world is Kevles (1995). Barkan traces the decline of scientific racism to before the Second World War (1992). The standard work on the history of eugenics and racial anthropology in Germany, including extensive materials on the Nazi era, is Weingart et al. (1992). Stefan Kühl (1997) looks at the eugenics movement as an international phenomenon. Material on race theory in fascist Italy can be found in Gillette (2002), notably the confusions around the relationships between the categories 'Italian', 'Aryan' and 'Mediterranean'. There is a wealth of material on racial anthropology and linguistics in Römer (1989). The myth of distinct languages is treated in Harris (1981, 2002). Studies of academic linguistics in Nazi Germany include Maas (1988), Hutton (1999), Knobloch (2002), and a set of detailed archival studies by Gerd Simon produced since the late 1970s (e.g. Simon 1985b, 2001). A range of important materials can be found at the website of the Gesellschaft für interdisziplinäre Forschung Tübingen (GIFT) including papers by Gerd Simon (http://homepages.uni-tuebingen.de/gerd.simon/gift.htm).

There are many excellent discussions of the *völkisch* movement and radical right in Germany. Important recent works include those by Breuer (2001) and Puschner (2001). An early work with a wealth of information is von See's *Barbar, Germane, Arier* (1994). Questions of space, territory and agrarian policy are treated in Mai's *Rasse und Raum* (2002). Weikart's *From Darwin to Hitler* (2004) traces the lines of thought from Darwin to National Socialism. Hossfeld and Brömer (2001) offers papers on 'Darwinism and/as ideology'. A detailed analysis of the Nuremberg Laws is available in Essner (2002). Schweizer gives an overview of psychiatry and eugenics in Switzerland and Germany in the National Socialist period (2002). Gerstner (2003) offers a discussion of racial elitism in *völkisch* thinking in the late nineteenth and early twentieth centuries.

German scholarship is particularly strong in the study of institutions and academic disciplines within Nazi Germany. Legal and administrative frameworks for the treatment of non-Germans by the Nazi regime are presented in Majer (2003). Academic-institutional politics are treated by Fahlbusch on the Volksdeutschen Forschungsgemeinschaften (1999); Hausmann on the *Aktion Ritterbusch* (1998); Hammerstein on the Deutsche Forschungsgemeinschaft (1999). One important genre is the study of particular universities within the Nazi period, e.g. Höpfner (1999) on Bonn University. Important institutional studies include Heinemann's study of the Rasse- und Siedlungshauptamt (2003) and Diana Schulle's analysis of the Reichssippenamt (2001). An earlier study of the Sippenamt is Seidler and Rett (1982). The general history of the Kaiser-Wilhelm-/Max-Planck-Gesellschaft, including the Nazi period, is treated in Vierhaus and vom Brocke (1990). The links between biological and genetic science and Auschwitz are discussed in Sachse (2003). The histories of psychology and psychiatry within Nazism is particularly complex, reflecting the pivotal position of these disciplines at the intersection of intellectual debates on heredity, environment and behaviour (see Ash 1995, 2002; Geuter 1992, 1999; Prinz 1985; Weber 1993; Schweizer 2002). The marginalization of Germanophilia in law is discussed in Stolleis (1998); on the failure of the 'Thing-movement' which aimed to revive a traditional communal-legal Germanic assembly (*Thing* or

Ding), see Mosse (1975: 115–18), Reichel (1993: 210–11), Van der Will (1995: 121–2). In language-planning policy, the state was more modernizing and centralizing than archaizing, see Simon (1979), Willberg (1998), Birken-Bertsch and Markner (2000).

General collections on science in the Third Reich include Olff-Nathan (1993), Renneberg and Walker (1994) and Szöllösi-Janze (2001). For discussion of the issue of scientific standards, see Schmuhl (2003a) and Massin (2003). On the role of the humanities in Nazi Germany, see the contributions in Hausmann (2002). Other important works include: Ingrid Richter's study of the relationships between Catholicism and eugenics (2001) and an edited volume on the University of Jena in the Nazi period (Hossfeld et al. 2003). Felbor looks at race biology and genetics in the medical faculty at the University of Würzburg from 1937 to 1945 (1995). The Lebensborn e.V. was analysed in Lilienthal (1985). Kröner (1998) looks at the Kaiser-Wilhelm-Institut after 1945 and addresses questions of continuity. Recent works include two collections on the Kaiser Wilhelm Institute (Schmuhl 2003b, Sachse 2003). Mai (1997) surveys the history of 'twin-research' in Germany up to 1945. The reception of the Baur-Fischer-Lenz volume is discussed in Fangerau (2000). A detailed guide to National Socialist terminology is given in Schmitz-Berning (1998). English renderings of 'Nazi-German' are found in Michael and Doerr (2002).

Plant biology and agricultural research are treated in Heim (2002). An important collection on German prehistorians is Steuer (2001), and an overview of the disciplines of prehistory and early history is given in Pape (2002). Questions of continuity and discontinuity are discussed in Kaupen-Haas and Saller (1999). The classical study of the Ahnenerbe is Kater (second edition, 1997); that of the Amt Rosenberg, Bollmus (1970). Lerchenmüller (1997) is a political-ideological history of Celtic studies in Germany from 1900 to 1945. Harten (1996) surveys questions of Germanization and education in Nazi-occupied Poland. The broad intellectual and ideological context of the relationship between National Socialism and the Slavic world is discussed in Schaller (2002).

Biographical studies include Rissom on Lenz (1983); Weber on Rüdin (1993), but see comments in Roelcke (2003) and in Wetzell (2003); Weingart on Ludwig Ferdinand Clauss (1995); Hossfeld on Heberer (1997); Völklein on Mengele (1999); Geisenhainer on Reche (2002); Gessler (2000) and Lösch (1997) on Fischer; Lüddeke on Saller (1995) and on Eickstedt (2000); Hagemann on Baur (2000); Föger and Taschwer on Lorenz (2001). Useful sources of biographical information on Nazi scholarship are Klee (2003) and Grüttner (2004).

APPENDIX II

Biographical Sketches

Ludwig Ferdinand Clauss (1892–1974)
German racial anthropologist. Clauss was awarded his doctorate in 1921 in Freiburg; between 1923 and 1931 he undertook anthropological expeditions. He was awarded the Habilitation in 1936, and taught 'race psychology' (*Rassenseelenforschung*) at the University of Berlin. Clauss was a student of Edmund Husserl and brought this phenomenological background into the study of race. Fieldwork in Palestine involved living with the Bedouins and applying his 'mimetic method' ('mimische Methode') and immersing himself into the lifestyle and psychology of his subjects ('Methode des Mitlebens'). Allegations about Clauss's relationship with his Jewish research assistant (Margarete Landé) and his self-appointed role as a popularizer of racial thinking led to conflict with Walter Gross of the Race Policy Office. In 1943, Clauss was expelled from the NSDAP and lost his teaching position, but was able to obtain support from the SS. Friends in the SS helped him rescue Landé. After the war his association with the SS meant that he was unable to resume his teaching career, though he was honoured by the state of Israel for saving Landé. (Reference: Weingart 1995.)

Egon, Freiherr von Eickstedt (1892–1965)
Anthropologist and ethnologist. Eickstedt studied physical anthropology, philosophy, psychology, ethnology, geography, prehistory and linguistics in Berlin and Freiburg. A decisive influence was Felix von Luschan in Berlin. He served as an assistant at the Museum of the Sea (Museum für Meereskunde) under Albrecht Penck, at the Ethnological Museum (Museum für Völkerkunde in Berlin) with

Luschan, at the Geographical Institute (Geographisches Institut) with Norbert Krebs and then at the Anatomical Institute (Anatomisches Institut) with Eugen Fischer in Freiburg. He subsequently worked in Vienna at the Museum of Natural History (Naturhistorisches Museum) and then at the Bavarian Academy of Sciences (Bayerische Akademie der Wissenschaften) in Munich, where Theodor Mollinson was professor. He published on a wide range of topics, including anatomy, an anthropological taxonomy of humankind, the reconstruction of Neanderthal man and biometrics of India. In the First World War he was a medical officer stationed in Romania, where he investigated the anthropometrics of prisoners of war, including non-Europeans, especially of the Sihks, the topic of his dissertation. India was the destination of his first organized research trip (1926–9). In 1929, he obtained an academic post in Breslau, where, on the initiative of H. von Eggeling, the anthropological department of the Anotomical Institute was made into an independent Anthropological Institute. Here, the Indian materials were organized and evaluated and an investigation of Silesia begun. He was awarded his Habilitation in anthropology in 1930, and obtained a teaching position in Breslau in 1933. The publication of his 1934 work *Rassenkunde und Rassengeschichte der Menschheit* made him widely known. He was editor of the *Zeitschrift für Rassenkunde und die gesamte Forschung am Menschen*. Between 1937 and 1939, he undertook a research trip to India, China and the Malay Archipelago, which resulted in his *Rassendynamik von Ostasien* (1944). After the 1945 destruction of the Institute in Breslau, Eickstedt failed to save the anthropological collections. In 1946, Eickstedt obtained a post at the University of Mainz, and founded the journal *Homo* in 1949. (References: Schwidetzky 1955; Lüddecke 2000.)

Eugen Fischer (1874–1967)
German anthropologist and anatomist. Studied medicine in Freiburg, where he completed a doctorate and then was employed as Assistant in the Anatomical Institute. He achieved his Habilitation in 1900, and in 1904 took up a post teaching anatomy and anthropology. A 1908 research trip to German Southwest Africa let to the publication of Fischer's influential study of racial mixing, *Die Rehobother Bastards* (1913). Fischer joined the Germany Society for Eugenics (Deutsche Gesellschaft für Rassenhygiene) and founded a branch in Freiburg in 1910. He also became a member of the German Society for Hereditary Science (Deutsche Gesellschaft für Vererbungswissenschaft). Fischer taught in Würzburg in 1912 before returning to teach in Freiburg. He served as a military surgeon in the First World

War. *Menschliche Erblichkeitslehre* (1921) (trans. as *Human Hereditary Teaching and Racial Hygiene*, 1921), co-written with Erwin Baur and Fritz Lenz, became the standard survey work of genetics, eugenics and racial anthropology. He was also the general editor of the publication series *Deutsche Rassenkunde* which began in 1929. Fischer was appointed to a chair at the University of Berlin in 1927, which he held until retirement in 1942. He was co-founder, with Hermann Muckermann, of the Kaiser-Wilhelm-Institut für Anthropologie, menschliche Erblehre und Eugenik in 1927. Fischer served as its director until 1942. Fischer was rector of the University of Berlin from 1933 to 1935, and in that capacity enforced Nazi exclusionary policies on university personnel. After the Nazi seizure of power, he acquiesced in the dismissal of Hermann Muckermann, a Jesuit, from the Kaiser-Wilhelm-Institut. Fischer came under fire from National Socialist ideologues for his views on racial mixing. In 1932, Fischer had been involved in deliberations of the Prussian State Health Council over a Law on Sterilization, and was an advisor in the sterilization of the mixed-race offspring of French troops who had served in the Rhineland, the 'Rhineland bastards'. He served as a medical advisor in the Higher Hereditary Health Court (Erbgesundheits-Obergericht) in Berlin from 1937 to 1945. Fischer had been a member of the völksich DNVP (the German National People's Party) from 1919 to 1926, and became a member of the NSDAP in 1940, and of the council of the anti-Semitic Reich Institute for the History of the New Germany (Reichsinstitut für Geschichte des Neuen Deutschlands) in 1941, and made many appearances at conferences organized by its Research Department for the Jewish Question (Forschungsabteilung Judenfrage). (References: Grüttner 2004: 48; Schmuhl 2003b: 330; Weiss 1998: 122–3; Lösch 1997.)

Walter Gross (1904–1945)
Gross studied medicine in Göttingen, Tübingen and Munich from 1923 to 1928. He joined the NSDAP in 1925, and was one of the founders of the Göttingen Nazi Student Union (NSDStB). He was awarded a doctorate in Göttingen in 1929, and worked as a doctor in Braunschweig from 1929 to 1932. From 1932, he was a member of the Nazi Doctors Union (NS-Ärtzebund). In 1933, Gross founded and directed the Education Office for Population Policy and Eugenics (Auflkärungsamt für Bevölkerungspolitik und Rassenpflege), which became the Race Policy Office of the Nazi Party (Rassenpolitisches Amt der NSDAP, RPA) in 1935. He taught courses in racial anthropology at the University of Berlin and became an honorary professor in 1938. The RPA was dissolved in 1942, and from 1942 to 1945

he was head of the Rosenberg Bureau (Hauptamtwissenschaft in der Dienstelle Rosenberg). In 1943, he left the Protestant Church. Gross was a formidable operator at the intersection of politics and race science. He was, with Gerhard Wagner, an influential medical advisor in the preparation of the Nuremberg racial laws, a consistent advocate of compulsory sterilization for undesirable elements and of other radical eugenic measures, including the murder of the mentally ill and mentally retarded, and a committed anti-Semite in the spirit of his mentor Alfred Rosenberg. Gross committed suicide in 1945. (References: Klee 1997a: 50–1; Grüttner 2004: 64–5; Weingart 1995.)

Hans F. K. Günther (1891–1968)
German anthropologist and race theorist. Günther studied modern languages in Freiburg and Paris. He was awarded his doctorate in Freiburg in 1914. He volunteered for military service in the First World War but was soon invalided out, and worked as a volunteer medical orderly from 1915 to 1919. In 1919, he left the Protestant Church. Between 1919 and 1930, he worked as a private scholar and freelance writer. With the backing of J. F. Lehmann, he began to publish works on racial anthropology. Günther lived in Norway and Sweden between 1923 and 1929. In 1930, he was appointed to a chair in racial anthropology (Sozialanthropologie) in Jena. The appointment was forced through against objections from the university professoriate by the Nazi State Minister of Education for Thüringen, Wilhelm Frick. He joined the NSDAP in 1932. In 1933, he joined the Expert Advisory Council of the Ministry of the Interior for Population and Race Policy (Sachverständigebeirat des Reichsministers des Innern für Bevölkserungs- und Rassenpolitik). From 1939 to 1945, he held a chair in Freiburg, a position from which he was dismissed in 1945. (Reference: Grüttner 2004: 66.)

Fritz Lenz (1887–1976)
German eugenicist, student of Alfred Ploetz. Lenz studied medicine in Berlin, Breslau and Freiburg between 1905 and 1912. He completed his doctorate in Freiburg in 1912, and his Habilitation in 1919 at the University of Munich. In 1913, took over the editorship of the Archiv für Rassen- und Gesellschaftsbiologie, and served until 1933. He obtained a teaching post in Munich in 1923 in eugenics, the first post with this title. *Menschliche Erblichkeitslehre* (1921) (translated as *Human Hereditary Teaching and Racial Hygiene*, 1921), co-written with Erwin Baur and Eugen Fischer, became the standard survey work of genetics, eugenics and racial anthropology. A single-authored companion volume *Menschliche Auslese und Rassenhygiene*

(Eugenik) was published at the same time. In 1933, he moved to the University of Berlin and became the dismissed Hermann Muckermann's successor as Head of the Department for Eugenics at the Kaiser-Wilhelm-Institut für Anthropologie, menschliche Erblehre und Eugenik. From 1933, he was a member of the Expert Advisory Council of the Ministry of the Interior for Population and Race Policy (Sachverständigebeirat des Reichsministers des Innern für Bevölkserungs- und Rassenpolitik); in 1940, he participated in official discussions on the drafting of a law on euthanasia. He joined the NSDAP in 1937. After the war he taught in Göttingen, obtaining a chair in human genetics in 1952. The focus of his research was the genetic inheritance of disease in the context of eugenics. (References: Grüttner 2004: 108; Kröner 1998; Schmuhl 2003b: 333; Rissom 1983; Weiss 1998: 296–7.)

Otmar, Freiherr von Verschuer (1896–1969)
Medical doctor and human geneticist. After military service in the First World War, Verschuer studied in Marburg, Hamburg, Freiburg and Munich. He participated in Marburg student action (Marburger Studentkorps) against the communist movement in Thüringen in 1920. Verschuer obtained his doctorate in 1923, and his Habilitation in genetics in Tübingen in 1927. In the same year, he became head of the Department of Human Genetics at the Kaiser Wilhelm Institute for Anthropology, Human Genetics and Eugenics. Like his colleagues, he was involved in official deliberations of the Prussian State Health Council over a Law on Sterilization. He served as a medical advisor in the Hereditary Health Court (Erbgesundheitsgericht) in Charlottenburg, Berlin. From 1933, he held a teaching post in Human Genetics and Eugenics at the University of Berlin. In 1934, he founded and edited the journal *Der Erbarzt*. In 1935, he was appointed to a chair in Frankfurt am Main and served as director of the Institute for Hereditary Biology and Eugenics, Frankfurt am Main (Institut für Erbbiologie und Rassenhgyiene) until 1942. Verschuer became a member of the NSDAP in 1940, and participated in conferences of the anti-Semitic Reich Institute for the History of the New Germany (Reichsinstitut für Geschichte des Neuen Deutschlands). He became director of the Kaiser-Wilhelm-Institut für Anthropologie, menschliche Erblehre und Eugenik in Berlin in 1942, as successor to Eugen Fischer. A specialist in twin research, Verschuer supervised Josef Mengele's doctoral thesis and allegedly received anthropological materials from Auschwitz. After the war Verchuer was attacked for his record under the Nazis. In 1951, he was appointed head of the Institute of Human Genetics (Institit für

Humangenetik) in Münster and served until his retirement in 1965. Proceedings against Verschuer for his involvement in crimes relating to concentration camps were cancelled in 1965. (References: Gausemeier 2003; Grüttner 2004: 177; Kröner 1998; Schmuhl 2003b: 342.)

APPENDIX III

Nazi Legislation (Selected Examples)

7 Apr. 1933 — Gesetz zur Wiederherstellung des Berufsbeamtentums ('Law for the Restoration of the Professional Civil Service') Reichsgesetzblatt [RGBl] I S. 175

The so-called 'Arier-Paragraph' (§3) excludes all citizens 'of non-Aryan descent' from the civil service (a person with one Jewish parent or grandparent counting as non-Aryan); excluded from this law are Jews who fought in the First World War or who entered the civil service before 1 Aug. 1914.

14 July 1933 — Gesetz zur Verhütung erbkranken Nachwuchses ('Law for the Prevention of Hereditarily Diseased Progeny') RGBl I S. 529

Compulsory sterilization for any person suffering from congenital madness, schizophrenia, manic depression, hereditary epilepsy, Huntington's chorea, hereditary blindness, hereditary deafness and grave physical deformities (§1.2).

30 Nov. 1933 — Reichserbhofgesetz ('Reich Hereditary Farm Law') RGBl I S. 549

§13 states that only a person of Aryan or related blood can become a farmer; excluding those with Jewish or black blood ('jüdisches oder farbiges Blut').

Date	Law	Description
26 June 1935	Gesetz zur Änderung des Gesetzes zur Verhütung erbkranken Nachwuchses ('Law for the Alteration of the Law for the Prevention of Hereditarily Diseased Progeny') RGBl I S. 196	§2 sanctions abortion within the first six months of pregnancy in cases of women categorized as 'hereditarily ill' by the Hereditary Health Courts; §4 stipulates sterilization or the termination of pregnancy if the physician has decided that this would forestall a threat to the life or health of the person concerned.
15 Sept. 1935	Reichsbürgergesetz ('Citizenship Law') RGBl I S. 1146	§2 limits citizenship in the German Reich to 'Germans or those of related blood'.
15 Sept. 1935	Gesetz zum Schutz des deutschen Blutes und der deutschen Ehre ('Law for the Protection of German Blood and German Honour') RGBl I S. 1146	'The purity of German blood is essential for the existence of the German *Volk* and the Reich possesses the unbending will to safeguard the German nation for the entire future'; law prohibits marriage (§1) and extramarital relations (§2) between Jews and people of German blood; bans Jews from employing German female domestic servants (under 45 years) and from hoisting the German flag (§3 and §4);
18 Oct. 1935	Gesetz zum Schutze der Erbgesundheit des deutschen Volkes (Ehegesundheitsgesetz) ('Law for the Protection of Hereditary Health of the German People/Marriage Health Law') RGBl I S. 1246	§1 prohibits marriage with a person who is mentally retarded or suffers from a hereditary disease (as set out in the 'Law for the Prevention of Hereditarily Diseased Progeny'); §2 introduces a certificate attesting the suitability of a marriage ('Ehetauglichkeit').

Date	Law	Description
14 Nov. 1935	Erste Verordnung zum Gesetz zur Ausführung des Gesetzes zum Schutze des deutschen Blutes und der deutschen Ehre ('First Supplementary Decree on the Law for the Protection of German Blood and Honour') RGBl I S. 1334	Prohibits marriage between a Jew and a Jewish *Mischling* or two Jewish *Mischlinge* (§2, §3, §4); a certificate (§7) attests the suitability of a marriage ('Ehetauglichkeit') [i.e. confirms that the two partners entering marriage have no hereditary disease or Jewish, black or Gypsy blood that would prevent a union].
14 Nov. 1935	Erste Verordnung zum Reichsbürgergesetz ('First Supplementary Decree on the Citizenship Law') RGBl I S. 1333	Defines a 'Jewish *Mischling*' as a person with one or two Jewish grandparents (§2.2) and a 'Jew' as a person with at least two Jewish grandparents and/or fulfilling other criteria such as being married to a Jew or born to a Jew (also extramarital) (§5); a Jew cannot be a 'Reichsbürger': s/he has no vote and cannot become a civil servant (§4).
26 Jan. 1937	Deutsches Beamtengesetz ('Civil Service Law') RGBl I S. 41	§25 stipulates that only a person 'of German or related blood' can become a civil servant and – if married – is married to a person of German or related blood; a civil servant must only marry a person of German blood (in some cases a second-degree *Mischling*); a person who incorrectly and without false intention has claimed to be of German blood/to be married to a person of German or related blood and is found to be otherwise, must retire from his duties at once (§72).

12 Nov. 1938	Verordnung zur Ausschaltung der Juden aus dem deutschen Wirtschaftsleben ('Decree for the Elimination of Jews from German Economic Life') RGBl I S. 1580	Jews are banned from possessing and running small businesses, import and export businesses, manufacturing works and industrial units (§1 and §2); Jews in leading managerial positions can be made redundant with six weeks' notice (§2); Jews are excluded as union members (§3).
1 Sept. 1941	Polizeiverordnung über die Kennzeichnung der Juden ('Police Decree for the Marking of Jews') RGBl I S. 547	Jews who have completed their sixth year must wear the 'Judenstern' at all times in public (§1); Jews are prohibited from leaving their residential area without authorization through the authorities (§2); excluded from §1 and §2 are Jews married to a German and having no children/non-Jewish children.
4 Dec. 1941	Verordnung über die Strafrechtspflege gegen Polen und Juden in den eingegliederten Ostgebieten ('Decree for the Legal Situation of Jews and Poles in the Newly Incorporated Eastern Territories')	Poles and Jews in the newly incorporated Eastern Territories are subject to German law: any act jeopardizing the sovereignty of the German Reich and the reputation of the German *Volk* is prohibited ('Sie haben alles zu unterlassen, was der Hoheit des Deutschen Reiches und dem Ansehen des deutschen Volkes abträglich ist.') (§1.1); they will suffer capital punishment (in less severe cases, imprisonment) if they attack a German citizen or German institution, utter anti-German sentiments, or are found in possession of weapons and ammunition (§1.2, §1.3, §1.4).

References

Archival references

[Report 1] Report of proceedings, Saturday, 20 December 1941, p. 22, German Federal Archives, Lichterfelde, Berlin, BDC OPG 3402000644 00235.

[Report 2] Akten des Obersten Parteigerichts Z Kammer Akt D Akten-Zeichen 163 1941. German Federal Archives, Lichterfelde, Berlin, BDC OPG 3402000644 00235.

[Report 3] Hecht, Günther and E. Wetzel (n.d.). Rassenpolitische Leitsätze zur Fremdvolkpolitik des deutschen Reiches. Entwurf von der Abteilung für Volksdeutsche und Minderheitenfragen (Dr G. Hecht) unter Mitarbeit der Abteilung für rechtsfragen (Amtsgerichtsrat Dr E. Wetzel). Heraus-gegeben von Prof. Dr W. Gross, Reichshauptamsleiter. Berlin, c.1939. German Federal Archives, Lichterfelde, Berlin, BDC PK 1030041481.

Primary printed sources (all pre-1945)

Abel, Wolfgang (1937). Über Europäer-, Marokkaner- und Europäer-Annamiten-Kreuzungen. *Zeitschrift für Morphologie und Anthropologie* 36: 311–29.

Aichel, Otto (1933). *Der deutsche Mensch: Studie auf Grund neuen europä-ischen und aussereuropäischen Materials.* Jena: Fischer.

Alnor, Karl (1935). *Geschichtsunterricht.* Osterwieck/Harz: A. W. Zickfeldt Verlag.

Ammon, Otto (1893). *Die natürliche Auslese beim Menschen: Auf Grund der Ergebnisse der anthropologischen Untersuchungen der Wehrpflichtigen in Baden und anderer Materialen.* Jena: Fischer.

Ammon, Otto (1900). *Die Gesellschaftsordnung und ihre natürlichen Grund-lagen: Entwurf einer Sozial-Anthropologie.* 3rd edition. Jena: G. Fischer. First published, 1895.

Anderson, James (1732). *Royal Genealogies: Or the Genealogical Tables of Emperors, Kings and Princes, from Adam to these Times.* London.

Anon (1913). The antiquity and evolution of man. *Nature,* 9 October 1913: 160–2.

Antonowytsch, Michael (1942). Das Schicksal der ukrainischen Gelehrten in der Sowjetukraine. In: Bolko Freiherr von Richthofen, ed., *Bolschewistische Wissenschaft und Kulturpolitik: Ein Sammelwerk.* Königsberg (Pruss.): Ost-Europa Verlag, pp. 45–130.

Arlt, Fritz (1938). *Volksbiologische Untersuchungen über die Juden in Leipzig.* 4. Beiheft zum Archiv für Bevölkerungswissenschaft und Bevölkerungspolitik Band VII. Leipzig: S. Hirzel.

Arntz, Helmut (1936). Herman Hirt und die Heimat der Indogermanen. In: Helmuth Arntz, ed., *Germanen und Indogermanen: Volkstum, Sprache, Heimat, Kultur. Festschrift für Herman Hirt.* Volume 2: Ergebnisse der Sprachwissenschaft. Heidelberg: Carl Winters, pp. 25–8.

Aschenbrenner, Helmuth (*c.*1935). *Überseekolonien: Das Ende der nordischen Rasse.* Berlin: R. Gahl.

Bahr, Richard (1933). *Volk jenseits der Grenzen: Geschichte und Problematik der deutschen Minderheiten.* Hamburg: Hanseatische Verlagsanstalt.

Banniza von Bazan, Heinrich (1937). Jüdische Zuwanderung in der Neuzeit. *Familie, Sippe, Volk* 3: 61–2.

Bartels, Adolf (1920). *Rasse und Volkstum: Gesammelte Aufsätze zur nationalen Weltanschauung.* 2nd edition. Weimar: Alexander Duncker.

Bavink, Bernhard (1934). *Eugenik.* Leipzig: Quelle & Meyer.

Baur, Erwin (1922). Der Untergang der Kulturvölker im Lichte der Biologie. *Deutschlands Erneuerung: Monatsschrift für das deutsche Volk* 6 (5): 1–12.

Baur, Erwin (1936). Menschliche Erblehre. In: Erwin Baur, Eugen Fischer and Fritz Lenz, eds, *Menschliche Erblehre.* Menschliche Erblehre und Rassenhygiene, vol. 1. München: J. F. Lehmann, pp. 3–94.

Baur, Erwin, Eugen Fischer and Fritz Lenz (1921). *Menschliche Erblichkeitslehre.* Grundriss der menschlichen Erblichkeitslehre und Rassenhygiene, vol. 1. München: J. F. Lehmann. Subsequent revised editions, 1923, 1932, 1936. 5th edition, with Kurt Gottschaldt, 1940.

Bayer, Maximilian (1905). Die Nation der Bastards. *Zeitschrift für Kolonialpolitik, Kolonialrecht und Kolonialwirtschaft* 9: 625–48.

Berger, Arthur (1938). *Kampf um Afrika.* Berlin: Büchergilde Gutenberg.

Bieberbach, Ludwig (1940). *Die völkische Verwurzelung der Wissenschaft: Typen mathematischen Schaffens.* Sitzungsberichte der Heidelberger Akademie der Wissenschaften. Mathematisch-naturwissenschaftliche Klasse. Jahrgang 1940. 5. Abhandlung. Heidelberg: Kommissionsverlag der Weiss'schen Universitätsbuchhandlung.

Blumenbach, Johann Friedrich (1795). *De generis humani varietate nativa.* Göttingen: Vandenhoek and Ruprecht. Trans: *On the Natural Varieties of Mankind.* New York: Berman, 1969.

Boas, Franz (1922). Report on the anthropometric investigation of the population of the United States. *Journal of the American Statistical Associa-*

tion 18: 181–209. Reprinted: *Race, Language and Culture.* Chicago: The University of Chicago Press, 1982, pp. 28–59.

Boas, Franz (1923). *Anthropology and Modern Life.* New York: Norton.

Böker, Hans (1934). Rassenkonstanz – Artenwandel. *Rasse: Monatsschrift der Nordischen Bewegung* 1: 250–1.

Böker, Hans (1937). Goethes Beziehungen zur Anatomie und zum Anatomischen Institut in Jena. *Sudhoffs Archiv für Geschichte der Medizin und der Naturwissenschaften* 29: 123–35.

Brandis, Ernst (1936). *Die Ehegesetze von 1935.* Berlin: Verlag für Standesamtswesen.

Broca, Paul (1864). *On the Phenomena of Hybridity in the Genus Homo.* Edited by C. Carter Blake. London: Longman, Green, Longman and Roberts. First published as *Recherches sur l'hybridité animale en général et sur l'hybridité humaine en particulier.* Paris: Imprimerie de J. Claye, 1860.

Büchner, Ludwing (1894). *Darwinismus und Sozialismus, oder: Der Kampf ums Dasein und die moderne Gesellschaft.* Leipzig: Günther.

Burgdörfer, Friedrich (1929). *Der Geburtenrückgang und seine Bekämpfung: Die Lebenslage des deutschen Volkes.* Berlin: Richard Schoetz.

Burgdörfer, Friedrich (1932). *Volk ohne Jugend: Geburtenschwind und Überalterung des deutschen Volkskörpers: Ein Problem der Volkswirtschaft, der Sozialpolitik, der nationalen Zukunft.* Beihefte zur Zeitschrift für Geopolitik, Heft 9. Vowinckel: Berlin.

Burgdörfer, Friedrich (1934). Bevölkerungsstatistik, Bevölkerungspolitik und Rassenhygiene. In: Ernst Rüdin, ed., *Rassenhygiene im völkischen Staat: Tatsachen und Richtlinien.* München: J. F. Lehmann, pp. 48–90.

Burgdörfer, Friedrich (1936). Bevölkerungspolitik. In: Heinz Woltereck, ed., *Erbkunde, Rassenpflege, Bevölkerungspolitik: Schicksalsfragen des deutschen Volkes.* 3rd revised edition. Leipzig: Quelle & Meyer, pp. 203–325.

Chamberlain, Houston Stewart (1922). *Lebenswege meines Denkens.* 2nd edition. München: F. Bruckmann.

Chamberlain, Houston Stewart (1932). *Die Grundlagen des neunzehnten Jahrhunderts.* 2 vols. München: F. Bruckmann. First published, 1899.

Chamberlain, Houston Stewart (1938). *Arische Weltanschauung.* 8th edition. München: F. Bruckmann. First edition, 1905. Subsequent editions, 1912, 1916.

Clauss, Ludwig Ferdinand (1933). *Semiten der Wüste unter sich: Miterlebnisse eines Rassenforschers.* Berlin: Büchergilde Gutenberg. Revised and expanded edition of *Als Beduine unter Beduinen.* Freiburg im Breisgau: Herder, 1933.

Clauss, Ludwig Ferdinand (1936). *Die nordische Seele: Eine Einführung in die Rassenseelenkunde.* München: J. F. Lehmann.

Clauss, Ludwig Ferdinand (1939). *Rasse und Seele: Eine Einführung in den Sinn der leiblichen Gestalt.* 15th impression. Berlin: Büchergilde Gutenberg. First edition 1926.

Clauss, Ludwig and Arthur Hoffmann (1934). *Vorschule der Rassenkunde auf der Grundlage praktischer Menschenbeobachtung.* Erfurt: Kurt Stengler.

Danzer, Paul (1937). *Geburtenkrieg*. 2nd revised edition. München: J. F. Lehmann.

Darré, Richard Walther (1930). *Neuadel aus Blut und Boden*. München: J. F. Lehmann. Subsequent editions, 1935, 1936, 1938, 1939, 1941.

Darré, Richard Walther (1933). *Das Schwein als Kriterium für nordische Völker und Semiten*. München: J. F. Lehmann. First published in *Volk und Rasse*, 1927.

Darré, Richard Walther (1934). *Das Bauerntum als Lebensquell der Nordischen Rasse*. 4th edition. München: J. F. Lehmann.

Darré, Richard Walther (1939). *Neuadel aus Blut und Boden*. München: J. F. Lehmann.

Darwin, Charles (1859). *On the Origin of Species by Means of Natural Selection*. London: John Murray.

Darwin, Charles (1871). *The Descent of Man, and Selection in Relation to Sex*. London: J. Murray.

Darwin, Charles ([1872] 1999). *The Expression of the Emotions in Man and Animals*. Edited by Paul Ekman. 3rd edition. London: Harper Collins, 1999. First published, 1872.

Debrunner, Albert (1932). Review of G. Schmidt-Rohr, *Die Sprache als Bildnerin der Völker*. Jena: Diederichs, 1932. *Indogermanische Forschungen* 50: 306–7.

Deniker, Joseph (1904). Les six races composant la population actuelle de l'Europe. *The Journal of the Anthropological Institute of Great Britain and Ireland* 34: 181–206.

Deniker, Joseph (1926). *Les races et les peuples de la terre: éléments d'anthropologie et d'ethnographie*. 2nd edition. Paris: Schleicher, 1926. First published, 1900.

Dobers, Ernst (1936). Beobachtungsschulung im rassenbiologischen Sehen und Verstehen. *Der Biologe* 5: 382–9.

Driesmans, Heinrich (1912/13). Zur Biologie der jüdischen Rasse. *Politisch-Anthropologische Monatsschrift für praktische Politik, für politische Bildung und Erziehung auf biologischer Grundlage* 11: 149–59.

Duncker, Hans (1934) Rassenmischung, biologisch gesehen. *Rasse: Monatsschrift der Nordischen Bewegung* 1: 265–79.

Dunlap, Knight (1944). The great Aryan Myth. *The Scientific Monthly* 59: 296–300.

Dünninger, Josef (1938). Der deutsche Volksgedanke und Johann Gottfried Herder. *Mitteilungen der Deutschen Akademie* 13 (3): 356–60.

Eickstedt, Egon, Freiherr von (1934a). *Rassenkunde und Rassengeschichte der Menschheit*. Stuttgart: Ferdinand Enke.

Eickstedt, Egon, Freiherr von (1934b). *Die rassischen Grundlagen des deutschen Volkstums*. Köln: Hermann Schaffstein.

Eickstedt, Egon, Freiherr von (1936). *Grundlagen der Rassenpsychologie*. Stuttgart: F. Enke.

Eickstedt, Egon, Freiherr von and Ilse Schwidetzky (1940). *Die Rassenuntersuchung Schlesiens: Eine Einführung in ihre Aufgaben und Methoden*. Breslau: Priebatsch.

Ekkehart, Winfried (1936). *Rasse und Geschichte: Grundzüge einer rassen-wertenden Geschichtsbetrachtung von der Urzeit bis zur Gegenwart.* Bochum: Kamp.

Exner, Franz (1939). *Kriminalbiologie in ihren Grundzügen.* Hamburg: Hanseatische Verlagsanstalt. 2nd edition, 1944. 3rd edition, Berlin: Springer, 1949.

Farrar, Frederic William (1878). *Language and Languages, being 'Chapters on Language' and 'Families of Speech'.* London: Longmans, Green, and Co.

Feldscher, Werner (1943). *Rassen- und Erbpflege im deutschen Recht.* Berlin: Deutscher Rechtsverlag.

Finger, Otto (1937). *Studien an zwei asozialen Zigeunermischlingssippen: Ein Beitrag zur Asozialen und Zigeunerfrage.* 2nd edition. Giessen: Justus Christ.

Firth, Raymond ([1938] 1956). *Human Types: An Introduction to Social Anthropology.* Revised edition. London: Thomas Nelson and Sons 1956. First published, 1938.

Fischel, Werner (1934). Abstammungslehre und Tierpsychologie. *Sudhoffs Archiv für Geschichte der Medizin und der Naturwissenschaften* 27: 511–15.

Fischer, Eugen (1910). *Sozialanthropologie und ihre Bedeutung für den Staat.* Vortrag gehalten in der Naturforschenden Gesellschaft zu Freiburg im Breisgau am 8. Juni 1910. Freiburg im Breisgau/Leipzig: Speyer & Kaerner.

Fischer, Eugen (1913). *Die Rehobother Bastards und das Bastardisierungs-problem beim Menschen.* Jena: Gustav Fischer. Reprinted with an intro-duction by Hans Biedermann. Graz: Akademische Druck- und Verlagsanstalt, 1961.

Fischer, Eugen (1914). *Das Problem der Rassenkreuzung beim Menschen.* Vortrag gehalten in der zweiten allgemeinen Sitzung der Gesellschaft deutscher Naturforscher und Ärzte in Wien, 1913. Freiburg im Breis-gau/Leipzig: Speyer & Kaerner, 1914.

Fischer, Eugen (1923). Spezielle Anthropologie: Rassenlehre. In: Gustav Schwalbe and Eugen Fischer, eds, *Anthropologie.* Leipzig and Berlin: Teubner, pp. 122–222.

Fischer, Eugen (1926a). Aufgaben der Anthropologie, menschlichen Erblichkeitslehre und Eugenik. *Die Naturwissenschaften* 14: 749–55.

Fischer, Eugen (1926b). Review of Günther, *Rassenkunde des deutschen Volkes.* München: J. F. Lehmann, 1926. *Zeitschrift für Morphologie und Anthropologie* 26: 190.

Fischer, Eugen (1927a). Das Preisausschreiben für den besten nordischen Rassenkopf, veranstaltet vom Werkbund für deutsche Volkstums- und Rassenforschung. *Volk und Rasse* 2: 1–11.

Fischer, Eugen (1927b). *Rasse und Rassenentstehung beim Menschen.* Berlin: Ullstein.

Fischer, Eugen (1933). Untersuchungen über die süddeutsche Brachykephalie. III: Die Gebeine aus dem kararolingischen Kloster Lorsch. *Zeitschrift für Morphologie und Anthropologie* 31: 283–98.

Fischer, Eugen (1934). Rassenkreuzung. *Volk und Rasse* 8: 247–51.

Fischer, Eugen (1935). Hans F. K. Günther: Der Rassen-Günther. *Mein Heimatland* 22: 219–21.

Fischer, Eugen (1936a). Rassenkreuzung und geistige Leistung. *Internationales Ärztliches Bulletin* March/April 1936: 35.

Fischer, Eugen (1936b). Die gesunden körperlichen Erbanlagen des Menschen. In: Erwin Baur, Eugen Fischer and Fritz Lenz, eds, *Menschliche Erblehre*. Menschliche Erblehre und Rassenhygiene, vol. 1. München: J. F. Lehmann, pp. 95–320.

Fischer, Eugen (1940). Die menschlichen Rassen als Gruppen mit gleichen Gen-Sätzen. *Abhandlungen der Preussischen Akademie der Wissenschaften.* Jahrgang 1940. Mathematisch-naturwissenschaftliche Klasse, Nr. 3. Berlin: Verlag der Akademie der Wissenschaften.

Fischer, Eugen and Hans F. K. Günther. (1927). *Deutsche Köpfe nordischer Rasse.* München: J. F. Lehmann.

Fischer, Eugen and Gerhard Kittel (1943). *Das antike Weltjudentum: Tatsachen, Texte, Bilder.* Hamburg: Hanseatische Verlagsanstalt.

Fleure, Herbert John (1927). *The Races of Mankind.* London: Ernest Benn.

Friedrichs, Karl (1934). Vom Wesen der Ökologie. *Sudhoffs Archiv für Geschichte der Medizin und der Naturwissenschaften* 27: 277–85.

Frisch, Karl von (1936). *Du und das Leben.* Dr.-Goebbels-Spende für die deutsche Wehrmacht. Berlin: Deutscher Verlag.

Fritsch, Theodor (1933). *Handbuch der Judenfrage.* 35th ed. Leipzig: Hammer-Verlag.

Fritz, Georg (1934). *Kolonien? Das koloniale Schicksal des deutschen Volkes, geschichtlich als Lehre, politisch als Aufgabe.* Berlin: Zentral-Verlag.

Fritz, Georg (1935). *Südwanderung: Das Ende der nordischen Rasse.* Berlin: Richard Gahl.

Frobenius, Leo (1921). *Paideuma: Umrisse einer Kultur- und Seelenlehre.* München: C. H. Beck.

Garbe, Heinrich (1938). Von Spengler zu Gobineau: Weg und Ziel der rassischen Geschichtswertung. *Rasse: Monatschrift der Nordischen Bewegung* 5: 441–52.

Gauch, Herman (1933). *Neue Grundlagen der Rassenforschung.* Leipzig: Klein.

Gerlach, Kurt (1929). *Begabung und Stammesherkunft im deutschen Volk: Feststellungen über die Herkunft der deutschen Kulturschöpfer in Kartenbildern.* München: J. F. Lehmann.

Gercke, Achim (1934). *Das Gesetz der Sippe.* Berlin: Verlag für Standesamtwesen.

Gerstenhauer, Max R. (1913). *Rassenlehre und Rassenpflege.* Leipzig: Armanenverlag Robert Burger.

Glässer, Edgar (1939). *Einführung in die rassenkundliche Sprachforschung: Kritisch-historische Untersuchungen.* Heidelberg: Carl Winter.

Gobineau, Joseph Arthur, Comte de (1853–5). *Essai sur l'inégalité des races humaines.* Paris: Didot.

Goetz, Walter (1932). Rasse und Geschichte. In: *Rasse und Geist, vier Vorträge in der Senckenbergischen naturforschenden Gesellschaft in Frankfurt/Main 1930/31.* Leipzig: Johann Ambrosius Barth, pp. 72–8.

Goldstein, Kurt (1913). *Über Rassenhygiene.* Berlin: Julius Springer.

Gottschaldt, Kurt (1942). *Die Methodik der Persönlichkeit in der Erbpsychologie.* Leipzig: Johann Ambrosius.

Grabe, Heinrich (1938). Der Ganzheitsgedanke als Grundforderung der rassenkundlichen Unterweisung. *Der Biologe* 7: 145–9.

Gradmann, Robert (1926). Volkstum und Rasse in Süddeutschland. *Volk und Rasse* 1: 135–48.

Graf, Jakob (1935). *Vererbungslehre, Rassenkunde und Erbgesundheitspflege: Einführung nach methodologischen Grundsätzen.* 3rd revised edition. München: J. F. Lehmann.

Grahmann, Rudolf (1936). Lag die Urheimat der nordischen Rasse in Sibirien? *Rasse: Monatsschrift der Nordischen Bewegung* 3: 337–46.

Grant, Madison (1916). *The Passing of the Great Race.* New York: Scribner.

Gross, Walter (1934). Nationalsozialistische Rassenpolitik: Eine Rede an die deutschen Frauen. Berlin: Rassenpolitisches Amt.

Gross, Walter (1935). *Rassenpolitische Erziehung.* Schriften der Deutschen Hochschule für Politik, Heft 6. Berlin: Junker und Dünnhaupt.

Gross, Walter (1936). *Rasse, Weltanschauung, Wissenschaft: Zwei Universitätsreden.* Berlin: Junker und Dünnhaupt.

Gruber, Max von (1927). Volk und Rasse: Die Rassenfrage. *Süddeutsche Monatshefte* 24 (10): 244–8.

Günther, Hans F. K. (1922). *Rassenkunde des deutschen Volkes.* München: J. F. Lehmann. Subsequent editions, 1926, 1930, 1934.

Günther, Hans F. K. (1924). *Ritter, Tod und Teufel: Der heldische Gedanke.* 2nd edition. München: J. F. Lehmann.

Günther, Hans F. K. (1925). *Der nordische Gedanke unter den Deutschen.* München: J. F. Lehmann. 2nd revised edition, 1927.

Günther, Hans F. K. (1926). *Rasse und Stil.* München: J. F. Lehmann.

Günther, Hans F. K. (1927). Der Nordische Gedanke. *Süddeutsche Monatshefte* 24 (10): 273–80.

Günther, Hans F. K. (1930). *Rassenkunde des jüdischen Volkes.* München: J. F. Lehmann. Originally published as an appendix to *Rassenkunde des deutschen Volkes,* 1922.

Günther, Hans F. K. (1933). *Kleine Rassenkunde des deutschen Volkes.* München: J. F. Lehmann.

Günther, Hans F. K. (1934). *Die nordische Rasse bei den Indogermanen Asiens.* München: J. F. Lehmann.

Günther, Hans F. K./Der Nordischer Ring (1936). Indogermanentun und Germanentum rassenkundlich betrachtet. In: Helmuth Arntz, ed., *Germanen und Indogermanen: Volkstum, Sprache, Heimat, Kultur. Festschrift für Herman Hirt.* Volume 1: Ergebnisse der Kulturhistorie und Anthropologie. Heidelberg: Carl Winters, pp. 317–40.

Günther, Hans F. K. (1940). *Formen und Urgeschichte der Ehe.* München: J. F. Lehmann.

Haas, Otto (1941). Pro and Con Evolution in Contemporary Germany. *Science* (New Series) 93 (2402): 41–1.

Haase-Bessell, Gertraud (1939). *Volk und Rasse in ihren Beziehungen zueinander.* Schriften zur Geopolitik, Heft 17. Heidelberg: Kurt Vowinckel.

Haeckel, Ernst (1899). *Über unsere gegenwärtige Kenntniss vom Ursprung des Menschen.* Vortrag gehalten auf dem Vierten Internationalen Zoologen-Congress in Cambridge am 26. August 1898. Bonn: Emil Strauss.

Haeckel, Ernst (1922). *Die Welträtsel: Gemeinverständliche Studien über Monistische Philosophie.* Leipzig: Alfred Kröner. First published, 1899.

Hamacher, Jakob (1942). Probleme der Entwicklungslehre. *Kosmos* 39 (1): 13–15, 26–8, 50–1, 72–3, 104–6.

Härtle, Heinrich (1941). Nationalsozialistische Philosophie? *Nationalsozialistische Monatshefte* 12: 723–41.

Hartnacke, Wilhelm (1937). Bemerkungen zu Ernst Krieck's '*Völkisch-politische Anthropologie*'. *Volk und Rasse* 12: 391–4.

Hartnacke, Wilhelm (1944). *Seelenkunde vom Erbgedanken aus.* 3rd edition. München: J. F. Lehmann.

Hauser, Otto (1924). *Rasse und Kultur.* Braunschweig and Hamburg: G. Westermann.

Hauser, Otto (1930). *Der blonde Mensch.* 2nd edition. Danzig and Leipzig: Verlag Der Mensch.

Heberer, Gerhard (1940). Die jüngere Stammesgeschichte der Menschen. In: Günther Just, ed., *Die Grundlagen der Erbbiologie des Menschen.* Handbuch der Erbbiologie des Menschen, vol. 1. Berlin: Julius Springer, pp. 584–644.

Heberer, Gerhard, ed. (1943). *Die Evolution der Organismen: Ergebnisse und Probleme der Abstammungslehre.* Jena: Gustav Fischer.

Hecht, Günther (1937). Biologie und Nationalsozialismus. *Zeitschrift für die gesamte Naturwissenschaft* 3: 280–90.

Heiss, Robert (1936). *Die Lehre vom Charakter.* Berlin/Leipzig: Walter de Gruyter.

Hellpach, Willy (1926). Rasse und Stämme im Deutschen Volkstum. *Neue Rundschau*, Heft 2, February 1926, pp. 113–38.

Helm, Carl (1923). *Arier, Wilde und Juden.* Wien: C.W. Stern.

Hennig, Hans (1933). *Ursprung der nordischen Philosophie: Die ältesten Kulturquellen nördlich der Alpen.* Berlin: Junker & Dünnhaupt.

Hennig, Richard (1931). *Geopolitik.* 2nd edition. Leipzig: Teubner.

Herder, Johann Gottfried von (1784–91). *Ideen zur Philosophie der Geschichte der Menschheit.* 4 vols. Riga: Johann Friedrich Hartknoch.

Herling, H. and Wilhelm Hildebrandt (1935). *Rassenmischung und Krankheit.* Stuttgart: Hippokrates.

Herpel, Martin (c.1933). Hermann Schwarz und die Nordische Gedanke. *Reden und Aufsätze zum nordischen Gedanken herausgegeben von Dr. Bernard Kummer*, Heft 8. Leipzig: Adolf Klein Verlag.

Herrmann, Albert (1934). *Unsere Ahnen und Atlantis: Nordische Seeherrschaft von Skandinavien bis nach Nordafrika.* Berlin: Klinkhardt und Biermann.

Herskovits, Melville J. (1934). A critical discussion of the 'Mulatto' hypothesis. *The Journal of Negro Education* 3: 389–402.

Hertwig, Paula (1940). Mutationen bei den Säugetiren und die Frage ihrer Entstehung durch kurzwellige Strahlen und Keimgifte. In: Günther Just, ed., *Die Grundlagen der Erbbiologie des Menschen*. Handbuch der Erbbiologie des Menschen, vol. 1. Berlin: Julius Springer, pp. 245–87.

Hertz, Friedrich (1925). *Rasse und Kultur: Eine kritische Untersuchung der Rassentheorien*. 3rd revised edition. Leipzig: Alfred Kröner.

Hervé, Georges (1912). Enquête sur les croisements ethniques. *Revue anthropologique* 22: 337–406.

Hesch, Michael (1934). Die nordische Rasse im Aufbau des deutschen Volkes. *Rasse: Monatsschrift der Nordischen Bewegung* 1: 57–69.

Hesch, Michael (1935) 'Vineta' in polnischer Beurteilung. *Rasse: Monatsschrift der Nordischen Bewegung* 2: 485.

Hildebrandt, Kurt (1935). Positivismus und Natur. *Zeitschrift für die gesamte Naturwissenschaft* 1: 1–22.

Hildebrandt, Kurt (1942). *Goethe, seine Weltweisheit im Gesamtwerk*. 2nd edition. Leipzig: Reclam.

Hitler, Adolf (1925–6). *Mein Kampf.* 2 vols. Munich: Franz Eher. Translated by Ralph Manheim, with an introduction by D. C. Watt. London: Pimlico, 1992.

Hoff, Richard von (1934). Rassenmaterialismus? *Rasse: Monatsschrift der Nordischen Bewegung* 1: 145–51.

Holler, Kurt (1934). Übersicht über die Nordische Bewegung im letzten Jahre. *Rasse: Monatsschrift der Nordischen Bewegung* 1: 31–48.

Holler, Kurt (1935a). 'Deutsche Rasse'. *Rasse: Monatsschrift der Nordischen Bewegung* 2: 31–2.

Holler, Kurt (1935b). Der Fall Saller. *Rasse: Monatsschrift der Nordischen Bewegung* 2: 115–17.

Holler, Kurt (1938). Aus den Richtlinien des Reichserziehungsministeriums für den Biologieunterricht. *Rasse: Monatsschrift der Nordischen Bewegung* 5: 468–70.

Hooton, Earnest (1935). Homo Sapiens – whence and wither. *Science* 82: 19–31.

Horkheimer, Max and Theodor W. Adorno ([1947] 1973). *Dialectic of Enlightenment*. Translated by John Cumming. London: Allen Lane, 1973. First published as *Philosophische Fragmente*. Amsterdam: Querido Verlag, 1947.

Hunke, Sigrid (1936). 'Verstehen'. *Rasse: Monatsschrift der Nordischen Bewegung* 3: 86–91.

Jakesch, Wilhelm (1909). *Die Schicksale der blonden Rasse: Die Kämpfe in Böhmen im Spiegel der Weltgeschichte. Zwei Vorträge, 1907*. Leipzig: Müller-Mannsche Verlagsbuchhandlung.

Johannes, Martin Otto (1934). Aufnordung. *Volk und Rasse* 9: 111–12.

Johannsen, Wilhelm (1909). *Elemente der exakten Erblichkeitslehre: Deutsche wesentlich erweiterte Ausgabe in fünfundzwanzig Vorlesungen*. Jena: G. Fischer.

Jones, Sir William (1786). The Third Anniversary Discourse, delivered by the President, February 2, 1786. *Asiatic Researches* 1: 415–31.

Jordan, Pascual (1935). *Physikalisches Denken in der neuen Zeit.* Hamburg: Hanseatische Verlagsanstalt.

Just, Günther, ed. (1940a). *Die Grundlagen der Erbbiologie des Menschen.* Handbuch der Erbbiologie des Menschen, vol. 1. Berlin: Julius Springer.

Just, Günther (1940b). Die mendelistischen Grundlagen der Erbbiologie des Menschen. In Günther Just, ed., *Die Grundlagen der Erbbiologie des Menschen.* Handbuch der Erbbiologie des Menschen, vol. 1. Berlin: Julius Springer, pp. 371–460.

Kant, Immanuel (1798a). *Anthropologie in pragmatischer Hinsicht.* In: *Kants gesammelte Schriften,* vol. 7. Berlin: Reimer, 1907. Trans. *Anthropology from a Pragmatic Point of View.* Translated by Victor Lyle Dowdell, with an introduction by Frederick P. Van de Pitte. Carbondale & Edwardsville: Southern Illinois University, 1978.

Kant, Immanuel (1798b). Der Streit der Fakultäten. In: *Kants gesammelte Schriften,* vol. 7. Berlin: Reimer, 1907.

Kaufmann, F. W. (1942). Fichte and National Socialism. *The American Political Science Review* 36: 460–70.

Kaup, Ignaz (1925). *Süddeutsches Germanentum und Leibeszucht der Jugend.* München: Verlag der Gesundheitsmacht.

Keiter, Freidrich (1936). *Menschenrassen in Vergangenheit und Gegenwart.* Leipzig: Reclam.

Keiter, Freidrich (1938–40). *Rasse und Kultur: Eine Kulturbilanz der Menschenrassen als Weg zur Rassenseelenkunde.* 3 vols. Ferdinand Enke: Stuttgart.

Keiter, Friedrich (1941). *Kurzes Lehrbuch der Rassenbiologie und Rassenhygiene für Mediziner.* Stuttgart: Ferdinand Enke.

Kern, Fritz (1927). *Stammbaum und Artbild der Deutschen und ihrer Verwandten: Ein kultur- und rassengeschichtlicher Versuch.* München: J. F. Lehmann.

Keudel, Karl (1935). Zur Geschichte und Kritik der Grundbegriffe der Vererbungslehre. *Sudhoffs Archiv für Geschichte der Medizin und der Naturwissenschaften* 28: 381–416.

Klages, Ludwig (1934). Vom Wesen des Rhythmus. *Sudhoffs Archiv für Geschichte der Medizin und der Naturwissenschaften* 27: 223–8.

Klages, Ludwig (1936). *Grundlegung der Wissenschaft vom Ausdruck.* 5th revised edition. Leipzig: Johann Ambrosius Barth.

Köhn-Behrens, Charlotte (1934). *Was ist Rasse? Gespräche mit den grössten deutschen Forschern der Gegenwart.* München: Eher.

Kossinna, Gustaf (1936). *Ursprung und Verbreitung der Germanen in vor- und frühgeschichlicher Zeit.* 3rd edition. Leipzig: Curt Kabitzsch. First published in two parts, 1926 and 1927.

Kranz, Heinrich Wilhelm (1940). Erbforschung über den angeborenen Schwachsinn. In: Johannes Schottky and Otmar von Verschuer, eds, *Fortschritte der Erbpathologie, Rassenhygiene und ihrer Grenzgebiete,* vol. 4. Leipzig: Georg Theime, pp. 1–48.

Kretschmer, Ernst (1931). *Körperbau und Charakter: Untersuchungen zum Konstitutionsproblem und zur Lehre von den Temperamenten.* Revised 9th and 10th editions. Berlin: Julius Springer.

Kretschmer, Ernst (1932). Genie und Rasse. In: *Rasse und Geist: Vier Vorträge in der Senckenbergischen naturforschenden Gesellschaft in Frankfurt/Main 1930/31.* Leipzig: Johann Ambrosius Barth, pp. 58–71.

Krieck, Ernst (1932). *Nationalpolitische Erziehung.* Leipzig: Aramanen Verlag.

Krieck, Ernst (1936). *Völkisch-politische Anthropologie.* Leipzig: Armanen.

Kuhn, Philalethes and Heinrich Wilhelm Kranz (1936). *Von deutschen Ahnen für deutsche Enkel: Allgemeinverständliche Darstellung der Erblichkeitslehre, der Rassenkunde und der Rassenhygiene.* München: J. F. Lehmann. First published, 1933.

Kulz, Werner (1939). Die politisch-weltanschauliche Bedeutung der Arbeiten Otto Reches. In: Michael Hesch and Günther Spannaus, eds, *Kultur und Rasse: Otto Reche zum 60. Geburtstag.* München: J. F. Lehmann, pp. 9–22.

Künkel, Fritz (1944). *Einführung in die Charakterkunde.* Leipzig: S. Hirzel.

Künneth, Walter (1935). *Antwort auf den Mythus: Die Entscheidung zwischen dem nordischen Mythus und dem biblischen Christus.* Berlin: Wichern.

Laing, Samuel (1895). *Human Origins.* London: Chapman and Hall. First published, 1862.

Lapouge, Georges Vacher de (1897). The fundamental laws of anthroposociology. Translated by Carlos C. Closson. *The Journal of Political Economy* 6: 54–92.

Lapouge, Georges Vacher de (1899). *L'Aryen: son rôle social.* Cours libre de science politique professé à l'Université de Montpellier (1889–1890). Paris: A. Fontemoing. Published in German as *Der Arier und seine Bedeutung für die Gemeinschaft: Freier Kursus in Staatskunde, gehalten an der Universität Montpellier 1889–1890.* Frankfurt am Main: M. Diesterweg, 1939. Quotations cited from 'Old and new aspects of the Aryan question'. Translated by Carlos C. Closson from *L'Aryen. The American Journal of Sociology* 5: 329–46.

Leers, Johann von (1936). Die Kriminalität des Judentums. In: *Judentum und Verbrechen.* Berlin: Deutscher Rechtsverlag, pp. 5–60.

Leers, Johann von (1938). *Rassen, Völker und Volkstümer.* Berlin and Leipzig: Julius Barth.

Lehmann, Ernst (1934a). Book notice: Heinrich Schmidt, *Ernst Haeckel: Denkmal eines grossen Lebens.* Jena: Frommannsche Buchhandlung, 1934. *Der Biologe* 3: 132.

Lehmann, Ernst (1934b). Protest. *Der Biologe* 3: 63–4.

Lehmann, Ernst (1935). Die Biologie an der Zeitenwende. *Der Biologe* 4: 375–81.

Lemmel, Herbert (1941). *Die Volksgemeinschaft, ihre Erfassung im werdenden Recht.* Stuttgart: Kohlhammer.

Lenz, Fritz (1923a). Die krankhaftem Erbanlagen. In: Erwin Baur, Eugen Fischer and Fritz Lenz, eds, *Menschliche Erblehre. Menschliche Erblehre und Rassenhygiene*, vol. 1. München: J. F. Lehmann, pp. 155–442.

Lenz, Fritz (1923b). *Menschliche Auslese und Rassenhygiene.* 2nd revised edition. München: J. F. Lehmann. Revised third edition, 1931.

Lenz, Fritz (1925). *Über die biologischen Grundlagen der Erziehung.* München: J. F. Lehmann.

Lenz, Fritz (1927a). Das Schicksal unserer Rasse. *Süddeutsche Monatshefte* 24 (10): 265–8.

Lenz, Fritz (1927b). Nordisch oder deutsch? *Süddeutsche Monatshefte* 24 (10): 287–90.

Lenz, Fritz (1934). Über Rassen und Rassenbildung. *Unterrichtsblätter für Mathematik und Naturwissenschaften* 40: 177–89.

Lenz, Fritz (1936). Die krankhaften Erbanlagen. In: Erwin Baur, Eugen Fischer and Fritz Lenz, eds, *Menschliche Erblehre. Menschliche Erblehre und Rassenhygiene*, vol. 1. München: J. F. Lehmann, pp. 321–773.

Lenz, Fritz (1937). Zur Frage der unehelichen Kinder. *Volk und Rasse* 12: 91–5.

Lenz, Siegfried (1940). Über Fortpflanzung und Ehehäufigkeit in Berlin. *Volk und Rasse* 15: 125–8.

Leonhardt, Ludwig (1934). Deutsche Rasse oder Nordische Rasse im deutschen Volk? *Volk und Rasse* 9: 188–90.

Lorenz, Konrad (1940). Durch Domestikation verursachte Störungen arteigenen Verhaltens. *Zeitschrift für angewandte Psychologie und Charakterkunde* 59: 2–81.

Marr, Wilhelm (1879). *Der Sieg des Judentums über das Germanentum: Vom nicht-confessionellen Standpunkt aus betrachtet.* Bern: Rudolph Costenoble.

Martin, Rudolf (1914). *Lehrbuch der Anthropologie in systematischer Darstellung mit besonderer Berücksichtigung der anthropologischen Methoden für Studierende Ärzte und Forschungsreisende.* Jena: G. Fischer. 2nd edition in 3 vols, 1928. 3rd edition in 3 vols, prepared by Karl Saller, 1957–66.

Merkenschlager, Friedrich (1927). *Götter, Helden und Günther: Eine Abwehr der Günther'schen Rassenkunde.* Nürnberg: Spindler.

Merkenschlager, Friedrich (1933). *Rassensonderung, Rassenmischung, Rassenwandlung.* Berlin: Waldemar Hoffmann Verlag.

Merkenschlager, Friedrich (1934). *Zwischen Hünengrab und Pfahlbau: Die Urlebensstile der europäischen Kultur.* Berlin: Waldemar Hoffmann.

Merkenschlager, Friedrich and Karl Saller (1934). *Ofnet: Wanderungen zu den Mälern der Deutschen Rasse.* Berlin: K. Wolff.

Merkenschlager, Friedrich and Karl Saller (1935). *Vineta: Eine deutsche Biologie von Osten her geschrieben.* Breslau: W. G. Korn.

Merle, Walter (1936). *Guttmanns medizinische Terminologie: Ableitung und Erklärung der gebräuchlichsten Fachausdrücke aller Zweige der Medizin und ihrer Hilfswissenschaften.* Berlin: Urban and Schwarzenberg.

Meyer, Adolf [= Adolf Meyer-Abich] (1934). Das Organische und seine Ideologien. *Sudhoffs Archiv für Geschichte der Medizin und der Naturwissenschaften* 27: 3–19.

Meyer, Erich and Karl Zimmermann (1942). *Lebenskunde: Lehrbuch der Biologie für die Höhere Schulen.* Volume 4. 2nd edition. Erfurt: Kurt Stenger.

[ML] (1936). *Meyers Lexikon.* 9 vols. 8th edition. Leipzig: Bibliographisches Institut.

Mollinson, Theodor (1913/14). Review of Eugen Fischer, *Die Rehobother Bastards.* Jena: Gustav Fischer, 1913. *Zeitschrift für Morphologie und Anthropologie* 16: 397–404.

Mollinson, Theodor (1934). Rassenkunde und Rassenhygiene. In: Ernst Rüdin, ed., *Rassenhygiene im völkischen Staat: Tatsachen und Richtlinien.* München: J. F. Lehmann, pp. 34–48.

Montriou, J. A. L. (*c.*1787). *Elements of Universal History: For Youth: Faithfully Extracted from the Best Authors, Carefully Abridged Agreeable to the most Exact Chronology.* London: printed for the author by Fry and Couchman.

Muckermann, Hermann (1932). *Rassenforschung und Volk der Zukunft.* Berlin: Alfred Metzner.

Muckermann, Hermann (1933). *Volkstum, Staat und Nation eugenisch gesehen.* 3rd unrevised edition. Essen: Fredebeul and Koenen. First published, 1932.

Muckermann, Hermann (1934a). *Eugenik und Katholizismus.* Berlin and Bonn: Ferdinand Dümmler.

Muckermann, Hermann (1934b). *Eugenik.* Berlin: Ferdinand Dümmler.

Muckermann, Hermann (1935). *Grundriss der Rassenkunde.* 2nd edition. Paderborn: Ferdinand Schöningh.

Mühlmann, Wilhelm (1936). *Rassen- und Völkerkunde: Lebensprobleme der Rassen, Gesellschaften und Völker.* Braunschweig: Vieweg.

Müller, Friedrich Max (1871–81). *Chips from a German Workshop.* 2 vols. New York: C. Scribner and Company.

Müller, Friedrich Max (1888). *Biographies of Words and the Home of the Aryas.* London/New York: Longmans, Green. Reprinted, 1912.

Nachtsheim, Hans (1936). *Von Wildtier zum Haustier.* Berlin: Metzner.

Nicolai, Georg Friedrich (1917). *Die Biologie des Krieges: Betrachtungen eines deutschen Naturforschers.* Zürich: Orell Füssli.

[NSLB] (1933). *Bekenntnis der Professoren an den deutschen Universitäten und Hochschulen zu Adolf Hitler und dem nationalsozialistischen Staat.* English title: *Vow of Allegiance of the Professors of the German Universities and High-Schools to Adolf Hitler and the National Socialistic State.* Überreicht vom Nationalsozialistischen Lehrerbund Deutschland/Sachsen: Dresden.

Opler, Morris Edward (1945). The bio-social basis of thought in the Third Reich. *American Sociological Review* 10: 776–86.

Padover, Saul K. (1943). Japanese race propaganda. *Public Opinion Quarterly* 7: 191–204.

Parsons, James (1767). *Remains of Japhet: Being Historical Enquiries into the Affinity and Origin of the European Languages.* London: printed for the author and sold by L. Davis.

Pastenaci, Kurt (1933). *Das viertausendjährige Reich der Deutschen: Ein Geschichtsbild der nationalen Revolution.* Veröffentlichung der Gesellschaft für germanische Ur- und Vorgeschichte. Berlin: Walter Kemmesies.

Pastenaci, Kurt (1935). *Das Licht aus dem Norden: Eine kurzgefasste Darstellung der frühesten Kulturschöpfungen des nordischen Menschen.* Berlin: Nordland.

Paul, Alexander (1940). *Jüdisch-deutsche Blutsmischung: Eine sozialbiologische Untersuchung.* Inaugural dissertation, Friedrich-Wilhelms-Universität zu Berlin. Schriftenreihe aus dem Arbeitsgebiet der Abteilung 'Volksgesundheit' des Reichsministerium des Innern. Berlin: Richard Schoetz.

Paul, Gustav (1936). *Grundzüge der Rassen- und Raumgeschichte des deutschen Volkes.* München: J. F. Lehmann.

Paulsen, Jens (1937). Der ewige Kampf der Westischen Rasse gegen die Nordische. *Deutschlands Erneuerung* 21: 652–6.

Pearson, Karl (1903). The law of ancestral heredity. *Biometrika* 2: 211–36.

Pearson, Karl (1936). On Jewish-Gentile relationships. *Biometrika* 28: 32–3.

Penka, Karl (1883). *Origines Ariacae: Linguistisch-ethnologische Untersuchungen zur ältesten Geschichte der arischen Völker und Sprachen.* Wien and Teschen: K. Prochaska.

Penka, Karl (1886). *Die Herkunft der Arier: Neue Beiträge zur historischen Anthropologie der europäischen Völker.* Wien and Teschen: K. Prochaska.

Petermann, Bruno (1935). *Das Problem der Rassenseele.* Leipzig: Johann Ambrosius Barth.

Pezron, Paul (1706). *The Antiquities of Nations: more particularly of the Celtæ or Gauls, taken to be originally the same people as our ancient Britains. Containing great variety of historical, chronological, and etymological discoveries, many of them unknown both to the Greeks and Romans.* London: Printed by R. Janeway. First published as *Antiquité de la nation et de la langue des Celtes, autrement appellez Gaulois.* Paris: Jean Boudot, 1703.

Pfahler, Gerhard (1938). *Warum Erziehung trotz Vererbung?* 3rd edition. Leipzig: Teubner.

Pfahler, Gerhard (1943). *System der Typenlehre.* 4th edition. Leipzig: Johann Ambrosius Barth.

Plate, Ludwig (c.1909). *Charles Darwin: Festschrift des Deutschen Monistenbundes zu seinem 100. Geburtstage.* Berlin: Im Verlag des Deutschen Monistenbundes.

Plate, Ludwig (1932). *Vererbungslehre.* Volume 1: *Mendelismus.* 2nd edition. Jena: Gustav Fischer.

Plate, Ludwig (1934). Umweltlehre und Nationalsozialismus. *Rasse: Monatsschrift der Nordischen Bewegung* 1: 279–83.

Ploetz, Alfred (1895). *Die Tüchtigkeit unserer Rasse und der Schutz der Schwachen: Ein Versuch über Rassenhygiene und ihr Verhältnis zu den humanen Idealen, besonders zum Sozialismus.* Berlin: Fischer.

Ploetz, Alfred (1911). Die Begriffe Rasse und Gesellschaft und einige damit zusammenhängende Probleme. *Schriften der deutschen Gesellschaft für Soziologie* 1: 111–36.

Ploetz, Alfred (1927). Rasse und Menschheit. *Süddeutsche Monatshefte* 24 (10): 248–53.

Rabes, Otto (1934). *Vererbung und Rassenpflege*. Versuche und Stoff für den Unterricht und Rassenpflege. Heft 1. Leipzig: Quelle and Meyer.

Rauschenberger, Walther (1938). Der Einfluss der fälischen Rasse auf die deutsche Kultur. *Rasse: Monatsschrift der Nordischen Bewegung* 5: 262–75.

Rauschenberger, Walter (1939a). Friedrich Nietzsches Rassenmerkmale. *Familie, Sippe, Volk* 5: 5–11.

Rauschenberger, Walter (1939b). Beethovens Abstammung und Rassenmerkmale. *Familie, Sippe, Volk* 5: 114–19.

Rauschenberger, Walter (1941). Rassenmerkmale Schillers und seiner näheren Verwandten. *Familie, Sippe, Volk* 7: 23–4.

Reche, Otto (1921). Rasse und Sprache. *Archiv für Anthropologie* NS 18: 208–18.

Reche, Otto (1933). *Die Rassen des deutschen Volkes.* Leipzig: F. E. Wachsmuth.

Reche, Otto (1936a). *Rasse und Heimat der Indogermanen*. München: J. F. Lehmann.

Reche, Otto (1936b). Entstehung der Norischen Rasse und Indogermanenfrage. In: Helmuth Arntz, ed., *Germanen und Indogermanen: Volkstum, Sprache, Heimat, Kultur. Festschrift für Herman Hirt.* Volume 1: Ergebnisse der Kulturhistorie und Anthropologie. Heidelberg: Carl Winters, pp. 287–316.

Reche, Otto (1943). Herkunft und Entstehung der Negerrassen. In: Günther Wolff, ed., *Koloniale Völkerkunde, koloniale Sprachforschung, koloniale Rassenforschung.* Berichte über die Arbeitstagung im January 1943 in Leipzig. Beiträge zur Kolonialforschung I. Berlin: Dietrich Reimer; Andrews & Steiner, pp. 152–67.

Rein, Adolf (1933). *Die Idee der politischen Universität.* Hamburg: Hanseatische Verlagsanstalt.

Richthofen, Bolko, Freiherr von (1942). Bolschewistische Wissenschaft und Judentum. In: Bolko Freiherr von Richthofen, ed., *Bolschewistische Wissenschaft und Kulturpolitik: Ein Sammelwerk.* Königsberg (Pruss.): Ost-Europa Verlag, pp. 289–318.

Riedel, Kurt (1937). Wer hat den Ausdruck 'nordische Rasse' geprägt? *Volk und Rasse* 12: 72–3.

Ripley, William Z. (1899). Deniker's classification of the races of Europe. *The Journal of the Royal Anthropological Institute of Great Britain and Ireland* 28: 166–73.

Ritter, Robert (1939). Die Zigeunerfrage und das Zigeunerbastardproblem. *Fortschritte der Erbpathologie, Rassenhygiene und ihrer Grenzgebiete* 3: 2–20.

Rittershaus, Ernst (1936). *Konstitution oder Rasse?* München: J. F. Lehmann.

Rodenwaldt, Ernst (1938). Das Rassenmischungsproblem. *Reichsgesundheitsblatt* 52 (Beiheft 4): 70–3.

Rodenwaldt, Ernst (1940). Allgemeine Rassenbiologie des Menschen. In: Günther Just *Die Grundlagen der Erbbiologie des Menschen*. Handbuch der Erbbiologie des Menschen, vol. 1. Berlin: Julius Springer, pp. 645–78.

Rosenberg, Alfred (1939). *Der Mythus des 20. Jahrhunderts: Eine Wertung der seelisch-geistigen Gestaltenkämpfe unserer Zeit*. München: Hoheneichen-Verlag. First published, 1930.

Rüsche, Franz (1937). *Blut und Geist*. Paderborn: Ferdinand Schöningh.

Ruttke, Falk (1937a). Erbpflege in der deutschen Gesetzgebung. In: *Bericht der 12. Versammlung der Internationalen Federation eugenischer Organisationen*. Konferenzsitzungen vom 15. bis 20. Juli 1936. London: IFEO Den Haag: W. P. van Stockum.

Ruttke, Falk (1937b). *Rasse, Recht und Volk*. Berlin: J. F. Lehmann.

Ruttke, Falk (1939). *Die Verteidigung der Rasse durch das Recht*. Berlin: Junker und Dünnhaupt.

Saller, Karl (1930). *Leitfaden der Anthropologie*. Berlin: Julius Springer.

Saller, Karl (1932). *Einführung in die menschliche Erblichkeitslehre und Eugenik*. Berlin: Julius Springer.

Saller, Karl (1933). Stand und Aufgaben der Eugenik. *Klinische Wochenschrift* 12: 1041–4.

Saller, Karl (1934). *Der Weg der deutschen Rasse*. 2nd edition. Leipzig: Felix Meiner.

Saller, Karl (1935). Erklärung an meine Hörer. Unpublished handout. Göttingen, 17 January 1935.

Sayce, A. H. (1888). Address to the Anthropological Section of the British Association at Manchester. *The Journal of the Anthropological Institute of Great Britain and Ireland* 17: 166–81.

Schaeppi, Hansjakob (1940/1). Über das Wesen der vergleichenden Morphologie. *Sudhoffs Archiv für Geschichte der Medizin und der Naturwissenschaften* 33: 173–86.

Schallmayer, Wilhelm (1918). *Vererbung und Auslese: Grundriss der Gesellschaftsbiologie und der Lehre vom Rassedienst für Rassehygieniker, Bevölkerungspolitiker*. Jena: Fischer.

Scheidt, Walter (1930a). *Rassenkunde*. Leipzig: Reclam.

Scheidt, Walter (1930b). Die nordische Rasse. In: Hans Friedrich Blunck, ed., *Die nordische Welt: Geschichte, Wesen und Bedeutung der nordischen Völker*. Berlin: Im Propyläen-Verlag, pp. 501–15.

Scheidt, Walter (1941). Die älteste bisher bekannte deutsche Schrift über Rassenhygiene 'De poluteknia eruditorum' von Joh. Paul Gumprecht aus dem Jahre 1717. *Sudhoffs Archiv für Geschichte der Medizin und der Naturwissenschaften* 34: 152–61.

Schmidt, Wilhelm (1927). *Rasse und Volk: Eine Untersuchung zur Bestimmung ihrer Grenzen und zur Erfassung ihrer Beziehungen*. München: Kösel and Pustet.

Schmidt[-Rohr], Georg (1917). *Unsere Muttersprache als Waffe und Werkzeug des deutschen Gedankens*. Tat-Flugschriften 20. Jena: Eugen Diederichs.

Schmidt-Rohr, Georg (1932). *Die Sprache als Bildnerin der Völker: Eine Wesens- und Lebenskunde der Volkstümer.* Jena: Diederichs.

Schmidt-Rohr, Georg (1933). *Mutter Sprache: Vom Amt der Sprache bei der Volkwerdung.* Jena: Diederichs.

Schmidt-Rohr, Georg (1934). Volkserziehung durch Sprachpflege. *Mitteilungen der Akademie zur wissenschaftlichen Erforschung und zur Pflege des Deutschtums* 3 (3): 378–81.

Schmidt-Rohr, Georg (1939a). Die zweite Ebene der Volkserhaltung. *Rasse: Monatsschrift für den Nordischen Gedanken* 6 (3): 81–9.

Schmidt-Rohr, Georg (1939b). Rasse und Sprache. *Rasse: Monatsschrift für den Nordischen Gedanken* 6: 161–8.

Schneider, Guido (1934). K. E. von Baer gegen Darwin. *Sudhoffs Archiv für Geschichte der Medizin und der Naturwissenschaften* 27: 494–8.

Schreiner, Helmuth (1934). Die Rasse als Weltanschauungsprinzip. In: Walter Künneth and Helmuth Schreiner, eds, *Die Nation vor Gott: Zur Botschaft der Kirche im Dritten Reich.* Berlin: Wichern, pp. 62–96.

Schultze, Walter (1934). Die Bedeutung der Rassenhygiene für Staat und Volk. In: Ernst Rüdin, ed., *Rassenhygiene im völkischen Staat: Tatsachen und Richtlinien.* München: J. F. Lehmann, pp. 1–21.

Schwab, Julius (1937). *Rassenpflege im Sprichwort: Eine volkstümliche Sammlung.* Leipzig: Alwin Fröhlich.

Schwidetzky, Ilse (1938). Soziale Siebung im Oberschlesien. *Zeitschrift für Rassenkunde und die gesamte Forschung am Menschen* 8: 167–92.

Seiler, Jakob (1928). Darwinsche Auslesetheorie und moderne Genetik. *Süddeutsche Monatshefte* 25: 405–9.

Shaler, Nathaniel S. (1904). *The Neighbor: The Natural History of Human Contacts.* Boston and New York: Houghton, Mifflin.

Siegert, Hans (1941/2). Zur Geschichte der Begriffe 'Arier' und 'arisch'. *Wörter und Sachen: Zeitschrift für indogermanische Sprachwissenschaft, Volksforschung und Kulturgeschichte.* NS 4: 73–99.

Siemens, Hermann Werner (1923). *Grundzüge der Rassenhygiene, zugleich Einführung in die Vererbungslehre.* 2nd edition. München: J. F. Lehmann. First published, 1916.

Siemens, Hermann Werner (1937). *Grundzüge der Vererbungslehre: Rassenhygiene und Bevölkerungspolitik.* 8th revised edition. München: J. F. Lehmann. Revised edition of Siemens (1923).

Spelter, Josef (1937). *Der deutsche Erzieher als Lehrer der Rassenkunde.* Landsberg (Warthe): Pfeiffer.

Spengler, Oswald [1922] (1993). *Der Untergang des Abendlandes: Umrisse einer Morphologie der Weltgeschichte.* München: C. H. Beck.

Spengler, Oswald (1933). *Jahre der Entscheidung.* Part 1: *Deutschland und die weltgeschichtliche Entwicklung.* München: Beck.

Staemmler, Martin (1935). *Rassenpflege im völkischen Staat.* Gekürzter Sonderdruck für das Rassenpolitisches Amt der NSDAP. 2nd edition. München: J. F. Lehmann.

Staemmler, Martin (1936). Rassenkunde und Rassenpflege. In: Heinz Woltereck, ed., *Erbkunde, Rassenpflege, Bevölkerungspolitik: Schicksals-*

fragen des deutschen Volkes. 3rd revised edition. Leipzig: Quelle & Meyer, pp. 97–202.

Steinthal, Heymann (1896). Dialekt, Sprache, Volk, Staat, Rasse. In: *Festschrift für Adolf Bastian zu seinem 70. Geburtstage.* Berlin: Dietrich Reimer, pp. 47–51.

Stengel von Rutkowski, Lothar (1936). *Grundzüge der Erbkunde und Rassenpflege.* Berlin-Lichterfelde: Langewort.

Stratz, Carl Heinrich (1904). *Naturgeschichte des Menschen.* Stuttgart: Ferdinand Enke.

Surén, Hans (1936). *Mensch und Sonne: Arisch-olympischer Geist.* 3rd edition. Berlin: Scherl.

Thomalla, Curt, ed. [*c.*1935] *Gesund sein – gesund bleiben: Ein volkstümliches Hausbuch für den gesunden und kranken Menschen.* Berlin: Peters.

Thierfelder, Franz (1932). Die Sprache – Ausdruck oder Inbegriff des Volkstums? *Mitteilungen der Akademie zur wissenschaftlichen Erforschung und zur Pflege des Deutschtums* 2: 255–8.

Tirala, Lothar Gottlieb (1934a). Rassenmischung. *Volk und Rasse* 9 (6): 185–8.

Tirala, Lothar Gottlieb (1934b). Rassenhygiene oder Eugenik. *Volk und Rasse* 9 (11): 353–7.

Tirala, Lothar Gottlieb (1935). *Rasse, Geist und Seele.* München: J. F. Lehmann.

Topinard, Paul (1885). *Eléments d'anthropologie générale.* Paris: Delahaye et Lecrosnier.

[UB] (1941). *Friedrich-Wilhelms-Universität Berlin: Personal- und Vorlesungsverzeichnis. Sommersemester 1941.* Berlin: Preussische Druckerei- und Verlags-Aktiengesellschaft.

Ullmann, Hermann (1936). *Das neunzehnte Jahrhundert: Volk gegen Masse im Kampf um die Gestalt Europas.* Jena: Eugen Diederichs.

Ulmenstein, Freiherr Christian Ulrich (1941). *Der Abstammungsnachweis.* Berlin: Verlag für Standesamtswesen.

Verschuer, Otmar, Freiherr von (1934). Die Rasse als biologische Grösse. In: Walter Künneth and Helmuth Schreiner, eds, *Die Nation vor Gott: Zur Botschaft der Kirche im Dritten Reich.* Berlin: Wichern Verlag, pp. 44–61.

Verschuer, Otmar, Freiherr von (1938a). Rassenbiologie der Juden. *Sitzungsberichte der zweiten Arbeitstagung der Forschungsabteilung des Reichsinstitut für Geschichte des neuen Deutschlands vom 5–7 Juli, 1938* 3: 137–51.

Verschuer, Otmar, Freiherr von (1938b). Eugen Fischers Werk über die Rehobother Bastards. *Der Erbarzt* 5: 137–9.

Verschuer, Otmar, Freiherr von (1941). *Leitfaden der Rassenhygiene.* Leipzig: Thieme.

Verschuer, Otmar, Freiherr von (1944). *Erbanlage als Schicksal und Aufgabe.* Preussische Akademie der Wissenschaften Vorträge und Schriften 18. Berlin: Walter de Gruyter.

Viernstein, Theodor (1935). *Die biologische Untersuchung der Erbhofbauern.* München: R. Oldenbourg.

246 References: post-1945

Voegelin, Eric ([1933] 1998). *The History of the Race Idea: From Ray to Carus*. The Collected Works of Eric Voegelin, vol. 3. Edited by Klaus Vondung; translated by Ruth Hein. Baton Rouge: Louisiana State University Press, 1998. First published as *Die Rassenidee in der Geistesgeschichte von Ray bis Carus*. Berlin: Junker und Dünnhaupt, 1933.

Vossler, Karl (1936). Sprache und Nation. *Mitteilungen der Deutschen Akademie* 11 (3): 355–62.

Wachler, Ernst (1916/17). Was ist ein Deutscher? *Politisch-Anthropologische Monatsschrift für praktische Politik, für politische Bildung und Erziehung auf biologischer Grundlage* 15: 48–9.

Webb, John (1669). *An Historical Essay Endeavoring a Probability that the Language of the Empire of China is the Primitive Language*. London: Printed for Nath. Brook.

Weidenreich, Franz (1932). Die physischen Grundlagen der Rassenlehre. In: *Rasse und Geist: Vier Vorträge in der Senckenbergischen naturforschenden Gesellschaft in Frankfurt/Main 1930/31*. Leipzig: Johann Ambrosius Barth, pp. 5–27.

Weinert, Hans (1934). *Unsere Eiszeit-Ahnen*. Volk und Wissen 19. Berlin: Brehm.

Weisgerber, Johann Leo (1933). Sprachwissenschaft als lebendige Kraft unserer Zeit. *Mitteilungen der Akademie zur wissenschaftlichen Erforschung und zur Pflege des Deutschtums* 2: 224–31.

Weisgerber, Johann Leo (1933/34). Die Stellung der Sprache im Aufbau der Gesamtkultur. *Wörter und Sachen* 15: 134–224; 16: 97–236.

Weisgerber, Johann Leo (1939). *Die volkhaften Kräfte der Muttersprache*. 2nd edition. Frankfurt am Main: Diesterweg. Originally published in *Beiträge zum neuen Deutschunterricht*. Edited by Ministerialrat Dr Huhnrhäuser. Frankfurt am Main: Diesterweg, 1939.

Weismann, August (1885). *Die Continuität des Keimplasmas als Grundlage einer Theorie der Vererbung*. Jena: Gustav Fischer.

Wichler, Gerhard (1937/38). Alfred Russel Wallace (1823–1913), sein Leben, seine Arbeiten, sein Wesen. *Sudhoffs Archiv für Geschichte der Medizin und der Naturwissenschaften* 30: 364–400.

Wirth, Albrecht (1914). *Rasse und Volk*. Halle (Salle): Max Niemeyer.

Wolf, Karl Lothar and Wilhem Troll (1942). Goethes morphologischer Auftrag: Versuch einer naturwissenschaftlichen Morphologie. 2nd edition. Halle (Saale): Maxh Niemeyer.

Woltmann, Ludwig (1905). *Die Germanen und die Renaissance in Italien*. Leipzig: Thüringische Verlagsanstalt.

Academic commentaries (including all post-1945)

Aly, Götz (2003). *Rasse und Klasse: Nachforschungen zum deutschen Wesen*. Frankfurt am Main: Fischer.

Aly, Götz and Susanne Heim (1997). *Vordenker der Vernichtung: Auschwitz und die deutschen Pläne für eine neue europäische Ordnung*. Frankfurt am Main: Fischer.

Aly, Götz and Kark Heinz Roth (2004). *The Nazi Census: Identification and Control in the Third Reich.* Translated by Edwin Black. Philadelphia, Pa: Temple University Press.

Anderson, Benedict (1991). *Imagined Communities: Reflections on the Origin and Spread of Nationalism.* 2nd edition. London: Verso.

Ash, Mitchell (1995). *Gestalt Psychology in German Culture, 1890–1967: Holism and the Quest for Objectivity.* Cambridge: Cambridge University Press.

Ash, Mitchell (1999). Kurt Gottschaldt and psychological research in Nazi and Socialist Germany. In: Kristie Macrakis and Dieter Hoffmann, eds, *Science Under Socialism: East Germany in Comparative Perspective.* Cambridge, Mass.: Harvard University Press, pp. 285–365.

Ash, Mitchell (2002). Psychologie. In: Frank-Rutger Hausmann, ed., *Die Rolle der Geisteswissenschaften im Dritten Reich, 1933–1945.* München: Oldenbourg, pp. 229–64.

Assion, Peter (1994). Eugen Fehrle and 'the mythos of our folk'. In: James R. Dow and Hannjost Lixfeld, eds, *The Nazification of an Academic Discipline: Folklore in the Third Reich.* Bloomington, Ind.: Indiana University Press, pp. 112–34.

Ballantyne, Tony (2002). *Orientalism and Race: Aryanism in the British Empire.* Basingstoke: Palgrave.

Barkan, Elizar (1992). *The Retreat of Scientific Racism: Changing Concepts of Race in Britain and the United States between the World Wars.* Cambridge: Cambridge University Press.

Bastian, Till (2000). *Homosexuelle im Dritten Reich.* München: Beck.

Bauman, Zygmunt (1989). *Modernity and the Holocaust.* Ithaca, NY: Cornell University Press.

Bäumer, Änne (1990). *NS-Biologe.* Stuttgart: S. Hirzel.

Bavaj, Riccardo (2003). *Die Ambivalenz der Moderne im Nationalsozialismus: Eine Bilanz der Forschung.* München: Oldenbourg.

Benz, Wolfgang, Hermann Graml and Hermann Weiss, eds (1997). *Enzyklopädie des Nationalsozialismus.* München: Deutscher Taschenbuch Verlag.

Beyerchen, Alan (1997). Rational means and irrational ends: thoughts on the technology of racism in the Third Reich. *Central European History* 30: 386–402.

Birken-Bertsch, Hanno and Reinhard Markner (2000). *Rechtschreiberform und Nationalsozialismus: Ein Kapitel aus der politischen Geschichte der deutschen Sprache.* Göttingen: Wallstein.

Bock, Gisela (1986). *Zwangssterilisation im Nationalsozialismus: Studien zur Rassenpolitik und Frauenpolitik.* Opladen: Westdeutscher Verlag.

Bock, Gisela (1991). Krankenmord, Judenmord und nationalsozialistische Rassenpolitik: Überlegungen zu einigen neueren Forschungshypothesen. In: Frank Bajohr, Werner Johe and Uwe Lohalm, eds, *Zivilisation und Barberei: Die widersprüchlichen Potentiale der Moderne.* Hamburger Beiträge zur Sozial- und Zeitgeschichte 27. Hamburg: Christians, pp. 285–303.

Bollmus, Reinhard (1970). *Das Amt Rosenberg und seine Gegner*. Stuttgart: Deutsche Verlags-Anstalt.

Bouquet, Mary (1994). Family trees and their affinities: the visual imperative of the genealogical diagram. *Journal of the Royal Anthropological Institute* NS 2: 43–66.

Bramwell, Anna (1985). *Blood and Soil: Richard Walther Darré and Hitler's 'Green Party'*. Bourne End, Bucks.: The Kensal Press.

Brechten, Magnus (1998). *'Madagaskar für die Juden': Antisemitische Idee und politische Praxis 1885–1945*. München: Oldenbourg.

Breuer, Stefan (2001). *Ordnungen der Ungleichheit: Die deutschen Rechte im Widerstreit ihrer Ideen*. Darmstadt: Wissenschaftliche Buchgesellschaft.

Bridgman, Jon and Leslie J. Worley (2004). Genocide of the Hereros. In: Samuel Totten, William S. Parsons and Israel W. Charny, eds, *Century of Genocide: Critical Essays and Eyewitness Accounts*. New York: Routledge, pp. 15–51.

Brumlik, Micha (2002). *Deutscher Geist und Judenhass: Das Verhältnis des philosophischen Idealismus zum Judentum*. München: Luchterhand.

Burleigh, Michael (1988). *Germany Turns Eastwards: A Study of Ostforschung in the Third Reich*. Cambridge: Cambridge University Press.

Burleigh, Michael (1994). *Death and Deliverance: 'Euthanasia' in Germany c.1900–1945*. Cambridge: Cambridge University Press.

Burleigh, Michael and Wolfgang Wippermann (1991). *The Racial State: Germany 1933–1945*. Cambridge: Cambridge University Press.

Call, Lewis (1998). Anti-Darwin, anti-Spencer: Friedrich Nietzsche's critique of Darwin and Darwinism. *History of Science* 36: 1–22.

Carey, John (1992). *The Intellectuals and the Masses: Pride and Prejudice among the Literary Intelligentsia 1880–1939*. London: Faber and Faber.

Chaudhuri, Nirad C. (1974). *Scholar Extraordinary: The Life and Times of Professor the Rt. Hon. Friedrich Max Müller*. London: Chatto and Windus.

Connelly, John (1999). Nazis and Slavs: from racial theory to racist practice. *Central European History* 32: 1–33.

Curran, Vivian Grosswald (2000). Herder and the Holocaust: a debate about difference and determinism in the context of comparative law. In: Frederick DeCoste and Bernard Schwarz, eds, *The Holocaust's Ghost*. Edmonton: University of Alberta Press, pp. 399–410.

Daim, Wilfried (1958). *Der Mann, der Hitler die Ideen gab: Von den religiösen Verirrungen eines Sektierers zum Rassenwahn des Diktators*. München: Isar Verlag.

Deichmann, Ute (1996). *Biologists under Hitler*. Translated by Thomas Dunlap. Cambridge, Mass.: Harvard University Press. First published: *Biologen unter Hitler: Porträt einer Wissenschaft im NS-Staat*. Frankfurt am Main: Fischer, 1995.

Dennett, Daniel C. (1996). *Darwin's Dangerous Idea: Evolution and the Meanings of Life*. New York: Touchstone.

Dickinson, Edward Ross (2003). Biopolitics, fascism, democracy: some reflections on our discourse about 'modernity'. *Central European History* 37: 1–48.

Dijkink, Gertjan (1996). *National Identity and Geopolitical Visions: Maps of Pride and Pain*. London: Routledge.

Dikötter, Frank (1992). *The Discourse of Race in Modern China*. Stanford, Calif.: Stanford University Press.

Eckart, Wolfgang U. (1997). *Medizin und Kolonialimperialismus: Deutschland 1884–1945*. Paderborn: Ferdinand Schöningh.

Ede, Emmanuel Chukwudi (1995). The color of reason: the idea of 'race' in Kant's anthropology. In: Katherine M. Faull, ed., *Anthropology and the German Enlightenment: Perspectives on Humanity*. Lewisburg, Pa: Bucknell University Press, pp. 200–41.

Efron, John M. (1994). *Defenders of the Race: Jewish Doctors and Race Science in Fin-de-Siècle Europe*. New Haven, Conn.: Yale University Press.

El-Tayeb, Fatima (2001). *Schwarze Deutsche: Der Diskurs um 'Rasse' und nationale Identität 1890–1933*. Frankfurt am Main: Campus.

Essner, Cornelia (2002). *Die 'Nürnberger Gesetze' oder die Verwaltung des Rassenwahns 1933–1945*. Paderborn: Ferdinand Schöningh.

Evans, Richard (2004). Editor's introduction. *Journal of Contemporary History* 39 (2): 163–7.

Fahlbusch, Michael (1999). *Wissenschaft im Dienst der nationalsozialistischen Politik? Die Volksdeutschen Forschungsgemeinschaften von 1931–1945*. Baden-Baden: Nomos.

Fangerau, Heiner (2000). *Das Standardwerk zur menschlichen Erblichkeitslehre und Rassenhygiene von Erwin Baur, Eugen Fischer und Fritz Lenz im Spiegel der zeitgenössischen Rezensionsliteratur 1921–1941*. Inaugural dissertation, Ruhr-Universität Bochum.

Felbor, Ute (1995). *Rassenbiologie und Vererbungswissenschaft in der Medizinischen Fakultät der Universität Würzburg 1937–1945*. Würzburg: Königshausen & Neuman.

Field, Geoffrey G. (1981). *Evangelist of Race: The Germanic Vision of Houston Stewart Chamberlain*. New York: Columbia University Press.

Fischer, Eugen (1955). Die Wissenschaft vom Menschen: Anthropobiologie im XX. Jahrhundert. In: Hans Schwerte and Wilhelm Spengler, eds, *Forscher und Wissenschaftler des Lebens im heutigen Europa: Erforscher des Lebens*. Oldenburg and Hamburg: Gerhard Stalling Verlag, pp. 272–87.

Föger, Benedict and Klaus Taschwer (2001). *Die andere Seite des Spiegels: Konrad Lorenz und der Nationalsozialismus*. Wien: Czernin.

Friedlander, Henry (1995). *The Origins of the Nazi Genocide: From Euthanasia to the Final Solution*. Chapel Hill: University of North Carolina Press.

Froggatt, P. and N. C. Nevin (1971). Galton's 'law of ancestral heredity': its influence on the early development of human genetics. *History of Science* 10: 1–27.

Gallagher, Hugh Gregory (2004). Holocaust: the genocide of disabled peoples. In: Samuel Totten, William S. Parsons and Israel W. Charny, eds, *Century of Genocide: Critical Essays and Eyewitness Accounts*. New York: Routledge, pp. 205–30.

Gansmüller, Christian (1987). *Die Erbgesundheitswesen des Dritten Reiches: Planung, Durchführung und Durchsetzung*. Köln/Wien: Böhlau.

Gausemeier, Bernd (2003). Rassenhygienische Radikalisierung und kolle-gialer Konsens. In: Carola Sachse, ed., *Die Verbindung nach Auschwitz: Biowissenschaften und Menschen Versuche an Kaiser-Wilhelm-Instituten.* Göttingen: Wallstein, pp. 178–98.

Geisenhainer, Katja (2002). *'Rasse ist Schicksal': Otto Reche (1879–1966) – ein Leben als Anthropologe und Völkerkundler.* Leipzig: Evangelische Verlagsanstalt.

Gasman, Daniel (1971). *The Scientific Origins of National Socialism: Social Darwinism in Ernst Haeckel and the German Monist League.* London: MacDonald/New York: American Elsevier.

Gellately, Robert and Nathan Stoltzfus, eds (2001). *Social Outsiders in Nazi Germany.* Princeton, NJ: Princeton University Press.

Gentile, Emilio (1993). Impending modernity: fascism and the ambivalent image of the United States. *Journal of Contemporary History* 28: 7–29.

Gerstner, Alexandra (2003). *Rassenadel und Sozialaristokratie: Adelsvorstell-ungen in der völkischen Bewegung (1890–1914).* Berlin: SuKuLTuR.

Gessler, Bernhard (2000). *Eugen Fischer (1874–1967): Leben und Werk des Freiburger Anatomen, Anthropologen und Rassenhygienikers bis 1927.* Frankfurt am Main: Peter Lang.

Geuter, Ulfried (1992). *The Professionalization of Psychology in Nazi Germany.* Translated by Richard J. Holmes. Cambridge: Cambridge University Press. First published: *Die Professionalisierung der deutschen Psychologie im Nationalsozialismus.* Frankfurt am Main: Suhrkamp, 1988.

Geuter, Ulfried (1999). Psychologie im nationalsozialistischen Deutschland. In: Renate Knigge-Tesche, ed., *Berater der braunen Macht: Wissenschaft und Wissenschaftler im NS-Staat.* Frankfurt am Main: Anabas, pp. 94–110.

Gillette, Aaron (2002). Guido Lamdra and the Office of Racial Studies in fascist Italy. *Holocaust and Genocide Studies* 16: 357–75.

Gilman, Sander L. (1985). *Difference and Pathology: Stereotypes of Sexual-ity, Race and Madness.* Ithaca, NY: Cornell University Press.

Gilman, Sander L. (1993). *Freud, Race and Gender.* Princeton NJ: Princeton University Press.

Gilman, Sander L. (1998). *Creating Beauty to Cure the Soul: Race and Psy-chology in the Shaping of Aesthetic Surgery.* Durham, NC: Duke University Press.

Goodrick-Clarke, Nicholas (1992). *The Occult Roots of Nazism: Secret Aryan Cults and their Influence on Nazi Ideology.* London: I. B. Tauris.

Gould, Stephen J. (1981). *The Mismeasure of Man.* New York: Penguin.

Graml, Hermann (1992). *Antisemitism in the Third Reich.* Translated by Tim Kirk. Oxford: Blackwell.

Graml, Hermann (1993). Rassismus und Lebensraum: Völkermord im Zweiten Weltkrieg. In: Karl Dietrich Bracher, Manfred Funker and Hans-Adolf Jacobsen, eds, *Deutschland 1933–1945: Neue Studien zur national-sozialistischen Herrschaft.* 2nd revised edition. Bonn: Bundeszentrale für politische Bildung, pp. 440–51.

Grosse, Pascal (2000). *Kolonialismus und bürgerliche Gesellschaft in Deutschland 1850–1918.* Frankfurt am Main: Campus.

Gruchmann, Lothar (1990). *Justiz im Dritten Reich: Anpassung und Unterwerfung in der Äre Gürtner.* 2nd edition. München: Oldenbourg.

Grunberger, Richard (1971). *A Social History of the Third Reich.* London: Penguin.

Grüttner, Michael (2004). *Biographisches Lexikon zur nationalozialistischen Wissenschaftspolitk.* Heidelberg: Synchron.

Haar, Ingo (2000). *Historiker im Nationalsozialismus: Deutsche Geschichtswissenschaft und der 'Volkstumskampf' im Osten.* Göttingen: Vandenhoeck and Ruprecht.

Hagemann, Rudolf (2000). *Erwin Baur (1875–1933): Pionier der Genetik und Züchtungsforschung.* Egling an der Paar: Kovar.

Hale, Christopher (2004). *Himmler's Crusade. The true Story of the 1938 Nazi Expedition into Tibet.* London: Bantam.

Hammerstein, Notker (1999). *Wissenschaftspolitik in Republik und Diktatur: Die Deutsche Forschungsgemeinschaft in der Weimarer Republik und im Dritten Reich.* München: Beck.

Hannaford, Ivan (1996). *Race: The History of an Idea in the West.* Baltimore, Md: Johns Hopkins University Press.

Harrington, Anne (1996). *Reenchanted Science: Holism in German Culture from Wilhelm II to Hitler.* Princeton, NJ: Princeton University Press.

Harris, Roy (1981). *The Language Myth.* London: Duckworth.

Harris, Roy, ed. (2002). *The Language Myth in Western Culture.* London: Curzon.

Harten, Hans-Christian (1996). *De-Kulturation und Germanisierung: Die nationalsozialistische Rassen- und Erziehungspolitik in Polen 1939–1945.* Frankfurt am Main: Campus.

Hau, Michael (2003). *The Cult of Health and Beauty in Germany.* Chicago, Ill.: University of Chicago Press.

Hausmann, Frank-Rutger (1998). *'Deutsche Geisteswissenschaft' im Zweiten Weltkrieg: Die 'Aktion Ritterbusch'.* Dresden: Dresden University Press.

Hausmann, Frank-Rutger, ed. (2002). *Die Rolle der Geisteswissenschaften im Dritten Reich.* München: Oldenbourg.

Heberer, Gerhard, Gottfried Kurth and Ilse Schwidetzky-Roesing (1959). *Anthropologie.* Frankfurt am Main: Fischer Bücherei.

Hecht, Jennifer M. (1999). The solvency of metaphysics: the debate over racial science and moral philosophy in France, 1890–1919. *Isis* 90: 1–24.

Hecht, Jennifer M. (2000). Vacher de Lapouge and the rise of Nazi science. *Journal of the History of Ideas* 61: 285–305.

Hecht, Jennifer M. (2003). *The End of the Soul: Scientific Modernity, Atheism, and Anthropology in France.* New York: Columbia University Press.

Heiber, Helmut (1991). *Universität unterm Hakenkreuz. Teil 1: Der Professor im Dritten Reich.* München: K.G. Saur.

Heim, Susanne, ed. (2002). *Autarkie und Ostexpansion.* Göttingen: Wallstein.

Heine-Geldern, Robert (1964). One hundred years of ethnological theory in the German-speaking world. *Current Anthropology* 5: 407–18.

Heinemann, Isabel (2003). *'Rasse, Siedlung, deutsches Blut': Das Rasse und Siedlungshauptamt der SS und die rassenpolitische Neuordnung Europas.* Göttingen: Wallstein.

Herf, Jeffrey (1984). *Reactionary Modernism: Technology, Culture, and Politics in Weimar and the Third Reich.* Cambridge: Cambridge University Press.

Herman, Arthur (1997). *The Idea of Decline in Western History.* New York: Free Press.

Hewitt, Andrew (1993). *Fascist Modernism: Aesthetics, Politics and the Avant-Garde.* Stanford Calif.: Stanford University Press.

Hirschfeld, Gerhard and Tobias Jersak, eds (2004). *Karrieren im Nationalsozialismus. Funktionseliten zwischen Mitwirkung und Distanz.* Frankfurt am Main: Campus.

Höpfner, Hans-Paul (1999). *Die Universität Bonn im Dritten Reich: Akademische Biographien unter nationalsozialistischer Herrschaft.* Bonn: Bouvier.

Hossfeld, Uwe (1997). *Gerhard Heberer (1901–1973): Sein Beitrag zur Biologie im 20. Jahrhundert.* Berlin: Verlag für Wissenschaft und Bildung.

Hossfeld, Uwe (2003). Von der Rassenkunde, Rassenhygiene und biologischen Erbstatistik zur Synthetischen Theorie der Evolution: Eine Skizze der Biowissenschaften. In: Uwe Hossfeld, John Jürgen, Oliver Lemuth and Rüdiger Stutz, eds, *'Kämpferische Wissenschaft': Studien zur Universität Jena im Nationalsozialismus.* Kölk: Böhlau, pp. 519–74.

Hossfeld, Uwe and Rainer Brömer, eds (2001) *Darwinismus und/als Ideologie.* Berlin: Verlag für Wissenschaft und Bildung.

Hossfeld, Uwe, John Jürgen, Oliver Lemuth and Rüdiger Stutz, eds (2003). *'Kämpferische Wissenschaft': Studien zur Universität Jena im Nationalsozialismus.* Kölk: Böhlau.

Hutton, Christopher (1999). *Linguistics and the Third Reich: Race, Mother Tongue, Fascism and the Science of Language.* London: Routledge.

Hyam, Ronald (1990). *Empire and Sexuality: The British Experience.* Manchester: Manchester University Press.

Jones, Cynthia Ann (2000). *The Misappropriation of Nietzsche in National Socialism: Myth and Reality.* PhD dissertation, the University of Missouri, Kansas City.

Junker, Thomas (2004). *Die zweite Darwinistische Revolution: Geschichte des synthetischen Darwinismus in Deutschland 1924 bis 1950.* Marburg: Basilisken-Presse.

Junker, Thomas and Uwe Hossfeld (2002). The architects of the evolutionary synthesis in National Socialist Germany: science and politics. *Biology and Philosophy* 17: 223–49.

Kalikow, Theodora (1980). Die ethnologische Theorie von Konrad Lorenz: Erklärung und Ideologie, 1938–1943. In: Herbert Mehrtens and Steffan Richter, eds, *Naturwissenschaft, Technik und NS-Ideologie.* Frankfurt am Main: Suhrkamp, pp. 189–214.

Kater, Michael (1989). *Doctors under Hitler.* Chapel Hill and London: University of North Carolina Press.

Kater, Michael (1997). *Das 'Ahnenerbe' der SS 1935–1945: Ein Beitrag zur Kulturpolitik des Dritten Reiches*. 2nd edition. München: Oldenbourg.

Kaupen-Haas, Heidrun (1986). Die Bevölkerungsplaner im Sachverständigenbeirat für Bevölkerungs- und Rassepolitik. In: Heidrun Kaupen-Haas, ed., *Aktualität und Kontinuität nazistischer Bevölkerungspolitik*. Nördlingen: Delphi Politik, pp. 103–20.

Kaupen-Haas, Heidrun and Christian Saller, eds (1999). *Wissenschaftlicher Rassismus: Analysen einer Kontinuität in den Human- und Naturwissenschaften*. Frankfurt am Main: Campus.

Kestling, Robert W. (1992). Forgotten victims: blacks in the Holocaust. *The Journal of Negro History* 77: 30–6.

Kestling, Robert W. (1998). Blacks under the Swastika: a research note. *The Journal of Negro History* 83: 84–99.

Kevles, Daniel (1995). *In the Name of Eugenics: Genetics and the Uses of Human Heredity*. New York: Knopf. First published, 1985.

Kiefer, Annegret (1991). *Das Problem einer 'jüdischen Rasse'*. Frankfurt am Main: Peter Lang.

Klee, Ernst, ed. (1997a). *Dokumente zur 'Euthanasie'*. Frankfurt am Main: Fischer.

Klee, Ernst (1997b). *Auschwitz, die NS-Medizin und ihre Opfer*. Frankfurt am Main: Fischer.

Klee, Ernst (1999). *'Euthanasie' im NS-Staat: Die 'Vernichtung lebensunwerten Lebens'*. Frankfurt am Main: Fischer.

Klee, Ernst (2003). *Personenlexikon zum Dritten Reich: Wer war was vor und nach 1945*. Frankfurt am Main: Fischer.

Knobloch, Clemens (2002). Sprachwissenschaft. In: Frank-Rutger Hausmann, ed., *Die Rolle der Geisteswissenschaften im Dritten Reich 1933–1945*. München: Oldenbourg, pp. 305–27.

Koonz, Claudia (2003). *The Nazi Conscience*. Cambridge, Mass.: Belknap Press of Harvard University Press.

Kröner, Hans-Peter (1998). *Von der Rassenhygiene zur Humangenetik: Das Kaiser-Wilhelm-Institut für Anthropologie, menschliche Erblehre nach dem Kriege*. Stuttgart: Gustav Fischer.

Krüger, Arnd (1991). There goes this art of manliness: naturalism and racial hygiene in Germany. *Journal of Sport History* 18: 135–58.

Kühl, Stefan (1997). *Die Internationale der Rassisten: Aufstieg und Niedergang der internationalen Bewegung für Eugenik und Rassenhygiene im 20. Jahrhundert*. Frankfurt am Main: Campus.

Lacoue-Labarthe, Philippe (1987). *La fiction du politique: Heidegger, l'art et la politique*. Paris: Christian Bourgois.

Leach, Edmund (1990). Aryans invasions over four millennia. In: Emiko Ohnuki-Tierney, ed., *Culture Through Time: Anthropological Approaches*. Stanford Calif.: Stanford University Press, pp. 227–45.

Leopold, Jean (1970). The Aryan theory of race in India 1870–1920: nationalist and internationalist visions. *The Indian Economic and Social History Review* 7: 271–97.

Leopold, Jean (1974). British applications of the Aryan theory of race to India, 1850–1870. *The English Historical Review* 89: 578–603.

Leopold, Jean (1987). Ethnic stereotypes in linguistics: the case of Friedrich Max Müller (1847–1851). In: Hans Aarsleff, Louis Kelly and Hans-Josef Niederehe, eds, *Papers in the History of Linguistics: Proceedings of the Third International Conference on the History of the Language Sciences (ICHoLS), Princeton, 19–23 August 1984*. Amsterdam: John Benjamins, pp. 501–12.

Lerchenmüller, Joachim (1997). *'Keltischer Sprengstoff': Eine wissenschaftsgeschichtliche Studie über die deutsche Keltologie von 1900 bis 1945*. Tübingen: Niemeyer.

Levinas, Emmanuel (1990). Reflections on the philosophy of Hitlerism. *Critical Inquiry* 17: 63–71.

Lewis, C. S. (2002). *Surprised by Joy*. London: Harper Collins. First Published, 1955.

Lewy, Guenther (1999). Gypsies and Jews under the Nazis. *Holocaust and Genocide Studies* 13: 383–404.

Lewy, Guenther (2000). *The Nazi Persecution of the Gypsies*. Oxford: Oxford University Press.

Lilienthal, Georg (1985). *Der 'Lebensborn e.V.': Ein Instrument nationalsozialistischer Rassenpolitik*. Stuttgart: Gustav Fischer.

Lilienthal, Georg (1993). Kinder als Beute des Rassenkriegs. Der 'Lebensborn e.V.' und die Eindeutschung von Kindern aus Polen, der Tschechoslowakei und Jugoslawien. *Dachauer Hefte* 9: 181–96.

Lindenfeld, David (1997). The prevalence of irrational thinking in the Third Reich: notes toward the reconstruction of modern value rationality. *Central European History* 30: 365–86.

Livingstone, David N. (1984). Science and society: Nathaniel S. Shaler and racial ideology. *Transactions of the Institute of British Geographers* NS 9: 181–210.

Livingstone, David N. (1987). Human acclimatization: perspectives in a contested field of inquiry in science, medicine and geography. *History of Science* 25: 359–94.

Lösch, Niels C. (1997). *Rasse als Konstrukt: Leben und Werk Eugen Fischers*. Frankfurt am Main: Peter Lang.

Lüddecke, Andreas (1995). *Der 'Fall Saller' und die Rassenhygiene: Eine Göttinger Fallstudie zu den Widersprüchen sozialbiologistischer Ideologiebildung*. Marburg: Tectum Verlag.

Lüddecke, Andreas (2000). *Rassen, Schädel und Gelehrte: Zur politis-chen Funktionalität der anthropologischen Forschung und Lehre in der Tradition Egon Freiherr von Eickstedts*. Frankfurt am Main: Peter Lang.

Lukács, Georg (1988). *Die Zerstörung der Vernunft: Der Weg des Irrationalismus von Schelling zu Hitler*. Berlin/Weimar: Aufbau-Verlag. First published, 1955.

Lusane, Clarence (2003). *Hitler's Black Victims: The Historical Experiences of Afro-Germans, European Blacks, Africans and African Americans in the Nazi Era*. London and New York: Routledge.

Lutzhöft, Hans-Jürgen (1971). *Der nordische Gedanke in Deutschland 1920–1940*. Stuttgart: Ernst Klett.

Maas, Utz (1988). Die Entwicklung der deutschsprachigen Sprachwissenschaft von 1900 bis 1950 zwischen Professionalisierung und Politisierung. *Zeitschrift für germanistische Linguistik* 16: 253–90.

Mai, Christoph (1997). *Humangenetik im Dienste der 'Rassenhygiene': Zwillingsforschung in Deutschland bis 1945*. Aachen: Shaker Verlag.

Mai, Uwe (2002). *'Rasse und Raum': Agrarpolitik, Sozial- und Raumplaning im NS-Staat*. Paderborn: Ferdinand Schöningh.

Majer, Dietmut (2003). *'Non-Germans' under the Third Reich: The Nazi Judicial and Administrative System in Germany and Occupied Eastern Europe, with Special Regard to Occupied Poland 1939–1945*. Baltimore, Md: Johns Hopkins University Press.

Malik, Kenan (1996). *The Meaning of Race: Race, History and Culture in Western Society*. New York: New York University Press.

Mallory, James P. (1989). *In Search of the Indo-Europeans: Language, Archaeology and Myth*. London: Thames and Hudson.

Marks, Jonathan (1996). The legacy of serological studies in American physical anthropology. *History and Philosophy of the Life Sciences* 18: 345–62.

Massin, Benoît (1993). Anthropologie raciale et national-socialisme: heurs et malheurs du paradigme de la *'race'*. In: Josiane Olff-Nathan, ed., *La science sous le Troisième Reich*. Paris: Editions de Seuil, pp. 197–262.

Massin, Benoît (1996). From Virchow to Fischer: physical anthropology and 'modern race theories' in Wilhelmine Germany. In: George W. Stocking, ed., *'Volksgeist' as Method and Ethic: Essays in Boasian Ethnography and the German Anthropological Tradition*. Madison: The University of Wisconsin Press, pp. 79–154.

Massin, Benoît (1999). Anthropologie und Humangenetik im Nationalsozialismus oder: wie schreiben deutsche Wissenschaftler ihre eigene Wissenschaftsgeschichte? In: Heidrun Kaupen-Haas and Christian Saller, eds, *Wissenschaftlicher Rassismus: Analysen einer Kontinuität in den Human- und Naturwissenschaften*. Frankfurt am Main: Campus, pp. 12–64.

Massin, Benoît (2003). Rasse und Vererbung als Beruf: Die Hauptforschungsrichtungen am Kaiser-Wilhelm-Institut für Anthropologie, menschliche Erblehre und Eugenik im Nationalsozialismus. In: Hans-Walter Schmuhl, ed., *Rassenforschung an Kaiser-Wilhelm-Instituten vor und nach 1933*. Göttingen: Wallstein, pp. 190–244.

Maw, Martin (1990). *Visions of India: Fulfilment Theology, the Aryan Race Theory, and the Work of British Protestant Missionaries in India*. Frankfurt am Main: Peter Lang.

Mees, Bernard (2004). Hitler and *Germanentum. Journal of Contemporary History* 39: 255–70.

Meinel, Christoph and Peter Voswinckel (1994). *Medizin, Naturwissenschaft, Technik und Nationalsozialismus*. Stuttgart: Bassum.

Michael, Robert and Karin Doerr (2002). *Nazi-Deutsch/Nazi-German: An English Lexicon of the Language of the Third Reich*. Westport, Conn.: Greenwood Press.

Milton, Sybil (2004). Holocaust: the Gypsies. In: Samuel Totten, William S. Parsons and Israel W. Charny, eds, *Century of Genocide: Critical Essays and Eyewitness Accounts*. New York: Routledge, pp. 161–202.

Mosse, George L. (1975). *The Nationalization of the Masses: Political Symbolism and Mass Movements in Germany from the Napoleonic Wars through the Third Reich*. Ithaca, NY: Cornell University Press.

Mosse, George L. (1998). *The Crisis of German Ideology: Intellectual Origins of the Third Reich*. New York: Howard Fertig. First published, 1964.

Müller, Gerhard (1978). *Ernst Krieck und die nationalsozialistische Wissenschaftsreform*. Weinheim: Beltz.

Müller-Hill, Benno (1988). *Murderous Science: Elimination by Scientific Selection of Jews, Gypsies, and Others, Germany 1933–1945*. Translated by George R. Fraser. Oxford: Oxford University Press. First published as *Tödliche Wissenschaft*, Reinbeck/Hamburg: Rowohlt, 1984.

Müller-Hill, Benno (1999). The blood from Auschwitz and the silence of the scholars. *History and Philosophy of the Life Sciences* 21: 331–65.

Münkel, Daniela (1996). *Nationalsozialistische Agrarpolitik und Bauernalltag*. Frankfurt am Main: Campus.

Murphy, David T. (1997). *The Heroic Earth: Geopolitical Thought in Weimar Germany 1918–1933*. Kent, Ohio: Kent State University Press.

Noll, Richard (1997). *The Aryan Christ: The Secret Life of Carl Jung*. New York: Random House.

Oesterle, Anka (1998). Verwischte Spuren – Robert Ritter: Eine biographische Rückblende. In: Ulrich Hägele, *Sinti und Roma und wir: Ausgrenzung, Internierung und Verfolgung einer Minderheit*. Tübingen: Kulturamt der Universitätsstadt Tübingen, pp. 36–74.

Olender, Maurice (1992). *The Languages of Paradise*. Translated by Arthur Goldhammer. Cambridge, Mass.: Harvard University Press.

Olff-Nathan, Josiane, ed. (1993). *La science sous le Troisième Reich*. Paris: Editions de Seuil.

Overy, Richard (2004). *The Dictators: Hitler's Germany, Stalin's Russia*. London: Allen Lane.

Paletschek, Sylvia (2001). The invention of Humboldt and the impact of National Socialism: the German University idea in the first half of the twentieth century. In: Margit Szöllösi-Janze, ed., *Science in the Third Reich*. Oxford: Berg, pp. 37–58.

Pape, Wolfgang (2002). Ur- und Frühgeschichte. In: Frank-Rutger Hausmann, ed., *Die Rolle der Geisteswissenschaften im Dritten Reich 1933–1945*. München: Oldenbourg, pp. 329–59.

Paul, Diane B. and Raphael Falk (1999). Scientific responsibility and political context: the case of genetics under the swastika. In: Jane Maienschein and Michael Ruse, eds, *Biology and the Foundation of Ethics*. Cambridge: Cambridge University Press, pp. 257–75.

Pietikainen, Petteri (1998). National typologies, races and mentalities in C.G. Jung's psychology. *History of European Ideas* 24: 359–73.

Pine, Lisa (1997). *Nazi Family Policy 1933–1945*. Oxford: Berg.

Poliakov, Léon (1974). *The Aryan Myth.* Translated by Edmund Howard. London: Chatto Heinemann for Sussex University Press. First published as *Le Mythe aryen: essai sur les sources du racisme et des nationalismes.* Paris: Calmann-Lévy, 1971. 2nd French edition. Bruxelles: Editions Complexe, 1987.

Poliakov, Léon and Joseph Wulf (1983). *Das Dritte Reich und seine Denker.* Frankfurt am Main: Ullstein.

Pollock. S. (1993). Deep orientalism? Notes on Sanskrit and power beyond the Raj. In: Carol A. Breckenridge and Peter van der Veer, eds, *Orientalism and the Postcolonial Predicament: Perspectives on South Asia.* Philadelphia: University of Pennsylvania Press, pp. 76–133.

Pommerin, Reiner (1979). *Sterilisierung der Rheinlandbastarde: Das Schicksal einer farbigen deutschen Minderheit 1918–1937.* Düsseldorf: Droste.

Prinz, Wolfgang (1985). Ganzheits- und Gestaltpsychologie und Nationalsozialismus. In: Peter Lundgreen, ed., *Wissenschaft im Dritten Reich.* Frankfurt am Main: Suhrkamp, pp. 55–81.

Proctor, Robert N. (1988). *Racial Hygiene: Medicine under the Nazis.* Cambridge, Mass.: Harvard University Press.

Puschner, Uwe (2001). *Die völkische Bewegung im wilhelminischen Kaiserreich: Sprache, Rasse, Religion.* Darmstadt: Wissenschaftliche Buchgesellschaft.

Puschner, Uwe (2002). 'One people, one Reich, one God': the *völkische Weltanschauung* and movement. *Bulletin of the German Historical Institute London* 24: 5–27.

Quinlan, Sean (1998). The racial imagery of degeneration and depopulation: Georges Vacher de Lapouge and 'anthroposociology' in fin-de-siècle France. *History of European Ideas* 24: 393–413.

Rabinbach, Anson (2004). Spirits for Hitler: Review of Treitel, *A Science for the Soul.* Baltimore, Md: Johns Hopkins, 2004. *Times Literary Supplement* 5203 (November 12), p. 36.

Reichel, Peter (1993). *Der schöne Schein des Dritten Reiches: Faszination und Gewalt des Faschismus.* Frankfurt am Main: Fischer.

Reindl, Josef (2001). Believers in an age of heresy? Oskar Vogt, Nikolai Timoféeff-Ressovsky and Julius Hallervorden at the Kaiser Wilhelm Institute for Brain Research. In: Margit Szöllösi-Janze, ed., *Science in the Third Reich.* Oxford: Berg, pp. 211–42.

Renneberg, Monika and Mark Walker, eds (1994). *Science, Technology and National Socialism.* Cambridge: Cambridge University Press.

Rensch, Bernhard (1979). *Lebensweg eines Biologen in einem turbulenten Jahrhundert.* Stuttgart: Gustav Fischer.

Richards, Robert J. (1998). The moral foundations of the idea of evolutionary progress: Darwin, Spencer, and the neo-Darwinians. In: David L. Hull and Michael Ruse, eds, *The Philosophy of Biology.* Oxford: Oxford University Press, pp. 592–609.

Richter, Ingrid (2001). *Katholizismus und Eugenik in der Weimarer Republik und im Dritten Reich.* Paderborn: Ferdinand Schöningh.

Rissom, Renate (1983). *Fritz Lenz und die Rassenhygiene*. Husum: Mattiesen.

Rockmore, Tom (1995). *Heidegger and French Philosophy: Humanism, Antihumanism and Being*. London: Routledge.

Roelcke, Volker (2003). Programm und Praxis der psychiatrischen Genetik an der Deutschen Forschungsanstalt für Psychiatrie unter Ernst Rüdin. Zum Verhältnis von Wissenschaft, Politik und Rasse-Begriff vor und nach 1933. In: Hans-Walter Schmuhl, ed., *Rassenforschung an Kaiser-Wilhelm-Instituten*. Göttingen: Wallstein, pp. 38–67.

Römer, Ruth (1989). *Sprachwissenschaft und Rassenideologie in Deutschland*. 2nd edition. München: Wilhelm Fink.

Rose, Paul Lawrence (1990). *German Question/Jewish Question: Revolutionary Antisemitism from Kant to Wagner*. Princeton, NJ: Princeton University Press.

Sachse, Carola, ed. (2003). *Die Verbindung nach Auschwitz: Biowissenschaften und Menschen Versuche an Kaiser-Wilhelm-Instituten*. Göttingen: Wallstein.

Saller, Karl (1949). *Art- und Rassenlehre des Menschen*. Stuttgart: Curt E. Schwab.

Saller, Karl (1961). *Die Rassenlehre des Nationalsozialismus in Wissenschaft und Propaganda*. Darmstadt: Progress-Verlag.

Schaller, Helmut (2002). *Der Nationalsozialismus und die slawische Welt*. Regensberg: Friedrich Pustet.

Schank, Gerd (2000). *'Rasse' und 'Züchtung' bei Nietzsche*. Berlin: Walter de Gruyter.

Schleunes, Karl A., ed. (2001). *Legislating the Holocaust: The Bernhard Loesener Memoirs and Supporting Documents*. Translated by Carol Scherer. Colorado: Westview Press.

Schmitz-Berning, Cornelia (1998). *Vokabular des Nationalsozialismus*. Berlin: Walter de Gruyter.

Schmuhl, Hans-Walter (1992). *Rassenhygiene, Nationalsozialismus, Euthanasie*. Göttingen: Vandenhoeck & Ruprecht.

Schmuhl, Hans-Walter (2002). Hirnforschung und Krankenmord: Das Kaiser-Wilhelm-Institut für Hirnforschung. *Vierteljahrshefte für Zeitgeschichte* 50: 559–609.

Schmuhl, Hans-Walter (2003a). Rasse, Rassenforschung, Rassenpolitik. In: Schmuhl, Hans-Walter, ed., *Rassenforschung an Kaiser-Wilhelm-Instituten*. Göttingen: Wallstein, pp. 8–37.

Schmuhl, Hans-Walter, ed. (2003b). *Rassenforschung an Kaiser-Wilhelm-Instituten*. Göttingen: Wallstein.

Schwidetzy, Ilse (1955). Egon Freiherr von Eickstedt: Begriff und Gestalt des lebendigen Menschen. In: Hans Schwerte and Wilhelm Spengler, eds, *Forscher und Wissenschaftler im Heutigen Europa*. Volume 4: Erforscher des Lebens: Mediziner, Biologen, Anthropologen. Oldenburg: Gerhard Stalling, pp. 317–24.

Schulle, Diana (2001). *Das Reichssippenamt: Eine Institution nationalsozialistischer Rassenpolitik*. Berlin: Logos.

Schweizer, Magdalena (2002). *Die psychiatrische Eugenik in Deutschland und in der Schweiz zur Zeit des Nationalsozialismus.* Frankfurt am Main: Peter Lang.

Seamon, David (1998). Goethe, nature and phenomenology: an introduction. In: David Seamon and Arthur Zajonc, eds, *Goethe's Way of Science: A Phenomenology of Nature.* Albany: State University of New York, pp. 1–14.

See, Klaus von (1994). *Barbar, Germane, Arier.* Heidelberg: C. Winter.

Segal, Sanford L. (2003). *Mathematicians under the Nazis.* Princeton, NJ: Princeton University Press.

Seidler, Horst and Andreas Rett (1982). *Das Reichssippenamt entscheidet: Rassenbiologie im Nationalsozialismus.* Wien: Jugend und Volk.

Semmel, Bernard (1958). Karl Pearson: socialist and Darwinist. *The British Journal of Sociology* 9: 111–25.

Sieg, Ulrich (2001). Strukturwandel der Wissenschaft im NS. *Berichte zur Wissenschaftsgeschichte* 24: 255–70.

Silvester, Jeremy and Jan-Bart Gewald (2003). *Words cannot be found: German Colonial Rule in Namibia. An Annotated Reprint of the 1918 Blue Book.* Leiden: Brill.

Simon, Gerd (1979). *Sprachwissenschaft und politisches Engagement.* Beltz: Weinheim.

Simon, Gerd (1985a). Die sprachsoziologische Abteilung der SS. In: Wilfried Kürschner and Rüdiger Vogt, eds, *Sprachtheorie, Pragmatik, Interdisziplinäres: Akten des 19. Linguistischen Kolloquims Vechta 1984.* Tübingen: Max Niemeyer, pp. 375–96.

Simon, Gerd (1985b). Sprachwissenschaft im III. Reich. In: Franz Januschek, ed., *Politische Sprachwissenschaft.* Opladen: Westdeutscher Verlag, pp. 97–141.

Simon, Gerd (1986a). Wissenschaft und Wende 1933: Zum Verhältnis von Wissenschaft und Politik am Beispiel des Sprachwissenschaftlers Georg Schmidt-Rohr. *Das Argument* 158: 527–42.

Simon, Gerd (1986b). Der 'Wandervogel' als 'Volk im Kleinen' und Volk als Sprachgemeinschaft beim frühen Georg Schmidt(-Rohr). In: Herbert E. Brekle and Utz Maas, eds, *Sprachwissenschaft und Volkskunde: Perspektiven einer kulturanalytischen Sprachbetrachtung.* Opladen: Westdeutscher Verlag, pp. 155–83.

Simon, Gerd (2001). Kontinuitäten und Brüche in der linguistischen Bedeutungsforschung. In: Georg Bolleneck and Clemens Knobloch, eds, *Semantischer Umbau der Geisteswissenschaften nach 1933 und 1945.* Heidelberg: C. Winter, pp. 175–81.

Simon, Gerd (n.d.) Nordistik: Der Modernisierer des nordischen Gedankens: Otto Höfler und die Skandinavistik im 3. Reich. http://homepages.unituebingen.de/gerd.simon/vorarbeiten.htm.

Smith, Woodruff D. (1991). *Politics and the Sciences of Culture in Germany 1840–1920.* New York: Oxford University Press.

Spencer, Hamish and Diane B. Paul (1998). The failure of scientific critique: David Heron, Karl Pearson and Mendelian eugenics. *British Journal for the History of Science* 31: 441–52.

Steigmann-Gall, Richard (2003). *The Holy Reich: Nazi Conceptions of Christianity, 1919–1945*. Cambridge: Cambridge University Press.

Stepan, Nancy (1982). *The Idea of Race in Science: Great Britain 1800–1960*. London: Macmillan.

Stepan, Nancy (2001). *Picturing Tropic Nature*. Ithaca, NY: Cornell University Press.

Stern, Fritz (1974). *The Politics of Cultural Despair: A Study in the Rise of the Germanic Ideology*. Berkeley: University of California Press.

Steuer, Heiko, ed. (2001). *Eine hervorragende nationale Wissenschaft*. Berlin: Walter de Gruyter.

Stocking, George W. (1968). *Race, Culture and Evolution: Essays in the History of Anthropology*. London: Collier-Macmillan/New York: The Free Press.

Stocking, George, W. (1987). *Victorian Anthropology*. New York: The Free Press/London: Collier Macmillan.

Stocking, George, ed. (1996). *Volksgeist as Method and Ethic: Essays on Boasian Ethnography and the German Anthropological Tradition*. Madison: University of Wisconsin Press.

Stolleis, Michael (1998). *The Law under the Swastika: Studies on Legal History in Nazi Germany*. Chicago, Ill.: University of Chicago Press.

Strohm, Harald (1997). *Die Gnosis und der Nationalsozialismus*. Frankfurt am Main: Suhrkamp.

Szöllösi-Janze, Margit, ed. (2001). *Science in the Third Reich*. Oxford: Berg.

Trautmann, Thomas R. (1997). *Aryans and British India*. Berkeley: University of California Press.

Treitel, Corinna (2004). *A Science for the Soul: Occultism and the Genesis of the German Modern*. Baltimore, Md: Johns Hopkins University Press.

Vierhaus, Rudolf and Bernhard vom Brocke, eds (1990). *Forschung im Spannungsfeld von Politik und Gesellschaft: Geschichte und Struktur der Kaiser-Wilhelm-/Max-Planck-Gesellschaft*. Stuttgart: Deutsche Verlags-Anstalt.

Völklein, Ulrich (1999). *Josef Mengele: Der Arzt von Auschwitz*. Göttingen: Steidl.

Walker, Mark (2003). Natural science in National Socialism. In: Uwe Hossfeld, John Jürgen, Oliver Lemuth and Rüdiger Stutz, eds, *'Kämpferische Wissenschaft': Studien zur Universität Jena im Nationalsozialismus*. Köln: Böhlau, pp. 993–1012.

Weber, Matthias M. (1993). *Ernst Rüdin: Eine kritische Biographie*. Berlin: Springer.

Wegner, Gregory (2002). *Anti-Semitism and Schooling under the Third Reich*. New York: Routledge Falmer.

Weikart, Richard (2004). *From Darwin to Hitler: Evolutionary Ethics, Eugenics, and Racism in Germany*. New York: Palgrave Macmillan.

Weindling, Paul (1985). Weimar eugenics: the Kaiser Wilhelm Institute for Anthropology, Human Heredity and Eugenics in social context. *Annals of Science* 42: 303–18.

Weindling, Paul (1989). *Health, Race and German Politics between National Unification and Nazism 1875–1945.* Cambridge: Cambridge University Press.

Weindling, Paul (2000). *Epidemics and Genocide in Eastern Europe 1870–1945.* Oxford: Oxford University Press.

Weingart, Peter (1995). *Doppel-Leben: Ludwig Ferdinand Clauss zwischen Rassenforschung und Widerstand.* Frankfurt am Main: Campus.

Weingart, Peter, Jürgen Kroll and Kurt Bayertz (1992). *Rasse, Blut und Gene: Geschichte der Eugenik und Rassenhygiene in Deutschland.* Frankfurt am Main: Suhrkamp.

Weiss, Hermann (1998). *Biographisches Lexikon zum Dritten Reich.* Frankfurt am Main: Fischer.

Weiss, Sheila Faith (1986). Wilhelm Schallmayer and the logic of German eugenics. *Isis* 77: 33–46.

Weiss, Sheila Faith (1990). The race hygiene movement in Germany. In: Mark B. Adams, ed., *The Wellborn Science: Eugenics in Germany, France, Brazil, and Russia.* New York: Oxford University Press, pp. 8–68.

Weiss-Wendt, Anton (2003). Extermination of the Gypsies in Estonia during World War II: popular images and official policies. *Holocaust and Genocide Studies* 17: 31–61.

Wetzell, Richard F. (2000). *Inventing the Criminal: A History of German Criminology, 1880–1945.* Chapel Hill: The University of North Carolina Press.

Wetzell, Richard F. (2003). Kriminalbiologische Forschung an der Deutschen Forschungsanstalt für Psychiatrie in der Weimarer Republik und im Nationalsozialismus. In: Hans-Walter Schmuhl, ed., *Rassenforschung an Kaiser-Wilhelm-Instituten.* Göttingen: Wallstein.

Will, Wilfried Van der (1995). Culture and the organization of National Socialist ideology. In: Rob Burns, ed., *German Cultural Studies: An Introduction.* Oxford: Oxford University Press, pp. 101–45.

Willberg, Hans Peter (1998). Fraktur and nationalism. In: Peter Bain and Paul Shaw, eds, *Blackletter: Type and National Identity.* New York: The Cooper Union for the Advancement of Science and Art, pp. 40–9.

Wise, Norton M. (1994). Pascual Jordan: quantum mechanics, psychology, National Socialism. In: Monika Renneberg and Mark Walker, eds, *Science, Technology and National Socialism.* Cambridge: Cambridge University Press, pp. 224–54.

Young, Robert J. C. (1995). *Colonial Desire: Hybridity in Theory, Culture and Race.* London: Routledge.

Young, Robert J. C. (1997). Hybridism and the ethnicity of the English. In: Keith Ansell-Pearson, Benita Parry and Judith Squires, eds, *Cultural Readings of Imperialism: Edward Said and the Gravity of History.* London: Lawrence & Wishart, pp. 127–50.

Zantop, Suzanne (1997). *Conquest, Family, and Nation in Precolonial Germany, 1770–1870.* Durham, NC, and London: Duke University Press.

Zmarzlik, Hans-Günther (1963). Der Sozialdarwinismus in Deutschland als geschichtliches Problem. *Vierteljahrshefte für Zeitgeschichte* 11: 246–73.

Index